Teaching Peace

Students Exchange Letters with Their Teacher

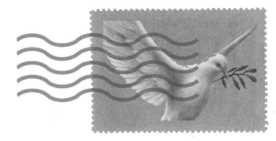

Colman McCarthy

VANDERBILT UNIVERSITY PRESS *Nashville*

This book is printed on acid-free paper.
Manufactured in the United States of America

Library of Congress Cataloging-in-Publication Data on file
LC control number 2014019563
LC classification number JZ5534.M44 2015
Dewey class number 303.6'6071—dc23

ISBN 978-0-8265-2038-8 (hardcover)
ISBN 978-0-8265-2039-5 (paperback)
ISBN 978-0-8265-2040-1 (ebook)

Teaching Peace

Also by Colman McCarthy

Disturbers of the Peace:
Profiles in Nonadjustment (1973)

Inner Companions (1975)

The Pleasures of the Game:
The Theory Free Guide to Golf (1977)

Involvements:
One Journalist's Place in the World (1984)

All of One Peace: Essays in Nonviolence (1994)

Solutions to Violence (Editor, 2001)

Strength through Peace:
The Ideas and People of Nonviolence
(Editor, 2001)

I'd Rather Teach Peace (2002)

At Rest With the Animals:
Thoughts Over Thirty Years (2008)

Peace Is Possible (Editor, 2012)

Baseball Forever (2014)

To my students, from Ariel to Yurina,

whose words grace these pages.

And, of course, to Mav McCarthy

Contents

Acknowledgments   ix

Foreword by Patrick G. Coy   xi

Preface   xv

Letters   1

Index   187

Acknowledgments

I owe some debts, both to those who have supported the Center for Teaching Peace, which my wife, Mav, and I founded in 1985, and to those whose friendship was a tailwind that helped make the going easier and the loads lighter.

Special and large thanks to the Helen Sperry Lea Foundation, the Olender Foundation, the Florence and John Schumann Foundation, the Nicholas B. Ottaway Foundation, the Morris and Gwendolyn Cafritz Foundation, Liz Wenger, Paul and Annie Mahon, the Nuclear Age Peace Foundation, the Barbra Streisand Foundation, the El-Hibri Charitable Foundation, the Penny and Ray Watts Trust, the National Student Leadership Foundation, the Lubsen Family Charitable Gift Fund, the Washington Post Company, the Public Welfare Foundation, the Lichtman Family Trust, Jim Monahan, Susan See, Grace Kelly, Morton Mintz, Nathaniel Mills, Katherine Hessler, John Storhm, Linda Smith, John Vincent, Kate Christianson, Joe and Joanne Steller, James Otis, Tara Foran, Charles Stevenson, Ayiesha Alizai Sadik, Maryanne Burke, Arthur Milholland, James Allen, Joanne Kim, Bernard Demczuk, Beth Blacklow, Eleftherios Michael, Joan Baez, Tommy Boone, Maria Shriver, Keith Sinzinger, Claire Nader, Ralph Nader, Kersti Columbant, Geri Critchley, Rep. Marci Kaptur, Claudia Levy, Barbara Zimmerman, Ruth Sherer, and many others of spirited nature.

Foreword

Patrick G. Coy

I have come to think of this creative and inspirational book as emblematic of Colman McCarthy's lived experiment with truthful teaching. Let me explain.

Gandhi titled his autobiography "My Experiments with Truth" in part because he knew he could never fashion a perfect mixture of heart-felt principles lived out in behavioral practices resulting in a truth-filled life. All he could hope for was to purposefully keep on experimenting each day to live out values-based principles in the face of constantly changing daily challenges. Those daily experiments not only were rooted in humility and a willingness to learn; they also required a self-reflexive spirit manifested in Gandhi's disciplined note-taking and journal writing (500 words almost every day from his law school days onward), which became the basis not only of his autobiography but also of his bountiful essays and articles.

Some of Gandhi's daily experiments were marked by failure. Other days—the good ones—his experiments might be deemed a partial success, but never more. The important thing to him was to stay committed to the daily experiments in truth and to never succumb to the false notion that he had achieved a truth-filled life. This was no easy feat considering the throngs nearby and worldwide who extolled his greatness, even his holiness. Yet Gandhi still managed to see each day as an experiment, to accept the encounters it presented as opportunities to grow toward the truth and to approximate it in some way.

Sadly, such an approach does not square well with the American spirit; it conflicts with entrenched national attitudes. That is why I often think of Gandhi's experiments with truth whenever one of my students mimes the tantalizing trope that the United States is the greatest country and the best democracy the world has ever seen. We've all heard this hegemonic maxim many, many times; it is often presented as a taken-for-granted expression of US reality.

But that notion is little more than the teat of the empire, the milk that every American school student suckles on from first grade through high school or risks going hungry and becoming a dissenting outsider. It is an attitude that slams the door shut on doubt, keeping humility at bay while allowing vainglory and the presumptuousness of empire in through every nook and cranny of the public house. If we have the greatest democracy ever and if we keep reminding ourselves of this so-called fact then that is the end of the story. Worse still, it is also the end of our daily experiments with improving democracy. We risk making democracy pro forma, only aping the tired motions rather than actually experimenting with new approaches to democracy and therefore embracing different results.

An admirer and serious student of Gandhi, McCarthy rejects this imperial presumptuousness both as a citizen and as teacher. He embraces each day and each class session as another opportunity to experiment in truth-seeking about democracy and its relations to peace and violence with his colleagues—his students. He not only gives them permission to be dissenting outsiders, he encourages it, presenting dissent as part of their experiments in acquiring knowledge through developing their own truths.

These are heartfelt letters from his students, often written in direct response to some provocative pedagogical tactic McCarthy deployed in a class session to invite his students into experimenting with truth. What makes these exchanges so fascinating and keeps us reading is that the letter-writers probe and poke at their teacher in the same ways that he no doubt probed and poked at the unexamined dimensions of their lives.

For example, in one of these fascinating exchanges, a student is puzzling over voting in elections and wants McCarthy to better explain his position because she was initially "outraged" that he did not vote. McCarthy's letter in response shows him to be not only a dissenter living out a daily experiment with the meanings of democracy but a patient and inspiring teacher in the classroom and beyond:

> People who vote are placing their faith in politicians who believe in violent solutions to conflicts. As a pacifist, it is only in political

elections that I decline to vote. I vote every day to get up at 6 am to teach my high school classes, I vote every day to buy healthy and cruelty-free food. I vote every day to commute by bicycle. I vote every day to spend time with my family. I vote every day to buy products that do no harm to the environment. To my mind, that is true voting power—occurring every day—that has nothing to do with electoral politics that involves passively pulling a lever once every four years.

This book about teaching is just as much about extending teaching beyond the classroom through letter writing. It works well because of the variety of approaches and tones that McCarthy takes in his responses to the letters from his students. Some of McCarthy's letters are witty and sharp, and he seems to have the knack of his Irish ancestors for using just the right amount of sarcasm, something that is too easily and too often overdone in hands less deft than his. In some letters he embraces the mentor role and guides the student into a deeper analysis through some engaging story. Elsewhere McCarthy seems more like a compassionate colleague, reciprocating the student's vulnerability by taking them into his confidence and relating his own struggles, his own daily experiments. In other letters he stands in solidarity with a moral choice a student has made, signaling the encouragement and support they seem to seek from their former teacher in order to live out a critical and ultimately dissenting life within the American experiment with democracy.

In still other instances McCarthy presents his personal positions without nuance and in a way that seems designed to goad. These provocations force his student, and now us readers, to think critically and to confront those many taken-for-granted presumptions about the meanings of individual freedom and the responsibilities of democratic citizenship in which we are awash in the United States. I should say that I don't often teach in the assertive, advocacy-based way that McCarthy does in his correspondence with students and that he also apparently habitually does in the classroom. But these letters from his students—which demonstrate the profound and long-lasting impact his approach has on them—are forcing me to be less cautious.

The book is brimming with a hard-won wisdom that is rooted in a lifetime of intentional choices the author has made as both a journalist and a teacher. In one recent semester McCarthy was teaching eight classes in six schools, ranging from high school to university to law school! He estimates that he has taught over ten thousand students in thirty years. Some of the high school teaching has been as a volunteer, while the university gigs are as an adjunct, for what he accurately calls "stoop wages." I suspect it is only his dedication to this avocation as a lived experiment in truthful teaching that moves it beyond being the exploitative labor that marks adjunct teaching in today's educational marketplace. While his love of teaching defines the book, McCarthy is no Pollyanna. He tells one student, "Grading is the foulest part of teaching. Grading is degrading. The second foulness is answering emails from students wondering, in mild but emphatic indignation, why I gave them a B instead of an A."

This is no cookbook for instruction, but it is laced with creative pedagogical techniques, some of which I intend to shamelessly lift and use because they are based on the best kind of teaching: cooperative, elicitive, and participatory learning that draws on the experiences and wisdom already in the room. In sharing with us these often deeply personal exchanges with his students, Colman McCarthy has once again expanded the walls of the classroom, this time letting us all in to join in the experiments. Were thousands of Americans to thoughtfully read these thoughtful letters, we may yet come to a collective understanding of what it takes to be the best the US should ever hope to be: a great experiment in democracy.

—Patrick G. Coy
Professor of Political Science and Conflict Management
Director, Center for Applied Conflict Management
Kent State University

Preface

Fortune and the kindness of the Jesuit fathers brought me to Spring Hill College in Mobile, Alabama, as its commencement speaker in May 1997. Excessively, the good priests spiced the day with an add-on, an honorary degree. Another recipient was on hand: Harper Lee.

Although it was not a long journey to Spring Hill from Miss Lee's home in nearby Monroeville, it had been years since she had traveled much at all. She wasn't quite in the J. D. Salinger league of eremitic living, but she was close. The college, where Flannery O'Connor spoke when I was an undergraduate in the early 1960s, felt blessed by the gods or at least the Holy Spirit to have landed so luminous a literary light as Harper Lee. It was rare for the iconic author of *To Kill a Mockingbird* to appear publicly for any kind of academic honor.

An Associated Press story carried in the *Tuscaloosa News* reported that "the appearance was not publicized and the reclusive author did not submit to any interviews, but Harper Lee graciously—and quietly—accepted an honorary degree and a standing ovation. . . . Miss Lee glanced from side to side, her eyes wide with surprise, as the crowd stood and applauded her Sunday. She has spent nearly four decades avoiding this kind of adoration."

Before the ceremony, in the wardrobe room where trustees, deans, professors, and the rest of us were suiting up in commencement regalia, I suggested to the Spring Hill president that it would be fine with me and definitely better for the graduates if Harper Lee, with her true star quality, gave the speech. Not a chance, he said. She had been asked months before but had emphatically refused. It took major persuasion to have her there at all for the degree.

I was paired with Miss Lee in the procession down the college's Avenue of the Oaks, and with four hundred giddy graduates and their families sitting on both sides, we had a few minutes for conversation: the luck of a sunny day, her trip from Monroeville, mine from Washington. Then a question, from me: "Are you writing much?" "All the time," she said. "Every day."

I needed to think. How had I missed her books? I couldn't remember a review in the *New York Times*, the *Washington Post*, the *Nation*, or anywhere. Did I miss her on C-SPAN's *Booknotes*? Apologetically, I confessed that I did not know the names of her latest books but would like to order them. "The titles?"

There are no books, she said. "I write letters to schoolchildren. They write to me about *Mockingbird* and I send back my thoughts."

I can't remember much of what I offered the graduates that day, and am certain they don't either, but I've never forgotten the purity of Harper Lee's line and the grace behind it: "I write letters to schoolchildren." How many thousands there must have been over the years. Her full writing life—an outpouring of words—had come one letter at a time, child by child.

The example of Harper Lee's commitment—the seriousness of it, the rarity—was an inspiration. Why don't I do that? In the years I was a columnist for the *Washington Post*, from 1969 to 1997, letters from children regularly came in. I would answer some, but not all. Diligence in letter writing had to be saved for what I mistakenly thought had a greater command on my time, such as answering readers who agreed with me.

On leaving the *Post*—editorially centrist and slinking to the right while I was edging further and further left—I increased my teaching commitments, which had originated in 1982 when I began volunteering at an impoverished public high school with fewer than three hundred students in downtown Washington. It lacked the basics: no auditorium, no gym, no cafeteria, no lockers, no athletic fields, and, for a time, no safe drinking water. Built during the administration of Ulysses S. Grant, it was certainly the poorest school in Washington, and perhaps the country, despite the intellectual richness of its stellar faculty. This was the School without Walls, a metaphorical name for an institution that specialized more in experiential learning outside the walls than on theoretical learning inside them. Students interested in politics could take on internships in Congress. If you saw yourself as a nurse, a physical therapist, or a physician, you could invest some time at the nearby George Washington University Hospital. If your enthusiasm was for the performing arts, you could spring for the Kennedy Center.

The School without Walls had another distinction beyond its poverty: it was five blocks west of the White House. No school was closer. Five blocks in the other direction was wealth: the Watergate apartments. Despite repeated invitations, no president had ever cared to hike the five blocks from the White House to visit the neighborhood school. They had time to roam the land orating on school reform—No Child Left Untested—but they couldn't make it five blocks. Students haven't minded. They aren't into big shots, they're into long shots. Seeing the odds against them, they know they better work twice as hard to make it.

As a columnist, I often wrote about the failures of schools and, with crass surety, flecked the columns with gimpy solutions. My weekly three-hour Wednesday seminar at Walls exposed me to how little I really knew about classroom education. At least now I could write columns with a measure of on-site credibility, rather than depend on clueless grandees on educational task forces dispensing their pedagogical insights on the failures of American schools. Early in their academic lives, students get the picture: schools trade in two kinds of knowledge, useful and useless. And much of it, groggily so, is the latter.

My Walls course was called "Alternatives To Violence." We read, discussed and debated the literature of peace, from the essays of Gandhi and Martin Luther King Jr., to Dorothy Day, Tolstoy, Gene Sharp, Emma Goldman, Emily Balch, Barbara Deming, Joan Baez, Daniel Berrigan, Scott and Helen Nearing, Howard Zinn, and a long list of others. Current events topics, taken off the front pages, included the death penalty, women's rights, animal rights, and militarism. After two years at Walls, I put together an anthology of peace essays: *Solutions to Violence*. Another collection followed, *Strength through Peace: The Ideas and People of Nonviolence*, and a third, *Peace Is Possible*.

As a pacifist as well as a journalist, I had been reporting, lamenting, and damning the world's violence, whether military violence across the ocean or domestic violence across the living room. To move beyond problem describing to solution finding, I accepted an invitation in 1984 to teach a peace studies course at American University, the first of its kind at the school. Within three years, more invitations came: the University of Maryland, Georgetown University Law Center, the Oak Hill, Maryland, juvenile prison, and the Washington Center for Internships and Academic Seminars. For three years, from 2002 to 2005, I was at Georgetown University. Those were afternoon or evening classes. Mornings I was volunteering at Wilson High School, and I taught daily 7:25 and 8:20 am classes at Bethesda–Chevy Chase High School. In the fall semester of 2012, I was teaching eight classes at six schools. I had the energy. Why not use it?

By rough count, I've taught more than ten thousand students in the past thirty years. A special joy of my teaching is being emotionally replenished by the energy of students as they move on and use the gifts I tried to nurture. It begins in the classroom when we create that rarest of delights between teachers and students: trust. We did away with the usual block to learning: the Powerful One lecturing the Powerless Many. Scrapping that, we debated, reflected, wrote, laughed, and risked, and way inside where all true spiritual growth occurs if we only dare it, together we loved to learn and learned to love.

With discussion-based, not lecture-based, classes we were able to talk heart to heart even if we didn't see eye to eye. Guest speakers came in, generously giving their time—more than four hundred over the years, of every stripe. They were capitalists, socialists, communists, militarists, internationalists, humanists, theists, atheists, traditionalists, nonconformists, environmentalists, theorists, anarchists, and pacifists. They were Nobel Peace Prize winners—Adolfo Pérez Esquivel, Mairead Corrigan and Muhammad Yunus. They were exonerated death row inmates; Vietnam, Iraq and Afghanistan war veterans; corporate lawyers and public interest lawyers; sentencing judges and sentenced defendants; warholics and peaceaholics; inner-city nurses and physicians; farmers; CEOs and COs; pastors; former Peace Corps, AmeriCorps, VISTA, and City Year volunteers; dissidents from the left and right; members of Congress, including Andy Jacobs, Elizabeth Furse, Connie Morella, Pat Williams, Harold Hughes, John Melcher, and Chris Van Hollen; heralded leaders, thinkers, and artists such as Sargent Shriver, Tim Shriver, Mark Shriver, Joan Baez, Howard Zinn, Peter Yarrow, Patch Adams, Si Kahn, George Pelecanos, and Ernesto Cardinal; Olympians and Special Olympians, Army psychiatrists; migrant workers; former prostitutes; school janitors; cops; historians; writers; parents and grandparents; the scorned and silenced; the homeless and the luckless.

At Bethesda–Chevy Chase, the most frequent guest speaker has been Lily Flores. I invite her every semester. For me, she ranks as the most accomplished and the most life-experienced teacher at the school, even though she never went past the eighth grade. Lily, now in her early forties and the single mother of three, including a boy with Down syndrome, is from El Salvador. She fled her village in the mid-1980s, at the height of the civil war in which both the Carter and Reagan administrations sided with the brutal Salvadoran government and its terrorizing military. In late 1979, Archbishop Oscar Romero of San Salvador pleaded with President Jimmy Carter not to send weapons to the Salvadoran military. Carter, the future Nobel Peace Prize winner, ignored the request and sent weapons. In the next decade, the sorry Reagan decade, seventy thousand died, including nuns, priests, labor leaders, social workers, and Romero himself during Mass on March 24, 1980. Much of the bloodletting was from thugs trained by the US Army at Fort Benning, Georgia, at what was then called the School of the Americas, also known as the School of Assassins.

Fleeing El Salvador at the age of fifteen, Lily made her way to southern Florida and labored as a field worker picking tomatoes and cucumbers. The pay was low, enslaving row bosses were ruthless, living conditions were squalid, and the companies to which the crops would be sold—McDonald's and Burger King among others—were uncaring about worker's rights. Lily endured for a year.

She then made her way north to Montgomery County, Maryland, outside Washington, where an older brother had settled. In time she found work at Bethesda–Chevy Chase, a jewel of a high school. Her job has been cleaning toilet bowls and urinals, scrubbing floors in the building's lavatories, picking up trash in the cafeteria after lunch, washing windows, buffing walls. Lily is one of the invisible people at the high school. Few students know her name, fewer still her background in El Salvador. Lily makes life easier for the students, cleaning up after them as they rush past her on the way to the next period's class.

Come talk to my students, I asked Lily. Tell them about your childhood, your days in south Florida, your children, your work in the bathrooms. Despite a hard life, Lily has not been hardened. She sprinkles her stories with humor, as when she asks the class why it is that the girls' bathrooms are always messier than the boys.' That stirs things up.

During Lily's talk one morning a few years ago, I noticed that one student, Hannah Flamm, was listening far more intently than the others. She took notes, the only one to do so. Hannah and Lily were connecting. At the end of the school day, at 2:10 pm, students headed to the parking lots, to after-school sports, the walk home. Every student left, except one: Hannah. Where did she go? To find Lily. And she did find her—in one of the bathrooms. She offered to help. She did so that afternoon and many more after. That summer, in 2004, Hannah went to El Salvador with a volunteer program, where she learned experientially about Lily's homeland. It would be the first of eleven visits to Hacienda Vieja, a village of some hundred families two hours by bus north of San Salvador, the capital. Her toils ranged from mentoring children to investigating the environmental and social effects of a proposed gold mining operation.

Following one of the trips, in the summer of 2005, Hannah wrote to me:

> I just returned from El Salvador. If you can't find me in four years, you know where to look. I am in love with that country. Living with the people and becoming so integrated in their lives and lifestyle makes it difficult to come back. This year's "peacemaking" consisted of building an after-school center for two weeks and then working for another week in the village I went to last year. We also spent several days in the capital, learning about the history of the country, the war, Oscar Romero, NAFTA and the current government. What was just as interesting as the information we were getting was the way the Salvadorans with us received it. They had never had the opportunity to learn their own history, and I watched them go from feeling ashamed that we, from the US, knew more about their country than they did, to feeling angry at their government for not trying to educate its people, to feeling energized to bring back what they had learned to their communities.
>
> Last year's village was more progressive than the new one this year. I had my first encounter with machismo. Guys came up to me on the worksite saying I couldn't carry the cement buckets. I shouldn't be working outside, I wasn't strong enough to lift blocks. The first time someone told me to put down the shovel, I was surprised, but didn't think to put up a fight. I handed him the shovel and felt defeated like I never have been before. And that was the last time anyone told me what to do. I've never felt defeated like that, and I've never started giving orders like that, either. The masons and "maestro de obra" (guy in charge of construction) were coming up to me asking me to

tell the guys to work or leave. By the second week women from the community were picking up shovels too! Some men changed—and even apologized for their earlier words—and others left, including one mason who couldn't handle me (a girl!) laying cinderblock for the walls. Oh well.

Hannah went on Tufts University, majored in political science, and graduated in February 2009. In the spring of 2014, she was completing her second year at New York University Law School and planning to become a public interest lawyer.

Other students at Bethesda–Chevy Chase had trouble understanding why Hannah helped Lily with her work. I saw it as true peacemaking—a genuine reaching out to lift another person's spirit, even if it was in the smallest of ways like moving a mop over a dirty floor. Years later when I catch up with former students from the school and we get talking about the class, a common question is, "How's Lily?" She left a mark, gifted teacher that she is.

Other speakers did also. What unified them was passion, whether for a cause, a mission, or a belief. That was the only requirement for being invited. Students hunger for role models, and to meet them in the close quarters of a classroom—to speak with them, to question them, to be leveled with—can be the purest and most lasting kind of learning.

From my own childhood, it was a classroom visitor who started me thinking about newspapering. Thomas J. Hamilton of the *New York Times* came to Glen Head Elementary School on Long Island's North Shore in 1948 when I was ten. His children, Anita and Bill, were schoolmates of mine. Georgia-born, a man of mettle who spoke softly with a slight southern accent, Hamilton said that the best journalists were almost always driven by immense curiosity: who, what, where, when, and why. Remember the five Ws, he advised us fourth graders, and you won't go wrong.

Hamilton was thirty-five at the time, just then picking up speed in a career that would go for three and a half decades with the Times and see him report from bureaus in Bonn, Geneva, London, Madrid, Washington, and the United Nations. Hearing this Timesman's stories in my classroom had me thinking that this could be the life for me. And why wait to get into the game? I started my class newspaper right then, with the first issue leading with the story of Hamilton's talk. Years later, in 1983, I paid back a bit of what I owed by visiting him in a retirement community in Southbury, Connecticut, to offer thanks for first shining a light in my life—one that keeps guiding me—and to pose the five Ws to write a column about him for the *Washington Post*. His son Bill, who married Jane Mayer of the *New Yorker*, became a national editor at the *Post* and a close colleague of mine.

Speakers who graced my classes would always receive thank-you letters from my students, guided by a two-line Ogden Nash–style poem: "If you have an attitude of gratitude, you gain altitude and fortitude."

One speaker who offered high and lasting value to my students was Joan Baez. I came to know her in the 1970s. Returning from concert tours in countries where men and women were stashed in dungeons and tortured, she would often pass through Washington on her way to her home in Woodside, California. She supplied me with column material: well-sourced information and documents about specific cases in various countries, from Chile and Argentina to Poland and South Africa. In 1983 I invited her to speak to my class at the School without Walls, one that met from 12:30 to 3:00 pm. Not possible: that was the time she was preparing for her evening concert, she said. Instead, bring the students to Constitution Hall and she would host a backstage seminar after the concert on nonviolence and human rights. She comped more than $1,000 worth of up-front tickets. Parents of some students—assorted lefties, Woodstock rebels, and Newport Folk Festival veterans with caches of Baez albums in the attic—had heartburn. Free tickets for my kids? What about us? The more creative moms and dads revived their old crashing skills and, to their children's red-faced embarrassment, slipped into the seminar.

Joan, sitting atop a dressing table and not far from a table holding sandwiches, fruit, and juices that she ordered for everyone, began with stories about her Quaker childhood, marching with Martin Luther King Jr. in the South, and her commitment to Gandhian nonviolence. Earlier, the students loved her singing. Backstage they connected quickly with her mind. She was not a star now. Better, she was a friendly, open-minded person coming on as a constellation of ideas, questions, opinions, and reconsiderations. In spirals of anecdotes and theories, she built a case that gradually peaked into the high ideal that radical nonviolence is the soundest and only answer worth offering to children: "I understand any kid who looks at the news and says, 'I wanna smoke dope for the rest of my life.' It's so huge what we are facing, so scary."

Joan said her commitment to nonviolence was to offer to young people alternatives to despair.

A few months after the backstage seminar, Joan wrote in her Humanitas International newsletter about the evening with my Walls students:

> Looking back on it, I think I got more out of that meeting than I did out of anything else during the tour. The students were racially, economically and politically mixed, and fairly knowledgeable, and very bright. Their discussion of social issues, viewed in the context of nonviolence, was honest, astute, intelligent but most striking of all, characterized by a sort of dignified cynicism and resignation. It seemed that these kids were all coping, each in his or her own private way, with the fear of a nuclear holocaust, which has to affect everyone's behavior, whether they accept or deny the reality of the situation—and the job of coping is taking up a lot of energy. One girl talked about her inability to read a newspaper or watch the news on television because it was too emotionally demanding. If she exhausted her feelings on the news, she feared she wouldn't have enough left to react to those things that ought to matter to her. Even the death of a relative, she confided, might not stir her from the indifference that seemed to consume her after watching the news.
>
> But of all that we talked about that evening, the one thought that struck me most, and which moved me to realize that it was time to reorganize my life once again, was a very simple one. It came from a 16-year-old boy whose "punk" styles included blond spikes in his hair, black jeans and a leather jacket. He sat casually near me on a couch, his motorcycle helmet in his lap. He called himself Dante, and he was clearly well-liked by the rest of the class. He had mused, participated, joked and now seemed to sum things up: "You see," he said, "you guys in the '60's had everything. You had the music, the issues, the symbols, the momentum. You had each other. You had glue. We are missing that. We don't have any glue."
>
> There was unanimous agreement in the room and I saw instantly that this statement rang true not only for young people but certainly for me, and, as I have found since that evening for practically everyone I meet. We are all so caught up in our individual problems and struggles that we have no attachment to others whose problems and

struggles are so very much like our own. We need some common bonding ingredient—some social and political "glue." Following that conversation, at the remaining concerts on the tour, I began testing this notion. "I know that there are intelligent people all over the world," I would say. "It's just that we have to discover each other." Audiences seemed to respond with enthusiasm.

～ ～ ～

Although awareness is growing that unless we teach our children peace someone else may teach them violence, a few foothills need to be ascended, and an Alp or two after, before peace education is promoted either by politicians nationally or by school boards locally. Is it imaginable that a presidential State of the Union address will call for peace universities to be built—an East Point Peace Academy across the Hudson River from the United States Military Academy at West Point—and given equal funding? I know of no American high school, public or private, that has a peace studies department equal in budget and staff to the math or science departments. Or how about an even wilder vision: as much money for peace studies as for the football team, and salaries for the teachers equal to those of coaches.

Higher education is sunnier. In 1970 only one school, Manchester College, a Church of the Brethren school in Indiana, offered a degree in peace studies. By last count, more than seventy schools had come around, with nearly three hundred sponsoring minors or concentrations. The schools with degrees in peace studies include American University, Notre Dame, Guilford, Hobart and William Smith, Goshen, the University of San Diego, Colgate, the University of Colorado, Goucher, Tufts, Manhattan, Earlham, and the University of Missouri.

To discover how knowledgeable students might be, I use the first minutes of class on a quiz—my $100 bill quiz. Identify six historical figures. I begin with Robert E. Lee. Hands rise on that one. Ulysses S. Grant. More hands. Napoleon Bonaparte. No problem there. Nearly everyone is three for three. Next name: Emily Balch. No response. Jody Williams. No hands. Jeannette Rankin. One or two hands, sometimes. I've done this quiz hundreds of times, in classes and during talks at high schools and colleges around the country. Even before teacher groups. It's risk-free, safe money. I can always count on American miseducation.

Students get the point of the quiz: they've been well taught about men who break the peace but know little or nothing about women who make the peace. Balch, a co-founder of the Women's International League for Peace and Freedom, won the Noble Peace Prize in 1946. Williams of Vermont won the prize in 1997 for her work to abolish land mines. Jeannette Rankin, a pacifist, was the only member of Congress to vote against US participation in World Wars I and II—on the basis of her view that you can no more win a war than win an earthquake.

After a few weeks into my course, whether it was called The Literature of Peace, Alternatives to Violence, or Journalism and Peace, students had a common plaint: why is it only now that we are learning that moral force can be superior to violent force for trying to manage or resolve conflicts They sensed they had been cheated, strung along. They weren't exposed to the thinking of Hannah Arendt: "Violence, like all action, changes the world but the most probable change is to a more violent world." Or to the thought of Theodore Roszak: "The usual pattern seems to be that people give nonviolence two weeks to solve their problem and then decide it failed. Then they go on with violence for the next hundred years." Or Desmond Tutu's belief: "The war against terrorism will not be won as long as there are people desperate with disease and living in poverty and squalor. Sharing our prosperity is the best weapon against terrorism."

Many students have endured or overcome violence in their own lives. Schoolyard bullying. Parents verbally abusing each other. Parental beatings. Neighborhood homicides. Date rape. Domestic violence. Gunplay. The violence of poverty. I've had students who survived war zones in their homelands: Iraq, Iran, El Salvador, Palestine, Israel, Northern Ireland, Afghanistan, Ivory Coast, Somalia, Serbia, Kosovo. At the end of every semester, I offered students a line from Woodrow Wilson when he served as president of Princeton: "The purpose of education is to make the young as unlike their elders as possible." Taking a course on pacifism and nonviolence all but ensures that the likenesses will decrease and, if we push it, vanish.

What follows in these pages is a sampling of the correspondence between my former students and me. A few other exchanges have been added—for example, correspondence with teachers looking to expand beyond the conventional. The teachers range from a faculty member at Phillips Exeter Academy to a Virginia death row inmate who held seminars on nonviolence while he and others awaited execution.

Many of the students' letters, nearly half, were handwritten. In this over-hurried digitalizing age, in which send buttons and password protection appear to have replaced fingers and hands tactilely moving pencils and pens slowly across pages, which are folded and placed in envelopes to be dispatched with forever stamps, I was heartened by the many students who clung to the epistolary ways of communicating. Opening a letter is physical. Intimacy is present: I touch the paper. A tonic is present: the writer took time for me, a gift in itself. Reading the first lines are moments tinged with soft excitement, a caressing that Katherine Mansfield felt when writing to a friend: "This is not a letter but my arms around you for a brief moment."

Minor editing—occasional excisions or additions—has been done. Some letters were written from the depths of pain, others sparkle with stories of what their writers were discovering about life beyond high school and college. Some writers were seeking advice, wondering about possible career moves or asking which tailwinds they should catch to be happy in their personal lives.

Because I was an unsalaried volunteer at two of the three high schools, and was paid little more than stoop labor wages at the third and as an adjunct professor at the universities, I came to see the letters as my real paychecks. It was genuine wealth, the pure gold of an undeserved windfall. I was touched by the appreciative and loving words many of the students expressed for having taken my classes. I had done nothing special to earn the students' affection. It would have been lavished on any teacher who gave them a voice, who cared to listen, who pushed them not merely to ask questions but to question the answers and to doubt the prevailing consensus, and who set them on fire with the kind of combustibles that will burn a lifetime.

The letters here are a small sampling of the thousand or so I've been blessed to receive in the past three decades. I tried to repay the students' gratitude by taking their letters seriously and never replying lazily with two- or three-sentence quickies. I can't imagine good Harper Lee doing that.

Colman McCarthy
Washington, DC
February 2014

To find the way to make peace with ourselves and to offer it to others, both spiritually and politically, is the most important kind of learning. To accept our abilities and limitations, and the differences of others: this is the contentment that gives life its highest value. It frees us to grow without restraint and to settle without pressure.

—WENDY SCHWARTZ

Speak your truth.
Listen when others speak theirs, too.
When you let go of fear, you will learn to love others,
and you will let them love you.
Open your heart to love, for that is why you are here.

—MELODY BEATTIE

Letters

Dear Mr. McCarthy,

There are two reasons for this letter. First, I have for some time followed your columns and have developed quite a respect for your abilities as a writer. That respect recently increased considerably when I opened my newest textbook to find a reproduction of your January 2, 1987, column. I read, instantly copied and almost as quickly memorized your list of 10 writing rules, promoted you to "mentor" from "writer-to-admire" and resolved to write you a letter gushing with praise and gratitude. I didn't write it because I soon doubted my ability to do so without violating one of more of the rules, and because there wasn't much to say except to announce myself as an amateur/admirer who aspires in her secret dreams to one day do what you do.

Well, that's one day. Today I am a midshipman at the United States Naval Academy, aspiring to the service of my country, and that, combined with a more recent column, is why I am writing now.

Sir, you have some crazy ideas about women and war. Rule #1: "say what you mean." In your January 14 column you said: "War is a male ritual based on a hyper-masculine ethic that violence is rational. Linda Bray in Panama [the first woman to lead US troops in combat, during the US invasion in 1983] was less a victory for female rights than for male wrongs. She bought into traditional masculinism: fists, guns, armies and killing are sensible solutions to problems."

As far as I can determine, the main thrust of your column is that "war is bad." Sir, I certainly do not disagree. I completely respect your right to be as anti-war and anti-military as you like. However, as a woman in the military, I take great offense at your using the premise that "war is bad" as a launching pad from which to attack Capt. Bray for doing her job. I agree that her role in the conflict—and the fact that she performed her job in a combat capacity—has been overplayed. But I would hardly accuse her of "leading the charge up Mt. Equality." She followed her orders, nothing more.

I cannot speak for Capt. Bray or for all women in the military. I only speak for myself. And you made several assumptions about me that I would like the opportunity to correct. By being in the military wearing a uniform and serving my country, I am not "buying into traditional masculinism," as you put it. I do not believe any more than you that "fists, guns, armies and killing are sensible solutions to problems." And no, I do not believe that Capt. Bray simply accomplishing her given mission provides eternally irrefutable proof that men and women should be side by side in the trenches forevermore. I am, however, unlike you, very much in support of Rep. Pat Schroeder's legislative proposal. Her proposed bill would allow a period of testing for combat roles for women. The issue of women in combat is not going to disappear, and Rep. Schroeder's bill is the first positive step I have seen anyone take toward resolving it.

I don't know the answers. The arguments you and several others have presented against women in combat are valid ones. But the "license to rape" issue that you mention is a problem of war and not a problem of women in war. The solution you offer in your column is the "abolition" of war, and frankly I'm all for that. However, while you columnists and politicians in Washington are working on that one, as a young woman about to become a military officer, I'd like to see more constructive work toward resolving our continuing problems of integration and less pointless prattle about the inequality of the sexes.

There are countless combat roles that women can do as well as men. I can learn to fly an F-14 as effectively as any of my classmates, but at the same time I am under no illusions about my physical limitations in other roles. I appreciate that my male counterpart can run faster and jump higher with a 20-pound pack on his back, and is therefore much better suited to certain combat roles. I am not asking for that kind of "job equality." Like most women in the military I would not want a job that physical limitations would prevent me from doing well. On the contrary, I hope that when the time comes, Congress does not prevent me from doing the job I have been trained to do, as Capt. Bray did in Panama. It cannot longer be a question whether or not women are capable of firing the guns, flying the planes, driving the ships and leading the troops. The question remaining is whether or not America is ready to accept that equality and begin to take advantage of the full resources of military women.

I'm honestly not sure if this country is ready. I am however more than ready to find out, and so is Rep. Pat Schroeder.

Why aren't you?

Sincerely,

Tara Lee

Dear Tara,

Half a ton of thanks for your letter, and a full ton for its impassioned language. When I was in college I dreamed, as you do now, of earning a living as a writer. Plenty of room is available for you in this calling, even if you have to call yourself, which is fine because usually no one will or should.

You're right that the "main thrust" of my column was, in your words, "war is bad." If you agree with that, as you say you do, why are you in a school dedicated to war preparation? The Naval Academy has its portion of quality professors, some of whom I came to know when I was invited to speak in writing classes. Many of the students have as high ideals as those in the classes I teach at the University of Maryland and Georgetown Law.

None of that alters what you are being trained to do: kill people and destroy property if the order is given. "Aspiring to the service of my country" is a pseudo-patriotic slogan. When commissioned, you won't be serving your country, you'll be serving those who run the country. A large difference. In *The Kingdom of God Is Within You*, Leo Tolstoy wrote, "Government is an association of men who do violence to the rest of us." Why serve those men? Government-sanctioned slaughter, otherwise known as war, has caused the deaths of eight million people in this century. Some 40,000 are killed a month in current wars and conflicts. Last December between 1,000 and 4,000 people were killed in the US invasion of Panama. The Pentagon doesn't know or care how many Panamanian civilians were killed, hence the estimates of between 1,000 and 4,000. Instead of a national debate on the morality of sending any US soldier—male or female—to slaughter Panamanians, the triviality of women's role in combat has been the preoccupation.

It's beneath both of us to be sucked into it. What we should be doing, instead, is examining our consciences to be as certain as possible that we are using our time and energy to decrease the violence of war. How is that done? By acting, in our personal and professional lives, on what David Dellinger said on entering prison in 1943 [as a conscientious objector]: "Very few people choose war. They choose selfishness and the result is war. Each of us, individually and nationally, must choose: total love or total war."

We are what we choose.* Perhaps my choices are flawed and someday I will come to my senses and abandon what you call my "crazy ideas." I've been tempted often, except that occasional events affirm my theories. Twenty years ago Gene Sharp wrote in *The Politics of Nonviolent Action*: "The essence of power is not in military might. People are ruled by the state to the degree that they cooperate with the state. The state loses its power to the degree that the people withdraw or sever their cooperation."

Yes, I've been told by the knowledgeable and worldly-wise, try selling that in Eastern Europe. But now that the dictatorships in Poland and Romania have fallen, Gene Sharp is seen to have been right. Such pacifists as Lech Walesa are cheered in Congress while his philosophy is ignored. He said: it is due "to nonviolence that I am where I am now. I am a man who believes in dialogue and agreement. I strongly believe that the 21st century will not be a century of violence. We've already tried and tested every form of violence, and not once in the entire course of human history has anything good or lasting come from it."

But we still don't get it. American politicians go on with our war preparation economy and arming the world. Weapon sales to Third World governments increased 66 percent in 1988 over the previous year. Yes, some parts of our system are worth fighting for, but how do we fight? Again, choices. There's George Patton: "I want you to remember that no dumb bastard ever won a war by dying for his country. He won it by making the other dumb bastard die for his country." Or Albert Einstein: "Our schoolbooks glorify war and conceal its horrors. They indoctrinate children with hatred. I would teach peace rather than war, love rather than hate. . . . [People] should continue to fight, but they should fight for things worthwhile, not imaginary geographical lines, racial prejudices and private greed draped in the colors of patriotism. Their arms should be weapons of the spirit, not shrapnel and tanks."

Thanks for your letter. The Naval Academy is lucky to have you. I wish it served you better by offering courses on nonviolence. But the militarists who run your school, and the military-supporting Congress that lavishly bankrolls it, fear academic freedom and intellectual choices. You'll have to study it on your own, which takes us back to where I began. The study of peace is a calling, and we end up calling ourselves.

In friendship,

Colman McCarthy

I invited Tara, then an English major in the spring semester of her third year at the Naval Academy, to take my course Law, Conscience, and Nonviolence in the fall semester at Georgetown University Law Center. Come as my guest, I said. Open-minded, adventurous, and the owner of a red convertible that she liked to drive, she was able to persuade her commandant to allow her to take a weekly leave of absence to cruise over from Annapolis to Washington for my weekly Tuesday afternoon seminar. She received no credit for the course. Her interest was intellectual exploration. The class was small, twenty-four second- and third-year students. Tara relished the give and take jousts of our debates and discussions, plus the inevitable digressions once law students get going. I suspected that it wasn't the way classes at the Academy were run.

Tara, engaging and naturally friendly, easily fit in, even as she dressed in midshipman whites. That was enough for one of the lads in the class. He began dating Tara, but, alas, as much as she savored his attentions she feared the relationship wouldn't survive her five-year obligation to the Navy after graduation. The student, Merrick Alpert, was obliging. After Georgetown Law, he went on to do well in business and in 2010 ran for an open Senate seat from Connecticut in the Democratic primary. He gave it full effort—walking across the state in a campaign reminiscent of Senator William Proxmire's reelection hikes across Wisconsin—but he was no match for the better known Richard Blumenthal, the state's attorney general, who won the primary and then the general election.

Halfway through the semester Tara confided to me that a bit of stereotyping was going on. At the Academy fellow midshipmen saw her as a secret hippie-liberal consorting with the enemy—the subversive, long-haired left at Georgetown Law—while at the law school some of her classmates viewed her as sunk in military conservatism. As they always are, the labels were hollow. Both sides had it wrong, Tara said: "I'm just me."

Tara's fidelity to the weekly commute was, for me, a touching example of desire-based learning.

More than once during the semester I wondered where the course and its literature would take Tara, if anywhere. Five years after leaving the Academy— she had invited me to her graduation to meet her parents—Tara called. Stationed at a southern California naval base, she had been going to law school at night and had earned her juris doctor degree from the University of San Diego Law School. She specialized in public interest law and worked at a children's advocacy institute. She won two awards: the Outstanding Future Trial Lawyer and the Outstanding Student in Public Interest Law. While volunteering at a shelter for homeless women with the law school's clinic, she represented abused children. "You can leverage change with a law degree," she said. "Kids are the most undefended people in America."

In the spring of 2012, Tara Lee, now married with four children and living in the Washington area, is a managing partner in DLA Piper, an international law firm with more than four thousand attorneys in forty-three nations. In 2007, working as a pro bono co-counsel with the Center for Justice and Accountability she made repeated and excessively dangerous trips to Somalia to gather evidence of war crimes and crimes against humanity committed by war lords in the 1980s. In the February 2010 *Journal of International Peace Operations*, she wrote:

> For a lot of Americans, awareness of Somalia and its violent history begins with "Black Hawk Down" and the humanitarian crisis that followed the fall of the Siad Barre regime—Somalia's last recognized government—and subjected its citizens in the north to an internationally recognized, well-documented pattern of human rights abuses, arbitrary detentions and extra-judicial killings. Those abuses reached a violent peak in June 1988 when the civilian population of Hargeisa was decimated by a month of indiscriminate aerial bombardment and artillery shelling. . . . During that same month hundreds of civilians in Hargeisa were rounded up and shot, their bodies dumped into mass graves around the cities. Planning to visit and document the mass gravesites, I expected to see mounds of dirt, solemnly marked and reverently kept. But at each site I visited in Hargeisa the only markers were the memories of those who had miraculously survived and the briar bushes locals dragged over to cover the mounds. Every few days they repositioned the briars to help protect the sites from animals that might drag away the human remains. Previously, locals had described to me how the rains washed away layers of dirt each year, exposing and sweeping away bones. I interviewed survivors of the mass executions, men who had somehow avoided death when they were lined up with the friends and brothers and shot in tight groups. Despite these descriptions, I was unprepared for what I saw. Exposed human bones littered the ground of Malko Dur-Duro. Spring rains

were especially destructive, deeply churning the soil. All around me white bone fragments jutted out of the dusty earth, through the tire tracks and in the gullies left by rainwater. Many of the bones lay loose and apart, unrecognizable at first as human remains. In some places there were so many, and I was so unsure of what I was seeing that it was hard not to step on the bones before I realized what they were. And then, 20 feet away, one piece was unmistakable: a human jaw bone half-covered in the dirt, many of its teeth still intact.

Tara's interviews of survivors led to the successful prosecution of Somalia's main war criminal. Under the Foreign Sovereign Immunities Act, she argued and won the case in the US Court of Appeals for the Fourth Circuit, a decision later affirmed 9-0 before the Supreme Court.

In late April 2012, I invited Tara to speak to my Peace and Social Justice seminar at American University. As relaxed and engaging as she was twenty years earlier in my law class, she detailed her work in Somalia of tracking down victims of violence in remote villages to gather evidence that would hold up in court.

I had my students write thank-you letters to Tara. One was from Grace Armstrong, a sophomore from northern California:

Dear Tara Lee,

Your visit to our class was the most fortunate thing that has happened to me all year. Your journey and accomplishments are truly inspiring. Having traveled to Africa as a blond, white female I connect with a lot of your trials and tribulations. The work you have done for the Somali people is amazing and gives me encouragement. Listening to your story encouraged me to pursue my passion: law and human rights. I am so glad to have met you and in one afternoon I see you becoming a role model in my life. Thank you so much for your time. Thank you. Thank you.

Best,

Grace Armstrong

Dear Colman,

Well, here I am, five years after resisting, arguing and disagreeing with you in Peace Studies class [at Bethesda–Chevy Chase High School]. Now I'm a firm believer and have committed two years to the Peace Corps

Of course I'm in a country [Bolivia] where the very same US government that I'm working for is promoting war and working in the exact opposite direction of the Peace Corps's three goals: (1) assist development by providing technical expertise, (2) improve other nation's citizens' knowledge of America, (3) improve Americans' knowledge of other nations.

The war on drugs, being waged in full effect here, (1) burns coca fields, kills/imprisons campesinos, encourages farmers to switch to other crops with which they go bankrupt; (2) creates an image of Americans among Bolivians as violently militant destructive imperialist dictators; (3) creates a complete shroud of ignorance in the US whereby most Americans probably don't even know where Bolivia is, let alone that last year over $120 million of their tax money came here, largely to fight this failed war on drugs that has ZERO impact on US drug consumption and destabilizing this already unstable democracy and trashing the world's perception of America and Americans.

The worst part of it is the current point man in the State Department for the war on drugs is a former ambassador to Bolivia and a firm believer that we can win this war. So even if the current ambassador tries to tell Washington that this effort is a failure (new acres of coca planted far exceed total acres eradicated, coca production is going up) and that it's having serious negative impacts on the country. There is no one in DC who will hear him because this other official has seniority and will say, "That's not true! I was there. I know we can win this war." I don't know his name but this same man is a returned Peace Corps volunteer.

Colman, if you wrote a column about this, if *60 Minutes* did a report, if somehow word got out in the US what is really happening, what our government is really doing, I don't think there would be any support in Congress for continuing the war on drugs here. As it is, congressmen themselves don't even know where Bolivia is. One congressman from Indiana, Dan Burton, suggested in official remarks before the House that we should put an aircraft carrier off the coast of Bolivia. Bolivia has no coast, it's landlocked! Every Bolivian gov't minister got a witty news bite out of that one.

The ignorance of the US government was the top story for a few days (e.g., they should figure out where Bolivia is on a map before they start dictating policy to us).

Did the *Washington Post* even run a blurb about it? According to my parents, it didn't.

Anyways, I'm looking forward to my work. I hope I can make some small contribution. Bolivia has a lot of needs: nutrition, health, education, transportation. I'll probably do a side project with gardens and nutrition. I've never seen a starving underfed Bolivian. But in the campo most children are severely malnourished. With all the starch they eat, they get plenty of carbs but are way short of protein, vitamins and minerals, and are often learning disabled as a result.

There's a program called World Wise Schools where the Peace Corps links up volunteers with teachers back home. If you're interested, I'd love to be linked up with you and your class next year and relay what's going on here and how my work is going. Let me know if you think it'd fit your class.

I hope all is well with you.

Tu amigo,

Fred Werner, Peace Corps Bolivia (1995–97)

JANUARY 20, 1996

Dear Fred,

Please forgive me for being a bit behind on things but finally some time to catch up. I can't tell you how overjoyed I am that you are the Peace Corps. It's really a program with all kinds of benefits—to those you are working with there and to yourself. Your couple of years in Bolivia will be a bankable resource period for you, with high interest rates in the years ahead. I've had more than a few students who have served, from Zaire to Fiji—and it's pretty much the same: they come home enriched, often embarrassingly so, because they went overseas, they thought, to give, not receive.

One of my former students at Georgetown Law, Mark Gearan, is now the Peace Corps director. I had Mark in class in 1990, his final year. He went on to work in the Bill Clinton campaign, one of the first to believe an obscure Arkansas governor could win the presidency. Clinton brought Mark to the White House, and delivering a plum of plums, asked him to run the communications shop. He accepted, and four years later Clinton, delivering another plum, appointed him the director of the Peace Corps. The joke around the White House was that Mark Gearan was joining the Peace Corps but would he be sent to Micronesia, Thailand, Hungary, where? No, it would be to K Street, a backward outpost in the undeveloped world where the natives spoke in strange tongues.

As your sister Susan may have told you, we read your letter aloud in class. It was a lively morning, with a spirited discussion. Your comment about the irony of working on local development while the US-inspired drug war is having its own negative effects miles away was telling. Thanks for spelling it out so graphically. I often suggest to my students to think about working abroad for a few years after college, a chance to see themselves and the US from a new angle. Your letter certainly gave some fiber to my words. Don't worry. I told the class you regularly disagreed with my view and were one of my prize dissenters.

You mentioned that you'd be willing to write occasionally to my B-CC students about your experiences there. Yes, definitely. Anything you could do would be a major plus. I start with the spring semester in a few days, so this is the right time.*

Many blessings to you. I go back a long way with the Peace Corps, having come to Washington to work for Sargent Shriver, the first director, a close friend all these years. My wife and I were at his 80th birthday party the other night at his home in Potomac. Hordes of Peace Corps alums were there.

Be well and do well,

Colman

*Weeks later, Fred Werner wrote to my class. This is an excerpt.

Queridos todos,

Greetings from Bolivia! I have just completed three months of intensive training and was officially sworn in as a Peace Corps volunteer last Friday at the posh ambassador's residence in La Paz.

Living with Dona Vicky and her four sons in their adobe home near a dirt courtyard was an experience in itself. They were very friendly, the kids especially, always wanting to play games, even if it meant trying to sneak a dead minnow into my dinner bowl. On food, I'm still struggling to get used to large quantities of dry, bland, starch eaten here. Boiled potatoes at every meal, sometimes with rice or pasta, occasionally with meat, chicken and guinea pig, and rarely with fava beans or some other veggie.

My two years' service begins in a few days. I'll be living and working in Miska Mayu, a high valley 15 km (10 miles) off the highway, four hours east of the city of Cochabamba in the department (state) of the same name. It's cold with snow and hard freezes on winter nights (June–Sept.). But unlike many other sites in the high Andes, or the altiplano for that matter, it's very moist and green because there's one tall mountain range below Miska Mayu and the lush Amazonian rainforests that stretch several thousand miles to the north and east.

There's no real town center. Adobe houses are strung along the dirt road that follows the river at the valley bottom. . . . Most people have no access to running water. There are a few communal spigots. They say they're five years away from receiving electricity, which means they'll probably get it in 15 years. There are no telephones. We communicate with the city by radio. Oh: it's a Quechua-speaking community, though most adults also understand Spanish.

So what am I going to do there? I'm officially charged with helping campesinos build terraces, organizing nurseries and reforestation projects, and teaching environmental education in two schools. Kids go to school K-5, but they go half day and there are frequent teachers' strikes. Schools have been closed for 6 weeks now. We figured out the average Bolivian kid spends the equivalent of 3 months of a US school year in class.

In other parts of Bolivia, terracing has been practiced for thousands of years. We saw some still standing strong, built 2–3000 years ago by ancestors of the Incas. But Miska Mayu has neither terraces nor a tradition of building them. Also, almost the only type of tree is the Australian eucalyptus.

So I'm here as a foreigner to reintroduce ancient technology and native species.

I'll write more when I get the chance. Please drop me a line. It always brightens my day to hear from those I care about and how things are going back home.

Con cariño,

Fred Werner

⌣ ⌣ ⌣

Dear Professor McCarthy,

With the number of students you've taught over the years, the chances of you remembering me from the last peace studies class you taught at Catholic University in the spring of '05 are probably pretty slim. Nevertheless, I offer you this letter as an all-too-belated thank you for introducing me to Gandhi, Tolstoy, King, Merton, Day and many of the other authors we read who challenged my notions about the practicality of peace. Since then, these writers have become both staples in my library as well as friends visited and revisited for advice, encouragement or a challenging word.

Even more valuable, however, is the personal commitment to nonviolence I began to cultivate during your class. Although it seemed to make sense, a question many of us asked that semester was "How practical is this?" Luckily, I didn't have to wait very long to find out and, to my surprise, I didn't find the answer in the hypothetical caught-in-a-dark-alley scenario that we had all imagined would someday test us.

After graduation, I decided to spend a few months volunteering at a Catholic Worker house of hospitality providing basic services to folks living on the streets in downtown Phoenix, Arizona. Though ostensibly I was there at the service of those who came in needing shade, a shirt, a shower, a phone call or a meal, I found myself repeatedly berated, cursed, spit at, screamed at and on two occasions violently attacked. Although these were perhaps the most personally and spiritually challenging encounters of my life, I never struck back but rather focused on meeting the abuse with love and patience. Of course, none of this is to my credit—I am indebted entirely to the grace of God. But my familiarity with the philosophies I learned in your class helped me see the good in these troubling experiences. I came away with the understanding that nonviolence is a work of mercy and forgiveness, begging us to forget ourselves in favor of the other when it is hardest to: when we have been injured.

I just thought that I would share some of my experiences since I believe you had a hand in shaping them. And maybe you would like to know that at least one of the seeds you planted in our class has taken root. As a side note, I've since returned to Washington, DC, and I work providing material and spiritual assistance to families living in project neighborhoods is Southeast DC. It's been a great blessing.

Thanks for everything, Colman.

Peace be with you,

Ryan Hehman

Dear Ryan,

How well and fully you are using yours gifts. And how quickly it has happened. Not many leave college and find a place, right away, to put their spirituality to work. From Catholic University to the Catholic Worker. I'd like to think that happened often but I'd need more evidence. From my years of teaching there I found only a few students who had read Dorothy Day or subscribed to the *Catholic Worker* newspaper. In a moment of giddiness I once suggested to a dean that a course should be offered on Dorothy Day. I might as well have proposed a course on Doris Day for all it mattered.

Perhaps I'm being harsh, because about 20 years ago some Catholic U students did indeed know about Dorothy Day and put her ideals into action. You'll be both heartened and surprised to know that it happened exactly where you are now living, at 939 T NW in Washington. In the mid-1980s Michael Kirwan, the grandson of Congressman Michael (Honest Mike) Kirwan of Youngstown, Ohio, was just beginning his apostolate to the city's hungry and homeless. Dorothy Day often stayed during her travels with the Kirwan family in Michael's boyhood. After the *Washington Post* wrote about his work, he received a donation, one large enough to buy the residence at 939 T. He called it the Llewellyn Scott Catholic House of Hospitality. At times, as many as 30 men and women were given space: alcoholics, drifters, prostitutes all trying to make it back up. Some stayed a night or two, others for long stretches, while Michael lived in a third floor garret no larger than a monk's cell. One year, an architecture professor at Catholic University and a believer in experiential learning, inspired his students to renovate the house. For months, they banged, scraped, painted, nailed, disinfected and spruced.

I wrote a column about their toils, one of many involving Michael Kirwan. The final one—his obituary—ran in November 1999. Dozens of times during the 1980s and '90s I brought my students to 939 T Street, to witness the work of Michael. Better to see a sermon than hear one.

That's all I've wanted to achieve as a teacher: offer students a few ideas about increasing peace and decreasing violence, and nudging them to use their moral and intellectual gifts to help make it happen. I'm heartened you have committed yourself to that.

Years, sometimes decades, must pass before our gifts are used. In the mid-1980s at American University I had a student who seemed the least likely ever to move beyond what looked to be ingrained self-absorption. She came from a family of wealth. The class was large, more than 150. A final-semester senior who no doubt had her fill of windy professors, she always took to one of the back rows. She rarely spoke. I'd look at her and ask myself the question that all professors pose when dispensing what we think are grand truths getting grander: Is she getting it? Of course she is, I'd con myself. Thirty minutes into the class her eyes would glaze, and I'd say to myself that she's not within six hemispheres of getting it. At semester's end, she graduated. I didn't hear from her until years later. A letter came. A poignant letter, handwritten. She had joined the Peace Corps and was sent to a remote desert village in northern Morocco. Of all the students in that class, she was the last one I'd have picked for the Peace Corps.

In the letter, she told of stopping in the school library after classes one afternoon. The only news from the outside world was an occasional copy of the *International Herald Tribune*. A villager would sometimes go to Rabat, the capital, and bring back a copy for the school. The teacher paged through and there, by chance, was a column of mine on the op-ed page. So reminded of my class, she wrote to say that she had been a water-treader that last semester of college. Confessionally, she said that as much as she wanted to think about nonviolence, and did try at least a bit, she couldn't connect with it. Her mind was elsewhere. But now that she'd been in Morocco these past two years, she wrote, and doing the works of peace in a modest way, it was all coming back to her: yes, nonviolence does make sense. I remember the letter because the moral of the story is obvious: every flower blooms when it's ready. Some bloom early, some late. My obligation is to teach with passion, and not think about, much less fret, who is or who is not getting it.

I remember your class at Catholic. It was to be my final one there. No dean or department head explained the reason for not inviting me back. I do have a hunch, though. It was that first moment of the first class. I asked a question about grades: is anyone taking this class for the sole reason of getting an A? If so, you can leave now and I promise to turn in an A at the end of the semester. Just tell me your name on the way to the door. You may remember that one lad, wide-eyed with disbelief but not letting the golden chance of a lifetime pass by, jumped up with noticeable glee. He slung on his backpack, told me his name—repeated it twice, just to be sure—and marched out. I did deliver the promised grade, but by then word had spread throughout the campus that a madcap prof was passing out A's like trinkets at Mardi Gras—and no attendance, no papers and no exams required. I did admire the boy for walking out, at least for his honesty. He was a grade-grubber, and when a moment came to grub he did. I was glad he left. The students who stayed were the ones I wanted to be with: for them a grade was secondary to learning.

I imagine that the boy who walked out with his guaranteed A came to college thinking that the more As you piled up the better chance of making it in life. If I could find the time, I'd like to check the college transcripts of corporate CEOs who were imprisoned for fraud of late. No doubt they had plenty of As and, brainy, were well on their way to success. But now they have Fs for character. For me, grading is the foulest part of teaching. Grading is degrading. The second foulness is answering emails from students wondering, in mild but emphatic indignation, why I gave them a B instead of an A. One came just yesterday, from a Georgetown Law student. Her 6,000 word term paper ran deep with ordinary language, dull footnotes and with not a sprightly metaphor in sight. The paper hovered between listless and lackluster. She missed three classes and was habitually late for class. The message came through: I offended her with a B.

Your letter touched my heart. I'm grateful you took the time to write. When I tell my future classes about former students who are truly other-centered, and not self-centered, be sure your story will be told.

In friendship,

Colman

Some five years later, Ryan Hehman wrote with an update, including his reflections about his time in Phoenix.

Dear Colman,

In the summer of 2006, I entered a school of Christian love. For three months, I helped the homeless at a Catholic Worker hospitality center in Phoenix. It was shortly after my graduation from college and a year after taking your Introduction to Peace Studies course.

Our hospitality center was in an area nicknamed "The Zone," a mostly abandoned industrial neighborhood near the railroad tracks. The Zone had a bad reputation, and we served people living on the streets there. They came to the neighborhood to buy drugs, "do business" (whatever that meant), and find help. The center offered free showers, laundry, clothes, phone calls, and dinner to almost 600 people every day. Many of our guests suffered from drug addiction or mental illness. Many suffered from bad choices and bad circumstances. All suffered from the heat, which rarely dropped below 100 degrees. The volunteers at the center were trying to perform the corporal and spiritual works of mercy for a pretty tough crowd.

When I arrived, I was eager to help the poor, and I firmly believed in nonviolence. It seemed to me that "love your enemies" and "turn the other cheek" were the most radical Christian teachings and the pinnacle of moral virtue. My experience in Phoenix would test that belief. To my surprise, the guests at the center were not initially happy to have me there. They jeered at me and told me to go back to the suburbs. One young woman even called me a chump.

I worked hard to be kind and patient with them, no matter how annoying, unreasonable or belligerent they were. Helping the guests involved daily squabbles over a multitude of mundane things: t-shirts, soap, an extra serving of macaroni, and one's place in line. At first, I found the work exhilarating. It demanded that I master my emotions, grow in patience, learn how to express myself clearly, return blessings for curses, and overall be more like Jesus. It was the hard, nitty-gritty work of love.

After only a few weeks, though, I became tired of the insults, thankless tasks, and inane arguments with the guests. In my former life, I had imagined myself to be a patient and virtuous person. My contact with the guests showed me that only the opposite was true. On a few occasions, guests had hit me. I didn't hit back because I wasn't allowed, not because I didn't want to. At times, I was filled with just as much anger as they were. But I thought my anger was justified because I was the do-gooder.

Nevertheless, the intensity of my anger after these altercations bothered me. I felt lost because my emotions conflicted with my ideals. Each night, I wondered why I had flown 3,000 miles to be cursed at, spit at and insulted. Then again, what did I expect. A hero's welcome?

The problem was that no really cared how good I was being. Because of this, I realized that my desire to volunteer did not come from a love of God, or even a love of the poor. It came from a strange sort of pride. I considered nonviolence to be Jesus' toughest teaching, and I wanted to see if I was up to the challenge. I wanted to be radical and different. I wanted to test my limits. This attitude made me more akin to an "extreme sports" athlete than a genuine Christian. I was so concerned with being peaceful that I was ignoring Jesus and actually missing the primary task of Christianity: following Him.

Only by getting to know Jesus personally can we know the type of peace He was talking about. It is a peace that we cannot manufacture for ourselves because it is a gift. Jesus did not want me to help the poor so others could recognize my goodness. He wanted me to help the poor so that I could recognize His goodness in others. Jesus counts Himself among the people I was trying to serve, and it was through them that I got to know Him. I eventually made a few friends among the guests, and this turned out to be the most valuable part of my experience.

Since I left Phoenix, I have been part of an inner-city ministry called A Simple House of Sts. Francis and Alphonsus. We are a small group of missionaries trying to spread the Good News through words, deeds and friendships with the poor living on the streets and in project neighborhoods. We have two missions located in Washington, DC, and

Kansas City. My wife, Laura, is also a Simple House missionary and we have seven-month-old son named Joseph.

Peace,

Ryan

AUGUST 8, 2009

Dear Professor,

I have been pondering something quite a bit lately and I was wondering if you could share with me some of your thoughts on the subject. Here goes.

I have always chosen to abstain from drinking and doing drugs because I have always known that I don't need intoxicants of that sort to enjoy myself. I also think that the way our society portrays teenage drinking and other drug-doing (I remember, of course, your decision to call it the "alcohol drug") is harmful in that it feels like everyone is telling teenagers, "Oh, experimentation of that sort is just a part of being a teenager. It's inevitable." The thing is, I've always thought it wasn't inevitable. People who are allergic to alcohol manage to find happiness in their lives (and they get through their teen years), and Buddhist monks end up pretty happy, though many never taste alcohol or experiment with drugs of any sort.

Essentially, part of my question is how you feel about intoxication, both of teenager and adults, and why.

Also—and this is something that I hope to figure out before I go to college—I do not know how best to explain my decision to abstain from these drugs to people who do not. Oftentimes I say nothing at all but when I am pressured to explain why I won't just have beer, my explanation comes off sounding condescending. Because of this it often seems like I am offending my friends who I care about. Also, I am often told "Don't knock it till you try it." Or: "How can you judge all of us when you've never even tried it?" But the thing is, I'm not interested in trying it and additionally there are plenty of things I know I'm not interested in without experiencing it. I know I do not want to fight in war or become a physicist or a bird watcher. This never seems to be a good argument though, and ideally, I don't want to argue with people I have just met in a collegiate setting.

Thus, the second part of my question is what you think the best way would be to explain sobriety without making it sound condescending or argumentative.

Essentially, I need your help. I have been trying to figure it out on my own for a while now but to be honest it is hard to find people my own age who understand where I'm coming from. Or anyone for that matter. I think I'm going a little crazy internally and I would love to hear your thoughts.

Thank you thank you thank you,

Hanna Mahon

Dear Hanna,

You may have come across it, that ambiguity-free line from T. S. Eliot: "In a world of fugitives, the person taking the opposite direction will appear to run away." That's you. By not running with the ruck, when it heads to the parties, bars or refrigerators for a fix of alcohol—or to the Rose Garden to slug a beer with Obama, the cop and professor—you're the mad one: daft in the head, slow to lighten up and assuredly not one to invite to the next kegger.

I'm not surprised you've taken a stand. You were the one student in [the Wilson High School] class last semester intent on making a difference in life—by being different. You were the one who had an eye for seeing through society's guff, including the kind heaved at high school students by the alcohol industry through relentless advertising. The typical teenager will have seen more than 100,000 beer commercials before turning 18. The Georgetown University Center on Alcohol Marketing and Youth looked at advertisements in 103 national magazines and their readership during 2001–2 and found that girls between 12 and 20 were exposed to those ads more than women between 21 to 34. The goal of the companies is brand loyalty. Research shows that once a person connects emotionally with a particular brand of beer, that loyalty remains in place for life. The results of advertising are impressive, grimly so: a recent study revealed that 77 percent of teenagers took up drinking by the end of 12th grade. In the late 1960s, seven percent of 10- to 14-year-old girls used alcohol. By the early 1990s it had risen to 31 percent.

For me, the alcohol industry ranks at the top for loathsomeness. I've wasted plenty of money in my life but not a penny has gone to buy liquor, wine, beer or whatever. I took a vow in high school never to drink, after my closest schoolboy pal, Bobby Trimble, was killed in an alcohol-related car crash. We grew up in Old Brookville, a subdued placid New York village through which the Long Island Railroad had tracks from Penn Station to Oyster Bay. At 16 Bobby was driving home one weekend night after drinking at a party. Evidently he saw the light of the train a half-mile down the tracks heading for the road crossing before the Glen Head station, and decided to race the train. He did but the train won. It took a day to clear the tracks of the wreckage. I loved Bobby all the years we were in school, and decided in his memory never to drink alcohol.

It's the worst of the drugs, whether measured in societal or person costs. I've never known a family that didn't have a life ruined because of drinking, whether a parent, grandparent or relative. It's a highly addictive drug, which is why I reject the drink-in-moderation argument. It's the same as telling children to play moderately with fire or teenagers to drive moderately above the speed limit. Moderation? What does it really mean, especially for those for whom the disease of alcoholism runs in the family. Then, too, it's worth asking what is so missing in one's life that the emptiness must be filled with a drug? Is filling it with alcohol the only way?

So how to explain to others your decision not to drink? You can probably have some fun on that one. Make up a story that you have a $100,000 book contract on what it's like to be a college non-drinker: *I Was a Nerd. And Worse, a Sober Nerd*. They'll make it into a movie! Or that you have a rich uncle who has promised you $1 million if you don't drink before 25. The last is not that bizarre. I recall reading a biography of Joseph Kennedy in which he pledged a hefty payoff to his children—eight of them including Jack, Robert, Teddy and Eunice—if they laid off until they were 25. I'll have to ask when seeing her again, but Eunice, I believe, was the only one who held on to collect.

The better way, and not a fantasy-driven way, to explain your stand is merely to tell people that you don't drink. Your close friends—and most of us, if we are blessed, have two or three people who are truly lifelong friends, with all the rest being acquaintances—will appreciate and respect you. The rest—those who move in and out of our lives—probably won't understand, much as they might be closed-minded about people who are slightly different. Why bother with them?

In my college classes, including Georgetown Law, I offer students the option of not drinking alcohol for the semester and writing a paper about it. Every year, a few do.

The papers carry the same theme: how the students came to realize that their social lives were built around alcohol, how they had no true friends but only drinking buddies, how they felt physically and spiritually better by not drinking, how their roommates or housemates thought they were having a nervous breakdown because suddenly they stopped.

I can almost assure you that the people who truly care about you, or even marginally care, will honor you for being resolute. In my own college years, when I was over-involved in athletics and decidedly un-involved in academics, I was the only member of my golf team—yes, I know, golf is a rich, white, Republican, country club game and I should do penance immediately—who didn't drink. I took all of the abuse, most of it lighthearted but some of it pointed, as if, as you said, I was posing as morally superior to the drinkers. Years later, many years later, I ran into one of my former teammates, Tommy Boone from Signal Mountain, Tenn. He said that he and a couple of others had secretly admired me for not drinking but they were too immature or too afraid of looking odd to say no to alcohol themselves.

Be sure that you have my deepest admiration for your choice. Don't be hard on yourself—"going a little crazy internally"—and certainly don't change. Take pride in your independence, from the corruptions of a society awash in drunkenness and from the predations of the alcohol industry. Seek the intoxications to be found in reading books—and soon enough for you, I suspect, writing books—or taking a year off before college to taste life, which you are doing.

On the nation's campuses, students are returning for the Fall semester—the beginning of the drinking season. For many—the estimated 1,700 who will die from alcohol-related causes—it will be their final semester. For many, many, it will mean alcohol-related injuries, not counting victims of rape or sexual assaults.

So continue on. Become a drinker, the kind you have been so far. One who swallows deeply of life's simpler joys: friendships, reading and writing, helping your parents, taking risks and bringing joy to your teachers, which you did every time you were in my class at Wilson. Even when you came late because you and Nell were getting out the Beacon.

Stay special, stay you—

Colman McCarthy

In the spring semester of 2011, Georgia Harper wrote a paper for my Journalism and Peace class at the University of Maryland. It deserved a wider audience than me, so with her permission, I offered it to the *National Catholic Reporter.* Titled "Challenge Accepted: Why I Quit Drinking," it ran in the November 11–24, 2011, issue.

Last year, the percentage of my friends that chose to binge drink at least four nights a week hovered somewhere between 99.5 and 100. They were the only people I would hang out with, because that is what I did too. I'm in a sorority. It's not an excuse, it's a lifestyle. A typical night out in the world of the Greek system at my university follows as such: generally, if we can get our act together on time, we get to "pregame" around 11 pm, which is usually at a local house being rented out for the year by a fraternity.

We'll have about four to seven shots, more if we don't want to spend money on drinks at the bar. We then go to the bars where a guy will usually buy a girl a drink or two if he doesn't think she's buzzed enough. After about an hour and a half, we go from the bar to the "postgame" where we don't know how much we're drinking because we all end up consuming it directly from the numerous half-gallon bottles being passed around until three or four in the morning. Then we walk home in the dark by ourselves or we black out.

I didn't always act like this. I was raised overseas where the legal drinking limit is non-existent. My parents always taught me how to control my alcohol. When we lived in Italy I was trained to enjoy my wine slowly and analyze it for its flavors. Was it fruity? Did it have a hint of oak? I never drank at high school parties in the US because I knew my parents would let me have alcohol in moderation at home if I chose to. The first semester in college, before I joined a sorority, I drank responsibly and I always made it to my dorm safely. After I joined, everything changed.

The way that my sorority sisters abuse alcohol is really a strange dynamic. We are encouraged, even applauded, to down as much as we can in one sitting, yet we are admonished when we are so drunk that we need to be walked home or taken to the hospital for it. We are expected to tread that fine line between "life of the party" and "that girl throwing up in the bathroom." Alcohol is involved in every one of our nighttime activities. It's impossible to avoid. This is why last spring, when I was challenged by my professor to give up alcohol, I accepted. It wasn't entirely his challenge that made me give it up but it was the final push I needed. Over the past two semesters, my body has not taken kindly to binge drinking. Since the spring of 2010 I can't even count the number of times I have hurt myself accidentally. I have been sexually assaulted twice, slipped and hit the back of my head on concrete, vomited on my sister's new futon, pulled out my friend's hair, smashed my knee and fell so hard head first on the sidewalk that I cracked open my forehead.

My sisters didn't want to get into trouble with the police so instead of taking me to the hospital to get stitches they took me back to the house to "patch me up" themselves.

I still have the dress covered in blood and the raised lump filled with scar tissue on my head to remind me of the incident.

I didn't want to gain weight by drinking too much, so, instead of drinking less I stopped eating. A morning after a night of heavy drinking without eating for 24 hours would result in me curling up on my bedroom floor shaking as my entire body fought back with everything it had. Drinking was hurting me more than when I was getting punched as a member of the boxing team.

But these are just the outward physical manifestations of my alcohol abuse.

These are things you can see. What are not visible are the hurtful words I have said to people while under the influence, the relationship that suffered because neither of us could spend enough time sober to make it work, the probable damage done to my liver, kidneys and heart. I have lost my phone, keys, money, ID and my entire purse to a night of hard partying because I wasn't coherent enough to hold on to it. It's all probably still under the chair on the floor of some dingy nightclub.

The eight weeks after giving it up were strange. The first part was excruciating. At first I tried to go out and not drink, which was just boring. Having drunk kids fall all over or try to grab you is not as fun when you're the only one who's not tipsy. My room in the sorority has five people I used to party with all the time. We would have our own "pre-pregame" where we'd drink our own alcohol before going out and getting even more wasted than everyone else. Now, on the nights when they go out, I try to go to bed early only to be inevitably woken up as they stumble in, drunken messes. They flip on the lights, drink some more, and then go to bed as I lie there, now wide awake. I always worry when one of them doesn't come back at night.

We don't talk anymore. We're different people. If we do talk, it's because they feel the need to tell me that I'm not fun anymore, that I've changed.

But I'm glad that I have, because for every night that my old friends go out and don't remember the night before, I'm spending quality time with the sisters in the house who don't drink—ones I never had the chance to get to know. The girls who, in all honesty, I never cared to get to know. When the partiers sleep in until four in the afternoon, I'm waking up at 8:30, going for a run, and getting my homework done. I take time to enjoy the sunlight. Colors are sharper. My skin is clearer, my hair is thicker and I'm not tired all the time. When I go home and see my mom, she no longer has to comment on how I smell like a distillery.

Someone made a comment to me about how I won't be able to keep this up forever.

That's another challenge I accept.

∽ ∽ ∽

MARCH 18, 2010

Dear Professor,

Yesterday's class affected me deeply. I've always been a vegetarian and profound lover of animals of all shapes and sizes. After my seminar finished at 10:40 last night, I went straight home and spent an hour playing with our cat, Coco. My three roommates and I give her a lot of attention and love, and we're often exasperated with her because she's barely a year old, ridiculously energetic and fond of raiding our recycling bags in the middle of the night to chase aluminum cans across our hardwood floors. Last week, after she waited behind the couch and leaped out to attack my tights as I was walking by, I jokingly said, "Coco, I'm going to sell you to the Chinese."*

Now I feel terrible about it. I spent a whole hour last night cuddling with her (she gets really affectionate in the late evening when she's tired), holding her, lying on the floor and letting her walk all over me (she loves this for some reason) and playing with her "teaser wand." After watching the abuse and torture of those cats, I wanted to remind at least one that she was loved very much.

After class I called my boyfriend, who eats meat, literally in tears over the cats in China. I've never been a proselytizing vegetarian and always accepted the fact that my boyfriend isn't. But I started asking him if he knew how his meat is obtained and processed. When I found out he did know, I asked him how he could eat it and not gag or get depressed. He was uncomfortable and said that during the three years he'd been with me, I'd introduced him to a whole new way of eating and he really didn't crave meat much at all anymore. I pressed him for reasons he was still okay with eating meat if he saw he could love his diet without it, and he just didn't want to talk about it.

Animals have always been a huge part of my life and even though I was raised without meat, I can't ever see myself "rebelling" and wanting to. Now I am a vegetarian for moral, environmental and practical reasons. The only pet I ever had who was really and truly only my buddy (I don't want to say he belonged to me) was a rabbit I got when I was eight. He was a tiny Netherlands dwarf, only two lbs. and for seven years he was a best friend. He was never once locked in his cage.

My Mom and I gave him the whole "mudroom" to run around in: a warm bunny condo, a cage that I changed twice a week with fresh cedar shavings, and constant fresh food and water. He had the run of the house when we were home. In the summer we let him roam around the yard. I spent hours sitting in his room, doing homework, reading books and talking to him. He had a real personality and was comfortable with me and almost no one else. Every morning when my Mom was getting ready for work, he would circle her feet, hindering her ability to move at all in the kitchen, until she gave him an apple slice. Whenever we opened the cupboard where the corn chips were kept, he'd come flying in from his favorite hiding spot under the desk, scrabbling across the slippery floor and sometimes running into the cupboards.

When he died, I was devastated. I cried for weeks and weeks and I still keep his picture by my bed. I feel that as children we're much more capable of loving animals and recognizing them as equals on different levels. Why is it that when we're older we start to think of them as property or objects? I find this subject depressing yet wholly necessary, and I thank you for being the only instructor I have ever had who examines this issue, marks it as important and forces others to look at it as well. I really enjoy learning from you and I'm glad I had the opportunity to be a part of this class.

Thank you for taking the time to read this.

Merissa

*In the two college classes I devote to animal rights and human wrongs, a staple is the seventy-five-minute HBO documentary *To Love or To Kill: Man vs. Animal*. One scene depicts a restaurant in southern China where cats and dogs are lifted from their cages to be killed and prepared for dinner. Customers choose. Workers are shown placing a cat into a tank of boiling water. After a few minutes, the tenderized body is taken out to be skinned and then dropped into cold water. The feline, still alive but barely, moves its jaws, gasping for breath.

MARCH 21, 2010

Dear Merissa,

Bring Coco to class! It's not so wild a notion. A few years ago a guest in my class at Wilson High was Abigail, a 25-lb. turkey and the only one ever celebrated with a page one profile in the *Wall Street Journal.* The story told of her being trucked south on I-95 from Pennsylvania to a slaughterhouse in Maryland, but not arriving because the truck crashed. Over a hundred turkeys were flopping around on the highway. By chance, two workers from the Poplar Spring Animal Sanctuary were driving by. They had room in their car for a bird. They named it Abigail. I saw the story and invited them and the turkey to my Wilson class—a week before Thanksgiving, as it turned out.

In the annals of secondary education, it was an historic moment: a lesson taught by a turkey was more relevant to the students' lives than anything the teacher, me, could have said even on his best day.

Half the class became vegetarians, suddenly making the connection between the lively and lovely Abigail and the corpses that would be centerpieces on the American table on Thanksgiving.

That's the puzzle about moving someone from a cruelty-based to a cruelty-free diet: arousing empathy. Students in the class could see Abigail poking and pecking around the room, her curiosity about chairs and legs as intense as the students' wonderment about the bird. Empathy came naturally. I asked the students if anyone would like to kill Abigail, perhaps get a gun from one of the cops in the hall and shoot her in the head and then eat her body the next Thursday. The question was greeted with shouts of disgust. Yet I knew that many in the class would soon be eating the body parts of another turkey.

That might be where your boyfriend is, locked into a state of mind disconnected from the pleasurable taste of flesh and the unpleasurable way the animal was killed. I am always careful when teaching animal rights not to come on too strongly, knowing that people become defensive when they feel you are accusing them of being cruel to animals. They are used to language that camouflages the reality. It's London Broil, a Chicken McNugget or a Burger King Whopper that's on the plate, not an animal body part.

I probably self-censor too much, knowing that I am in no position to judge anyone. If complicity with violence to animals is the issue, who is really innocent? Definitely not me. Until college, I dined on animal flesh. I'm sure I took drugs that were tested on animals. I wrote for the *Washington Post*, a newspaper whose earnings were enhanced by ads from the dairy, egg, meat and fur industries. I live in a home, like most American homes, that displaced animals; I pay taxes to a federal government that through the Department of Agriculture sanctions the slaughter of billions of animals annually. I've traveled in cars with leather seats, on roads unfenced to prevent road kill. I've praised members of Congress whose voting records never challenge the hunting lobby—or as the pliant pols call it, "the sportsman lobby." I've been in houses of worship that practice religions that give human beings, we upright primates, full dominion over animals and where the clergy bless parishioners' pets every Oct. 4 in honor of Francis of Assisi, the patron saint of animals, but don't dare tell the faithful to stop eating meat or fish.

It was, oddly enough, in a sermon by Father Zossima in *The Brothers Karamazov* by Fyodor Dostoyevsky that the message is stated in a way to open minds and stir hearts, as it did mine: "Love all God's creation and every grain of sand in it. . . . Love animals. God has given them the rudiments of thought and joy untroubled. Do not trouble their joy, don't harass them, don't deprive them of their happiness, don't work against God's intent. Man, do not pride yourself on superiority to animals. They are without sin, and you, with your greatness, defile the earth by your appearance on it, and leave traces of your foulness after you. Alas, it is true of almost every one of us."

So keep letting Coco walk all over you. Don't be discouraged that your boyfriend isn't with it. I suspect he is, just taking more time than you'd like.

We'll have a memorable class next week. Michael Weber from FARM (Farm Animals Rights Movement) is coming in. He's 25, a vegan, knowledgeable, dogged and a graduate of Evergreen State College which is among the most progressive campuses in the country. By the way, did you know that PETA ranks American U in the top three vegetarian friendly schools, along with Wesleyan and Oberlin? No wonder you thrived here.

Bless you and Coco—

Colman McCarthy

~ ~ ~

DECEMBER 28, 2010

Dear Mr. McCarthy

I am writing from Oberlin to, first of all, thank you for an extraordinary class at Wilson last semester and, second, to check in with you to see how you've been and to update you on what I've been up to. I also wanted to reimburse you for the *Solutions to Violence* textbook that I never returned. I hope the loss of it from your class wasn't too much trouble. I have it and will be making full use of the book for myself as a peacemaker.

The Wilson course gave me a chance to learn and become knowledgeable on issues I strongly care about. It also offered information that every person must learn if we are ever to achieve a peaceful existence. Your kind and patient attitude was always appreciated by our class, especially when some students weren't making the most of it and essentially wasting your time. It is inspiring that you were able to continue teaching and not lose your patience up against so much apathy in the classroom. Many students eventually began to really care about the class, even ones who did not seem to care at the beginning of the year. I also really appreciate that you teach at Wilson, because many kids may feel hopeless due to situations at home. They are in desperate need of a class like yours that truly educates them about the world we live in. I think that when you trust a student enough to teach them about what's actually going on in our world it makes them feel respected and can inspire them. It definitely felt that way for me.

I am also very thankful that you are committed your causes. Many of your class discussions by you and the guest speakers helped shape my personal morals and philosophy. I am definitely more committed to pacifism now than I was before your class. I have continued to eat vegetarian and try to inform my family and friends what I know about being a peaceful responsible eater.

I do think my favorite guest speaker was Paul Chappell whose book I read and loved after he gave me a copy.* I have remained in contact with Paul and found out that he is coming to Oberlin in May.

So far I am really enjoying Oberlin. I had a nice summer before leaving for school, during which I worked at the Friendship Place Community Council for the Homeless. Volunteering there was a great experience. It was good to be able to help solve the problem of homelessness in my community.

But back to Oberlin. This is really a great place for me with so many music and activist opportunities. I am taking Intro to Peace and Conflict Studies. My other notable class is my freshman seminar "Selfishness or Altruism: the Evolution of Sociality in Humans and Other Animals." I'm learning a lot about the nature of human life and life itself. I learned in the Peace and Conflict class that war only began 10,000 years ago, making it evident that humans are not inherently warlike but that something about the way our society is structured can lead to war. I have also gone to a few meetings for the Oberlin Peace Activists League and the Oberlin Animal Rights Group.

Thanks again Mr. McCarthy. You truly are one of my heroes and I really enjoyed being able to learn from you and hope to be able to continue to do so.

Take care,

Peter Hartmann

Will War Ever End: A Soldier's Vision of Peace for the 21st Century (rev. ed., Westport, CN: Easton Studio Press, 2011). Paul Chappell, a 2002 West Point graduate and Iraq War veteran, is the director of the Peace Leadership Program at the Nuclear Age Peace Foundation, Santa Barbara, California.

JANUARY 1, 2011

Dear Peter,

What a lovely and lovingly written letter. I was touched by it, of course, in much the appreciative way I so cherished having you in class. Sometimes teaching is as easy as breathing, when students like you are there. Other times, it's as hard as gasping for air, as when students like you are not there. If I were more on my game, it shouldn't matter. I'd be able to let the limpers limp, the slackers slack and the sleepers sleep and be content that I supplied all the energy I could. When the limping, slacking and sleeping becomes too much, as it came close to doing more than once in your class when it was your ill luck and mine to be stuck with students dumped onto us by over-busy counselors, I'd remember the line from good Pope John XXIII, "See everything, overlook much, improve a little."

John, a northern Italian from the small Lombardy city of Bergamo, whose birth name was Angelo Roncalli, held the papacy for only five years, 1958–63. But what a five years they were, as he put through reforms at the Second Vatican Council that made the Church less judgmental and more human, less secretive and more collegial. It could be argued that he went way beyond improving things only a little, but progress, or least the kind that lasts and doesn't stumble, is almost always a matter of pushing forward little by little. And then there's that story about the day John's brother, an illiterate farmer, came to the Vatican and the pope was showing him around the place. He asked John, "how many people work here?" "About half," the pope said.

My current Wilson class, freshman to seniors, is a model of diversity: six international students (Colombia, El Salvador, China, Germany, Eritrea and England), four or five whose parents went to the Ivies, a dozen from African American families, five athletes, a couple of musicians and a Latino boy who every class hands me a document from the DC Superior Court and wordlessly points where to sign my name and where to write the date to show he is here.

For guest speakers, we've had a bracing mix: Eddie Ellis, the former prisoner who came to your class; an Episcopalian priest who is now getting a masters in conflict resolution from Eastern Mennonite University; an organizer from the Farm Animal Rights Movement; Steve Mowbray (Remember him? The former businessman from Kansas who has chosen voluntary poverty and has no house, no car, no job, no money, no insurance, no credit card but NO WORRIES); a Buddhist monk from Oregon; a Muslim who converted to Catholicism; a former Peace Corps volunteer who did health work in the interior of Ecuador; and a lad named Zaccai Free who went to Maret, was accepted at Brown but turned it down for North Carolina A&T, one of the historically black colleges, where he thrived but then spent four years living in Belize trying to sort out the big questions. Now he works for Code Pink, the antiwar sisterhood Medea Benjamin founded ten years ago. I had Medea speak to my Georgetown Law class in October when we were having a couple of classes on civil disobedience. She has a sparkling arrest record, from disrupting congressional hearings on the military budget to standing a bit too long holding signs in front of the Bush White House against the commands of Secret Service bullies to move on.

One of the law students who savored Medea and her stories was a second year law student, Charity Ryerson. She went to a Jesuit high school in Indianapolis and then a Jesuit university in Illinois. Along the way she was swayed by the writings of Daniel Berrigan, the Jesuit priest whose ministry including defying the militarism of the American Empire. Charity's own defiance came in the Fall of 2003 at Ft. Benning, a massive Army base near Columbus, Georgia. She was arrested, along with busloads of others, in a nonviolent protest against what the Army called "the School of the Americas" but which is more accurately known as the School of the Assassins. During the 1970s and '80s, it trained the soldiers of dictators who would return to countries like El Salvador, Colombia, Honduras and Nicaragua to murder, torture and abduct nuns, priests, labor organizers and others who sided with the poor. It was the era of death squads. On March 24, 1980, Archbishop Oscar Romero was gunned down by killers trained at Ft. Benning. Later that year four American women—three nuns and a social worker—were killed by SOA graduates.

Every third weekend in November, thousands of protestors show up at the gates of the base. Their host is Fr. Roy Bourgeois, a Maryknoll priest who has overseen the protest for more than 20 years. In 2003 Charity was arrested for crossing the line. A trespasser on federal property, she was sentenced to six months in federal prison. The main requirement for my Georgetown Law class was a 6,000 word paper. I encouraged Charity to write about her crimes against the state. Evidently she didn't learn her lesson. Six weeks ago she was back at Ft. Benning—to be arrested again, with a pending trial in March. I probably push it too far but I keep telling my law students to write papers about their own experiences with law, conscience and nonviolence—which happens to be the title of the course. If Charity writes with only a touch of literate language, she is in for the coveted A, although I think she deserves blessings far more meaningful than a letter on a transcript.

Large numbers of the protestors are from US colleges. I know that for many years Oberlin students piled into vans and headed south to the base. Check with one of the chaplains if groups still go.

It's a delight to know that you are getting your dollars' worth at Oberlin. From my two visits to the college as a guest speaker, I had the feeling it has a caring faculty that focuses on classroom teaching, as against a research-driven faculty that looks on interactions with students as bothersome distractions. Alas, Oberlin does not yet offer a degree in peace studies. You'd think it would, wouldn't you, given its past agitations in the civil rights movement. I was heartened that after my visit four years ago a couple of professors—Stephen Crowley and Stephen Mayer—are teaching the Intro course you are taking and are using *Solutions to Violence*.

Speaking of that, thanks for the check. You're in luck. It comes at the right moment: It's buy-one-get-two-free-week at the Center for Teaching Peace. I'm sending you *We Who Dared to Say No To War*, a collection of essays by and about conscientious objectors to America's wars, from 1812 to Afghanistan, and *The Mind of Mahatma Gandhi*.

The first one comes to you by way of Ralph Nader, the man of passion whom I've known and supported since the 1960s. He called from his office near 16th and P Sts. some months back to say that he had 1,200 copies of *We Who Dared to Say No To War* and could I use them. Ralph keeps track of remaindered books, ones that are left over from the first or second printings and which publishers unload—harsh word, considering the sensibilities of authors—at steep discounts to free up space at the warehouses. Send them on, I said gratefully. Ralph paid for the shipping from a plant near Knoxville. I use the book for classes, and I imagine there will be enough for a few years. It tells you something about the disinterestedness of the American media that an antiwar book like this could be published and receive so few reviews that the public knew little about it.

The Gandhi book is traceable to James Otis. In the mid-1980s he was in my Honors course at the University of Maryland. He was leaving class one day, after we had discussed the life and thinking of Gandhi. James was noticeably eager to learn more. I took him aside and suggested a few titles of books he might read, including Erik Erikson's *Gandhi's Truth*. It wasn't something I remembered more than a few minutes after. Fifteen years later, James Otis phoned. "You told me to read some Gandhi on my own," he said, recalling the class. "I took the advice and it's time I thanked you. I have a gift and will send it." The next morning a FedEx truck is at my door, with the driver unloading ten large boxes weighing over 40 lbs. each and hauling them inside on a dolly.

I checked the sender's name and address: James Otis, Beverley Hills, California 90210. Inside the boxes, now parked in my living room, with space for little else, were the collected works of Gandhi: 95 thick volumes in all. The Mahatma wrote more than 500 words a day after finishing law school in London. The Navajivan Publishing House in Ahmedabad, India, gathered them in 95 books. I asked the FedEx driver what the overnight pre-noon delivery cost: "At least a couple thousand dollars."

I called James to thank him. It turns out he has done well as a documentary film maker, specializing in topics of nonviolence. One of the residuals of teaching is that students occasionally do send gifts after taking the course. James, let it be noted, is at the top of the leader board with the 95 Gandhi books. Where are they now? I wanted to build bookshelves on the walls of our living room, there to read through them one by one. My wife, who once hosted a dinner at our home for Arun Gandhi, who is the second son of Gandhi's second son, was somewhat less carried away than I: a wide audience should benefit. She prevailed. We donated the books, in James Otis's name, to the library at American University.

To make a long story longer—sorry—James has another distinction among my former students: he's the only one ever to make the front page of the *New York Times*, with a picture and a 1,200 word story. It seems that his interest in Gandhi ran deep, well beyond books. Over the years and many, many trips to India, he collected a trove of Gandhi belongings: his eyeglasses, walking stick, sandals, soup bowl, clock, notebooks. James decided to sell the collection at a New York auction house, with the money not for himself but, as the *Times* story noted, as "a means to promote pacifist causes." The winning bid was $1.8 million, put up by an Indian millionaire who promised to put the items on display in India. The *Times* story, by the way, ran on March 6, 2009, if you want the details.

Last week, more books came from James: this time, six boxes of Gandhi biographies and collections of essays. This time the US Postal Service did the lifting, at about $30 a box. James is economizing.

Enjoy both Ralph's and James's books, if you ever have time for reading for pleasure, which few collegians do. Speaking of reading, special thanks for taking a look at my column the other day in the *Post* on ROTC at US campuses. You're a pal for pumping it on Facebook. I was told it drew more than a thousand comments on the *Post*'s website, with only 20 favorable and the rest scolding, damning, fuming and venting. Not an assault I'm not used to.

You and I have been blessed by the gods to know Hanna Mahon. I remember when she introduced me to you at the Wilson High graduation, and thinking "well at least there's something right in the world, that the paths of these two loveable and idealistic children have crossed." Hanna, now at Middlebury, is arranging for me to speak there in the Spring.

You have three years to shake up Oberlin and get a peace studies program in place, one that's as well-funded and staffed at the music department. If the administrators give you the brush-off—odds on they will—remember the fundamental rule of social reform: when the other side doesn't see the light, make 'em feel the heat. Start a sit-in in the president's office, then the provost's, and then—now it gets nasty—lie down and block the faculty parking lot.

Peace and a little extra,

Colman McCarthy

P.S. Some sad news. My trusty Raleigh 3-speed, after more than 30,000 miles in weather from 20 below freezing to the scorchers of July and August, has expired. Death came on the operating table at Big Wheel Bikes in Bethesda. It was down to a single gear, which I was holding together with two rubber bands, not far from the Scotch tape which kept the two rear baskets from falling off. The gear gave out when the lad in the store took off the rubber bands and tried to stretch the wire to reach the rear hub. It snapped. If you know of anyone who has a Raleigh—the British-made vintage kind that the Bobbies used to ride with three speeds, not one of those contraptions with 18 gears—I'm in the market.

Dear Colman,

Let me introduce myself. My name is Joe Wolfson and I teach mathematics at Phillips Exeter. As it turned out, Ryan Morgan was in my class last term (and a wonderful class it was), so it was with appreciative surprise that I realized he was the one who brought you to campus.

In any case, I wanted to ask you a few questions about some thoughts you offered during Assembly. Specifically, you talked about homework, tests and grades as being violent toward students. For many years now (15?) I have returned papers without grades and without thinking about them. I came to the conclusion that grades interfered with learning. Unfortunately Exeter demands grades at term's end, so I ask students what grade I should enter for them, and occasionally negotiate, though usually agree with them or raise them a bit higher. I also give tests infrequently, mostly because I think they are, at best, crude instruments and, at worst, invoke fear and other emotions that preclude learning. I haven't given them up altogether, although I do tell students that they are no more than one day's work, weighed no more heavily than any other day in my thoughts about their work. I also give partner tests and group tests: fun activities in that they encourage communication. However, I do see that tests can be used (and I often have to fight against this myself) as a way for the teacher to assert his/her superiority. So although I'm not sure I'd use the word "violent" to describe tests and grades, I certainly see that their use in general is counterproductive to learning and can be damaging.

Then there's the matter of homework. Now I can see that assignments can be used to punish or to exercise control, but I do not clearly see how my assigning problems 3-10 on page 72 does either of these things (never mind being violent) given the following stipulations which I attach to all assignments:

- These problems will be at the heart of tomorrow's conversations.
- You don't owe it to me or your classmates or yourself to spend more than an hour and fifteen minutes on them.
- We will go over all the problems tomorrow so that any uncertainties can be resolved, whether or not you've found solutions.

I am curious about your thoughts on these issues.

Having spent the years 1972–1987 (the pre-Exeter years) in Washington, and having read the *Post* for my daily news fix, I am familiar with your writing, and being an old lefty myself (or at least the son of an old lefty, who praised the likes of Lenin and Martin Luther King around the house when I was growing up), I typically agree with what you have to say. So it was good to see you on the Exeter stage, better yet to have you invited and praised by a student who I don't think is naturally inclined to the political left. Do come again.

Sincerely,

Joe Wolfson

Dear Joe,

Some loose moments, finally. Thanks for your patience.

It was a special moment to be visiting Exeter, my second time to speak at the school. Too bad we didn't catch up on either visit.

My first question for you would have been on longevity. How have you lasted so long at the academy, rebelling as you do against grading and testing. I can see you fitting in well at Simon's Rock or some other liberated haven, but Exeter? Maybe they can't find a math teacher to replace you? Maybe you gave a million bucks last year? Or you've been lucky that your students don't snitch to the headmaster that you believe "grades interfere with learning."

We're on the same ball field on this one, although I imagine the risks for you are far greater than mine. At two of the three high schools where I teach, I'm a volunteer. I can't be fired because I haven't been hired. At one school, Bethesda–Chevy Chase, which *Time* magazine once called the best public high school in America, I give no homework, no tests or exams, and students know coming in that they'll likely be getting an A at the end of the course. Five principals have come and gone since I started in 1988. None has ever raised a negative eyebrow about this, especially not to demand that I stop flouting the school's academic standards—if flouting is what it is.

This semester I have two classes, one at 7:25 am, the next at 8:20; about 40 students in each, all seniors. On the no testing, no homework and all As, my head is neither in the sand nor in the clouds. I'm aware that some students blow off the course and that others see it as the mother of all gut courses. No so fast, I tell them the first day of class: this will be the most difficult course you've ever taken. You'll need to make genuine demands on yourself rather than respond to artificial demands from your teacher. Self-made people tend to be self-demanding people.

Scotching homework, tests and grades decreases, as you suggested, fear-based learning and replaces it with desire-based learning. Most students learn quickly, starting even in pre-school, that the teacher has power over them and that pleasing authority is the way to get ahead in both the classroom and beyond. Grade mongering soon sets in. Schools might as well become factories processing students as if they were slabs of cheese going to Velveeta High and onto Mozzarella U and Cheddar grad school. Midway through my Assembly talk, if I recall, I asked if anyone in the hall could raise his or her hand and tell everyone, in totally honesty, "I have never cheated in school." Only a few hands rose, out of 350 students.

Dishonesty becomes a coping tool. It's the same at every school where I'm invited to speak. A study was done a few years back on what students talk about when the conversation turns to teachers. More than 75 percent of it is on how a teacher grades: not on what the teacher's politics might be, the availability of the teacher, his or her academic background or class-room skills. It's mostly about power, which is what students link grades with. How does this person, the teacher, have power over me? Quality teachers don't want power over students, they want power with students. For what? To bring about a more just and peaceful society, which I is why I teach and, I'm sure, why you and any conscientious teacher teaches.

Students who play it safe get to play again. Break ranks and risk being broken. Had I more time in my talk, I would have done my counting cars experiment, the one I did this morning in Bethesda high school. In an earnest tone of voice, I asked the students to leave the room and go to the parking lot. Stand there for five minutes and count as best they can all the red cars they see and all the green cars. Come back and I'll have two questions for you. Dutifully, even happily, they marched out. Five minutes and they were back. Question one: did anyone think it was stupid, standing there counting red and green cars? Plenty of yeses on that. Question two: if you thought it was stupid, why'd you do it? Few brains cells were needed to figure out the point of the experiment: when power tells you to do something obviously and insultingly stupid, refuse.

When it tells you to believe in wars as the way to create peace, don't count the cars. When it tells you that death row executions help solve the crime problem, don't count the cars.

I understand your feelings about homework, that it can be useful. It probably would be if other teachers weren't also demanding it the same nights. If it were just for one class and for one teacher it might be helpful. But for five or six classes? How can students not see it as anything more than busywork, a chore to push through and not an intellectual exercise to be enjoyed? If teachers do a worthy job in class, students won't need homework. They'll engage in home-thinking. Mark Twain had it right: work is what you do when you'd rather be doing something else.

It's a magic moment, and I'm sure you have had them, when teachers run into the parents of a student and the Mom or Dad give the ultimate compliment: "we often talk about your class during dinner."

I should tell you that Ryan Morgan added much to my class last summer at Georgetown. He was one of two high school students in the course, the other a girl from Venezuela. The two usually sat together. The class of 18 included a girl from Poland, two recovering alcoholics, a gentle and giving girl from the royal family of Abu Dhabi and the granddaughter of the emir. The topics of the course—it was called The Literature of Peace—were new to Ryan, ranging from capital punishment to animal rights, with Gandhi, Tolstoy, Dorothy Day, Thomas Merton and others in between. For papers, I asked the students to stay clear of the library: get off campus and explore an issue you never looked at before. Ryan did that, heading into one of the city parks well away from George-town to interview some homeless people and writing about the experience movingly.

Thanks for sending your thoughts.

Colman McCarthy

∽ ∽ ∽

At the end of the fall 2009 semester a student was rankled at my occasional failure to remember everyone's name—this student's especially. My reply:

Largest of thanks for your letter. In addition to you, David, Max, Kia, Magnus, Blair, Judson, Charles, Josephine, Shoshanna, Ian, Evan,

Luis, Philip, Stephanie, Jamilah, Maria, Kelsey, Isadora, David, Elliott, Owyn, Jeremy, Ian, Elvis, Paul, Christopher, Teckla, Shayne, Jennifer, Susana, Daniel, Leah, Alison, Ivana, Taylor, George, Alexander, Kofi, Julius, Langston, Maya, Catherine, Kelly, Lia, Tyler, Gregory, Jonathan, Cecelia, Khircelle, Evan, Nakissa, Filip, Gregory, Ilyah, Jack, Damon, Carly, Zubaydah, Sarah, James, Patrick, Nazret, Margaret, Miroslava, Gabriela, David, Josephina, William, Travis, Kajal, Scuyler, Grady, Emily, Lauriane, Mason, Emily, Brad, Hanna, Brandon, Peter, Zachary, Lindsay, Derrick, Krista, Megan, Meghan, Sara, Lauren, Nina, Amanda, Yang, Kristina, Eugene, Ashley, Ryo, Ari, William, Trevor, Natalie, Amy, Timothy, Zachary, Rachel, Natalie, Amy, Alison, Jenna, Laura, Ian, Sarah, Marie, Eric, Ferda, Rachel, Anna, Ashley, Elizabeth, Francisco, Elizabeth, Kelsey, Shelley, Hosam, Kevin, Samantha, Emily, Chika, Brianna, Erin, Jessica, Valerie, Christopher, Pratik, Scoti, Philip, Rebecca, Andrea, Alicia, Nora, Elizabeth, Rutvij, Daniel, Mark, Rachel, Eric, Samantha, Najeff, Hilary, Ben, Erick, Jeffrey, Destiny, Michele Ann, Michah, Carrie, Kevin, Benjamin, Ryan, Kimberly, Sean, Amanda, Matthew, Tionna, Theresa, Carrianne, Alyssa, Lea, Emma, Adeolu, Meghan, Kimberley, Leandra, Georgia, Eli, Billy, Dakota, Nick, Driss, Jing Jing, Riyong, Menquin and Niall are my students this semester in the eight classes I'm teaching at two high schools, three universities and one law school.

Sometimes I slip up and falter when attempting to correctly place 170 names with 170 faces. My apologies to you.

Keep on,

Colman McCarthy

∽ ∽ ∽

Dear Mr. McCarthy

You are very cool. I am Sophie. I am nine years old and love to write. I am in Roots and Shoots, and one of our activities is an ongoing peace class. We have learned about various people including Mahatma Gandhi, Riane Eisler, Henry David Thoreau, Bruno Hussar, Dalai Lama, Thich Nhat Hanh and many more. We also learned about you. I like how you teach peace to everyone. Here is a poem that I wrote about you. I hope you like it.

To Teach Peace Is To Live Peace

To teach peace is to live peace
To live peace is to love peace
To love peace is to teach peace.
Round in a circle
The words spin together,
Living and laughing
We all sing together.

To live peace is to love peace
The dove coos from the branch.
To love peace is to teach peace
From the ant upon the sand.

To teach peace is to live peace
They merrily agree
When they finish speaking
They gently come to me.
Peace changes my life
Says the quietly sitting cat.
Peace changes your life
Says the wet and shivering rat.

From our friend McCarthy
Teach peace at an early age.
Says the prisoner
Tis much better than a life trapped in a cage
And their voices blend together
As they read a peaceful page.

Peace is the answer
Cries the brightly blushing tree.
Quoth the vet.
If there was peace I might still have knees.
And their tears run together
As they read of dear Gandhi.

All around the world
Even in your hometown
There are problems to discover.
There are tasks to be found

All over the country
And in your hometown
The story of Colman McCarthy's unwound
The tale of peace
And the calling he found.

To teach peace is to live peace
To live peace is to love peace
To love peace is to teach peace
Round in a circle
The words spin together
Living and laughing
We all sing together.

Love,

Sophie E.

Dear Friend Sophie

It isn't often that a handwritten letter comes saying in the opening line
that I am "very cool." It's never happened before, whether in the first
line of the letter, or the second or third or last line. But here's the aston-
ishment: it's true that I am cool. The current weather in Washington
has ranged between 10 and 25 degrees below freezing. Every weekday
morning at 6:45 I ride my Raleigh 3-speed bicycle five miles to Bethesda–
Chevy Chase High School to teach two Peace Studies classes to about 75
students. On arrival I am assuredly cool. After the second class, which
ends at 9:10, which is long enough to benefit from if not global warming
then at least schoolhouse warming, I ride to the next school, Wilson
High, four miles away. I'm a cool guy again—or as one of my students
from the hood puts it, "You a cool cat, bro."

It isn't often either that a letter arrives from some who is nine, who loves to write, who is in "Roots and Shoots" and who is up on Gandhi, Thoreau and the other north stars that help us navigate to peace. What do you owe it to—winning the birth lottery, lucking out in having a teacher who values peace education?—that you are in a progressive program like Roots and Shoots?

You'll be delighted to know that I have a 28-minute film titled *New Shoots For Peace* which I play for all my high school, college and law classes. There's a story behind the film. In the mid-1980s I had a student at American University who was a second semester senior limping to the finish line of graduation. His grades were wretched, borderline flunking out. Three credits behind, and trembling in fear that he wouldn't graduate, he asked after class one day if I could cook up a work-study project that would supply the three credits. I knew the lad was a gifted photographer. His passion was cameras. He would cut classes to go on shoots, which likely explained the three-credit deficit and low grades. I suggested that he make a slide show about peace education: take some pictures, write a script and find some music for the background.

Can you do it? I asked. Give me two weeks, he announced, clasping my hand like a drowning man about to sink. Before bounding off, he asked about the music. Get some folk songs from the 1960s and '70s, I said: Joan Baez, Pete Seeger, John McCutcheon, Peter, Paul and Mary. "Do you know about the '60s?" I asked. "Sure," he replied. "We've been studying it in my ancient history class, it's right between the Pleistocene and Neanderthal era." Smart boy.

The film came back: stunning pictures, striking scenes, quotes from Dorothy Day, Tolstoy, Gandhi, King, Jeannette Rankin, Maria Montessori, a workable script that needed only a second or third draft for polishing. For songs: Joan Baez opening with "Where Have All the Flowers Gone" and "Forever Young" for the closing. In between was "Shenandoah" and Eric Bogle's anti-war song, "The Green Fields of France."

I've shown it hundreds of times, before audiences from Cyprus to Seattle. Three years ago, one of my former teaching assistants, Katherine Hessler, and her husband, John, converted the slide show to a DVD which I can send you sometime if you'd like.

So what happened to the boy who made the film? I gave him three credits—he deserved 30—and he did graduate, much to the relief of his parents. The last I heard, he left the East for the West Coast and the mandatory mid-20s San Francisco phase. He settled down, went to graduate school and is now a philosophy professor.

I loved your poem. My wife, Mavourneen, did too—reading it aloud when the mail came yesterday, right after we played Scrabble. She had two seven-letter words and her score was 542, which is high. I was way behind, not even above 400.

You must tell me when and where you discovered that you had a gift for language. All writers carry the memory of that time and place within themselves, the moment that brightened like a double rainbow in the sky of opportunity.

I'd also like to know about your teacher who runs Roots and Shoots. A story is there. I'm sure you can tell it well.

If you ever come to Washington with your parents or teachers, please come to my classes. Don't travel right now. It's freezing. Or maybe you'd like to come, if you want be "very cool."

All the best and be the best of all—

Colman McCarthy

JANUARY 5, 2011

Dear Mr. McCarthy,

You are cooler than I thought. Wow! You might say that I am cool, too, because I ride my bike every day except Friday, Saturday and Sunday. I think you might be interested to know that I am having one of my stories published in a magazine!! Here is a copy of it.

Your book is great. A++. May I please have a copy of *New Shoots For Peace*? I would like to share it with the other Roots and Shoots kids. My R&S teacher, Miss Julie, is very interesting, although I do not know her story. I will ask her, though, and write to you about her soon. I am taking a peace class with her called Great Peacemakers. When we read about you, we made a book about teaching peace. You are amazing! You are great! You are A+. You are wonderful!

Love,

Sophie E.

P.S. Thank you for your book.

P.P.S. All I know is that I was talking in paragraphs when I was two.

Dear Friend Sophie,

If I'm so amazing, great, A+ and wonderful, how come I'm a year late in answering your letter. Instead of amazing, let's try lazy. Instead of great, let's try graceless. Instead of A+, how about an F? Instead of wonderful, woebegone.

Please accept my apologies for taking so long. At the same time, please accept my praise and gratitude for sending your story, "A Fair Day." I love it. What a clever title, followed by the narrative of your day at the New Mexico State Fair and your showing of Dooley, your alpaca. Congratulations on placing third, not at all bad for your first time at the fair.

For me, you earn first place for pushing ahead and getting your story published. I treasure the booklet you made of it, complete with 34 color photographs. You can be sure that I have been showing it to my peace classes when we take up animal rights and human wrongs.

Now that you are a published writer, what's next? Easy question: get published again. Bringing that about is the trick. I taught a writing course a few years ago, and offered the class 10 suggestions for improvement and which later became a column for the *Washington Post*. As a teacher, I can no more define quality writing than a horse can define a beautiful meadow. I can sense it, and like the horse before the grassland, I want to bound through a piece of fine writing for the exhilaration it promises. Scrubland we both avoid.

1.   Write in a location safe from noise and interruption.
2.   Begin with a definite goal of how long your writing period will last. If five minutes, fine. If five hours, fine. Just know. Then regularize. Gandhi, who wrote more than 10 million words in his life, put down at least 500 words a day for 50 years. He regularized.
3.   Learn new words. Have a vocabulary program. Add a new word a day, a week, a month, whatever. Keep adding, that's all. Master the one and two-syllable words. Five and six-syllable Latin-Greek derivatives are for showoffs. Study idioms, metaphors and similes, which are the rainbows coloring the prose landscape.
4.   Spray disinfectants on clichés, bromides. Eliminate weak words:

very, nice, quiet, rather, presently, brilliant. Go over each story word by word and cut each that doesn't work. Otherwise readers are narcotized.

5. Never begin a piece of writing with "the." Writers who do so are yawning in print, at you.

6. If you are not in the mood to write, write anyway. Writing is often more sweat than sweetness, more fidelity than feelings. If you need to be in the mood to write, the only topic you'll ever master is moods.

7. When not writing, don't bore people by quoting yourself. Don't boast or preen, even covertly, about where you've just been published. And don't quiz friends on whether they have (a) read your latest literary effort, (b) caught its "full meaning," (c) taped it on the refrigerator door.

8. Comfort other writers. Read their latest effort, strive to catch its "full meaning," and make room among the recipes and kids' drawings on the refrigerator door.

9. Spend as much time reading and as writing, but read only writers who heed Samuel Johnson's edict: "What is written without effort is read without pleasure."

10. Be a fanatical reviser. When I was visiting the Iowa Writers' Workshop at the University of Iowa, I asked Paul Engle, the director, for his definition of good writing: "Writing is rewriting what you have rewritten." Never trust a first draft. Never be satisfied with a second. Never think that a third is your best. Tolstoy wrote seven drafts of "War and Peace." Ernest Hemingway once spent all morning putting in a comma and all afternoon taking it out.

Maybe you have your own rules for writing. If so, send them along.

Here is a copy of my newest book I've edited: *Peace Is Possible*. I wish it could have been titled *Peace Is Probable*, but humanity is not there yet. Maybe in the year 10,000, if we hurry.

My best to your Mom and Dad and, of course, Dooley—

Colman McCarthy

In mid-November 2013 I wrote to Sophie asking her to sign a consent form allowing her letters to be published in this book. She returned the signed form, along with this:

NOVEMBER 26, 2013

Dear Mr. McCarthy,

Thank you for the letter. I had hoped to write to you sooner, but had to put it off, so this is a perfect memory jog. I have certainly been doing well lately. I am in 7th grade at Jefferson Middle School in Albuquerque where I am in gifted classes, and a rock band (Rock and Rhythm). I have continued to practice peace, and try to be as nice as possible at school, even when others aren't that way to me. I am also pleased to say that Jefferson has a strong bully-prevention program, and I have seen no problems so far.

I am now an avid actress, and I do non-competitive wushu (kung fu) which is fun. I am also writing a novel, *A World of Sand*, which is coming along fairly well. I just finished reading *Oliver Twist* which I enjoyed immensely.

I hope that you are doing well, and along with you, the Center for Teaching Peace.

I still hope to visit someday.

You certainly seem to be just as cool as you were when I first wrote to you, if not more so. I am deeply honored that you want to include my letters in your book.

Thank you again for being awesome, and I hope that you can continue to teach peace for years to come.

Sincerely,

Sophie E.

P.S. I apologize for the numerous typing and punctuation problems, but I am writing this on a typewriter, and the correction tape doesn't work.

Dear Colman,

I'm an English teacher at Niles West High School in Skokie, a suburb just north of Chicago. I'm writing to let you know that our district, somewhat miraculously, approved a peace studies course. Here is the full story.

I have had a lifelong interest in peace studies and peace education, most likely due to my father who is a World War II veteran and retired English professor. He is a lifelong liberal in the Howard Zinn and Jonathan Kozol mold. To what my father gave me, I added an interest in liberation theology (I am Roman Catholic) and Buddhism.

From that, I was driven to learn about human rights violations in Central America and elsewhere. Buddhism has taught me to focus on inner peace. In Chicago I have had the privilege of knowing Kathy Kelly of Voices for Creative Nonviolence, and I have brought her to my school several times. For years I was the faculty moderator of a student peace group, which has become a student chapter of Amnesty International.

Due to your book, *I'd Rather Teach Peace*, I had the idea of starting a peace course in our district. I ordered your two collections of peace essays several years ago. You wrote back an encouraging letter.

It takes a long time to get a course started here, with many institutional hoops to jump through. Two other teachers and I put a proposal together which at first was rejected. It was too "social studies" oriented. We are all, incidentally, English teachers. Our second proposal, titled The Literature of Peace, was accepted by the school board. This was the miraculous part. Because the course is part of the English curriculum, we will be teaching more literature—poetry, short stories, drama—than you would in yours.

We begin teaching the course this Fall. With two high schools in our district, we will have one course in each. I would love to keep in touch with you as we go through this process. The three of us are new at this and we want to do the best we can to make sure the courses become popular and continue. I would love to see it blossom into a school-wide peace studies program involving our entire curriculum. We are at the first step.

In closing, I want to thank you from the bottom of my heart for your work, because your writing inspired me to get this course going.

Peace,

Paul Wack

Dear Paul,

Until I check the AAU indoor record book for the fastest time anyone has created a peace studies course, I'm guessing you are close to medaling. It's usually years and years between a proposal and the day students walk into class. I needed seven years to win approval of my book *Solutions to Violence* for use in Bethesda–Chevy Chase High School.

Not to get carried away with anything grandiose, but in a rational world schools would be putting peace courses into classes at all levels. Yet here we are in the US where only a few of the nation's 78,000 elementary schools, 31,000 high schools and 4,000 colleges and universities offer courses in alternatives to violence.

You've done well in Skokie. But watch out. You know the line, "The trouble with a good idea is that it soon degenerates into hard work."

Enjoy your degeneracy—

Colman McCarthy

JULY 7, 2004

Dear Colman,

I don't know if you remember me so I'll start with an introduction. My name is Beth Blacklow and I took your Peace Studies class at Bethesda–Chevy Chase six years ago. It was you who first put in my head the idea of volunteering for the Peace Corps.

That's exactly what I did after graduating from Barnard College. I've been living in Ecuador for two years and I'll be returning home in a month. Although the first months in my town here were some of the most difficult, lonely and depressed points in my life, the following year and a half has more than made up for that. I'm working in the health program promoting basic hygiene, nutrition, family planning, alcohol awareness and other subjects. I've made some close friends in my town and always have a group of children playing in my house. I feel I've been able to help the community or some individuals with small changes. I still want to be a teacher and I'm now considering bilingual education so I can put my Spanish to use and I can work with immigrants.

This letter is to thank you for the time you put into my high school Peace Studies class. Your own dedication has inspired me to change my life and still affects me. I've been a vegetarian for six years. You may not hear from your past students frequently but you are one of the great teachers we never forget.

Thanks again,

Beth Blacklow

AUGUST 2, 2004

Dear Beth,

Much praise to you for digging in and persevering through the rough early months.

We never know what our principles are until they are tested. You passed the test.

Of course I remember you. Although it was a large class, I had no trouble sensing that you had a caring heart and gentle spirit—the gifts that brought you to the Peace Corps and ones you shared with the local people. I've been close to the Peace Corps all these years, having come to Washington to work for Sargent Shriver, the first director. Every year at B-CC I push the program, half-wishing that maybe a few will remember it during their college years and join after graduation. I was moved to receive your letter. Assuredly it will encourage me to keep promoting the Peace Corps. That's where you come in. Please come speak to my classes this Fall when you return to Bethesda. And here's hoping you don't go through a re-entry crisis: emerging from the poverty of your village to the wealth of Bethesda, one world far removed from the other.

You may remember Claire Moody, a year ahead of you at B-CC. She spoke to my classes in April, spiritedly telling of her Peace Corps work in Benin, West Africa. The liveliness of her stories reminded me of Sargent Shriver's belief of how volunteers are affected by the land in which they serve. Those who went to Asian countries return as mystics. Those sent to Africa come home singing and dancing. Those from Latin America become revolutionaries.

So read up on liberation theology, Paulo Freire, Dom Hélder Câmara and Oscar Romero and keep the revolution blazing.

Many blessings to you, not that you are running short.

Colman

Dear Professor McCarthy,

My name is Casey and I was in your Principles and Practices of Peace class this past semester. I was just writing to ask about my grade. I was quite shocked and slightly offended that I received a B+. I came to every class, read every assignment, helped with videos, joined discussions where I could, and even gave up a crucial part of my former diet for this class. I am still not eating meat. For a class that I have learned so much from, I did not expect a B+ Also, I was not aware that the grade for my second paper would be put down so low. We were never made aware of that lateness policy. I know you don't think I should be worrying about my grades but until my parents put Bs on the same level as As, I will be. Thank you very much for your time and for an extremely rewarding semester.

Cassandra Gugoff

MAY 12, 2007

Dear Cassandra,

Thanks for your inquiry. It isn't often that students tell me that they are "quite shocked and slightly offended" about a B+, especially when I am told—by friends and critics—that I am an overly generous grader. If I were as strict as many other professors routinely are when it comes to grading essays—and which I could be because I am a writer by trade— Cs, and rarely As and only a few Bs would be given.

Your B+ was generous. The first paper was an A-. The second was a B. It was a late paper, which means it would have been an A if turned in on time. You say that "we were never made aware of that lateness policy." Check the syllabus, where it says: "grade deduction for late papers." You said you couldn't find your syllabus, a problem I don't know how to solve. Some professors won't accept late papers. In our class, about 10 students were late for the second paper. I accepted them all. On the exam, your grade was a B-, the result of four incorrect answers. Put together, the A-, B and B- comes to a B. I raised it to a B+. And now you are shocked and offended.

Grading students is the worst part of teaching. Fretting about grades is commonplace among students.* Parents, the strapped bill-payers, have their moments too. I prefer a pass/fail system which is how I teach one of my classes at the University of Maryland, but at American few students would opt for pass/fail courses. At one of my high schools, I assign no homework, give no exams and another teacher grades. That's about as pure as it gets. Universities are nowhere near that. Too often, artificial learning prevails.

I care deeply about my students, especially someone like you who took the class seriously, was appreciative of the material and discussions, and took to heart—and to the dinner table—some of the ideas in the readings. I'm enormously grateful for your thoughtful and kind comments in the [unofficial] evaluations, and I think you know how delighted I was to have you in class. I wish it had been smaller so I could have gotten to know you and your thinking a bit better.

If it would help matters at home, I'd be glad to write a letter to your parents—to tell them what an exemplary student you are.

In friendship,

Colman McCarthy

*A student to whom I gave an A- wrote to tell me that the grade would ruin all chances to graduate with a 4.0 GPA, and is there any extra work that could be done to raise it up to an A.

I replied:

Dear ———,

Good to hear from you, just as it was a delight to have you in class. You livened up the place, and I wish more students had followed your example.

I understand your disappointment in the A- rather than an A, even though a grade of A- would have more than a few students at the university shouting and jumping with joy on the rooftops on the tallest dorm on campus, and possibly waving a florescent banner painted with the A-.

I appreciate your offering to do something to raise the grade, and I wish I could take you up on it. But if I did, then I and every other professor would have to say yes to all students out to jack their grades by performing one academic handstand or another.

I do my best to advise students not to stress out about grades, citing the telling line from a Walker Percy novel that you can make all As in school but go on to fail at life. I've seen it happen. I try, too, to persuade students that when life's plusses and minus are finally toted, grades don't really matter. When you have a moment, take a look at the obituary pages of the *Washington Post* and *New York Times*. Whether the obits are written by staff reporters or are paid announcements (at up to $700 an inch in the *Post*, more on Sundays and more with color photos), nowhere will you find mention of the GPA of the departed nor a syllable on how many As they scored in high school or college or gold stars in pre-K. I have yet to find an obituary that said the death bed words of the deceased were "I wish I'd made more As in school."

Now head to the wedding pages, which both papers run on Sundays. You'll be told about the couples' parents—mandatory mentions in the *Times* if they are CEOs who summer in the Hamptons or winter in Gstaad—and be informed on where the couples met and where educated. I have never seen a wedding story or paid wedding announcement that included the GPAs of the happily betrothed.

You have to wonder, then, if grades are that crucial why no reference to them at these important moments? Why don't obituaries start off with this: "Mary Smith, whose 4.0 GPA in college was acclaimed throughout the Western world, died at home yesterday of a heart attack after her 911 call failed to get through to her town's ambulance rescue squad." Why don't wedding announcements begin: "Millie Jones and Bubba Carter, whose GPAs respectively were 3.9 and 1.7, were married yesterday at Our Lady of Academic Excellence, the chapel at the Deep South Catholic college where they met. The chapel is next to the campus library, where Millie spent scads of time studying and Bubba rarely entered."

It's possible that you'll remember me, if you remember me at all, as the guy who ruined your chances for a 4.0. But suppose I did up the

A- to an A. You might remember me as the guy you conned into feeling sorry for you. Either way, it looks like a lose-lose deal.

Let's think about winning. I remember your saying you were thinking of law school. I'd be glad to write a letter of recommendation for you.* I've been at Georgetown Law for 25 years, and I can see you easily fitting in and doing well there. And the same for any law school.

Be worry free,

Colman McCarthy

*The student asked and I wrote, glowingly.

⌣ ⌣ ⌣

Dear Mr. McCarthy

I wish to thank you for taking the time to write your Dec. 17 letter to us, Chris Neumeyer's parents. We will treasure your generous and kind words about our son [who took your course in the Fall of 2006]. I also send thanks for mentioning Chris and me in your *Washington Post* article on the death of Father [Robert] Drinan.

Because our paths have now crossed, I need write you this: in 1968 I had just finished serving 5 years in the Marine Corps and started under-graduate studies at the University of Maryland. Not that I am any less confused now about the world than I was then. Way back then, though, I discovered your column in the *Washington Post*. As simply, and I hope as clearly as I can, I want to thank you. I honestly feel my reflecting on what you stated in your columns contributed more to my education than a lot of that gained in formal schooling. I suppose some evidence of what I relate is I not only clearly read any thought that you wrote, I clipped from the newspaper your words. Saved them to read again.

Lastly, I also want you to know this. After school I finally ended up as a counselor of military veterans for the US Department of Veterans Affairs for 25 years. Rewarding but sometimes difficult work. There were times I had to stop and think: how can I best help who is sitting across my desk? I relied on my own thinking of course, but as well, sometimes

I ranged over the wisdom I know from others. Mostly from what I read. You surely were not the only one, but sometimes I would think, "What would McCarthy do with this?"

Sincerely,

Norris F. Neumeyer Jr.

Dear Norris (please call me Colman),

Sorry for the delay, have been gadding about.

I'm grateful for your kind words about my columns back in your college days at Maryland. You are owed debts for helping veterans. Perhaps you worked for the VA when Max Cleland was the director. Overall I thought he was competent and level-headed and showed great empathy for veterans. He was a triple amputee himself. I came to know him well, because the mistreatment of Vietnam veterans was one of the beats I carved out for myself—at the encouragement of my editor at the *Post*, Philip Geyelin. Along with Max, Bobby Muller was another source—not only for information but for justified anger. Both men came home from Vietnam with shattered bodies, destined for wheelchairs, while the war's architects wheeled themselves off in limousines to write their self-serving memoirs.

It's happening again. In my classes, I get discussions started on the similarities between the Vietnam and Iraq wars. We are up to 15 now, including the one of Robert McNamara and Paul Wolfowitz both leaving the Pentagon for the World Bank, going from killing poor people to saving them—sort of saving. Another possible similarity, and one which I'm not yet sure of, are the funerals at Arlington Cemetery. I do know that Bush has never been to one, though it's almost daily these past years that the horses and buglers are called out for another funeral. I can't remember Nixon or Johnson ever appearing.

In 20 years of teaching at Georgetown Law, I need little time to sense who is the most informed student in the class and the one most likely to pull the intellectual rug from under me. Chris was the puller this past semester, especially when I'd drop an historical fact or two—or what I thought was fact. He knew how to correct me gracefully, speaking to the class as a wise person, not a wiseguy. I really controlled my digressions when he owned up to being a former high school history teacher.

Chris called the other day and asked for an extension on his paper. The school asks for 6,000 words, which can be marathonic for some students. Chris may have told you that he's writing the paper about your journey from a Marine to the person you are now, and planning to interview you during the spring break. I'm guessing that you are in the bracing company of such former soldiers turned peacemakers as Philip Geyelin, Andy Jacobs, Howard Zinn, Philip Berrigan, Mark Hatfield, Kurt Vonnegut, Heinrich Böll and, again, good Bobby Muller. I encourage students to interview their parents, rather than grind footnoted, endnoted and overnoted research jobs that they were loath to write and I was bored to read. So much goes on in families that sometimes children learn little or nothing from it, or are even curious to find out—and often these are the children who turn out to be history majors in college. They are swaddled in every history but their own parents' and grandparents.' Howard Zinn came to my high school class one morning—at 7:25 am, which didn't bother him a bit—and told the students that history is the winner's version of what happens. Sometimes it's worthwhile to get a parent's version.

I was glad to include your words in the piece I wrote for the *Post* on Bob Drinan. You may have read it online, which means you were denied the pleasure of a huge gasp at the way the editors placed it: above the fold on the front page of the heralded Style section. But it was beneath a similar story—"an appreciation"—on the death of Barbaro, plus a picture of the horse. The message of the placement was clear. Devote your life as a Jesuit priest in a ministry of 60 years to the works of mercy and rescue, to teaching legal ethics, to working for human rights and civil rights, but if you happen to die at the same time as a three-year-old horse who was forced to run around in circles for the enrichment of millionaire owners and the delight of besotted gamblers in the grandstand, you can expect to get second billing in the newspaper.

Leave a bit of time for a visit when you come East for Chris's graduation this spring. In addition to writing letters to the parents of my law students, I like to meet them in person also. One funny tale about the letters. A mother of a student in Chris's class wrote back to say how mightily relieved she was that her daughter was praised by her professor: she "was an only child who was a major challenge to raise throughout her teenage years, so to see that we all made it is a real miracle." And this was a girl who had the deepest spirituality of anyone in the class.

Have to go now. The evening news is coming on. And I expect it will be momentous news: a fourth man has announced that he's the father of Anna Nicole Smith's love child. You don't think that will be the lead for ABC, CBS, NBC—plus Larry, Greta, mouthy Chris and more mouthy Mary Grace?

Be well—

Colman

∿ ∿ ∿

MARCH 6, 2012

Dear Professor,

Hello, it's Sam Roberts from our Wednesday Peace and Social Justice class. I spoke to you last week about losing my book and asking if I could borrow one from you for the rest of the semester. I am writing you now at a very late hour, both literally and in the context of my message because I have some questions and am also looking for your input.

Not to make any excuses but just to give a little information from my perspective, I am a senior this year hopefully graduating in May. To do so I am having to take 19 credits this semester (six classes) and all but one of them block SIS classes. I severely underestimated the difficulty of this and have been really struggling just to keep up with all my classes and the volume of their assigned readings and workloads. For some reason, even though it says March 7th on the syllabus [for the first paper due date] I thought this was the end of the semester final paper and as a result I was not prepared for it.

I realize this is late to be bringing all this up, but all this week I have at least one paper or exam (sometimes both) on every day. Last week was more of the usual, trying to keep up and do all the readings for all my classes. Please do not think that I do not consider your class when I say this, as your class is very light on the readings and a joy to relax and have discussion-based lectures in class.

As it stands, it's the truth I have to accept. And I was not able to prepare a paper. This saddens me because when [the syllabus] suggested the kind of papers we might want to write you gave many interesting and cool ideas on what previous students had written and now I simply do not have the time to conduct the type of experiments with my own life that some of your past students did. I have to admit that I am very bad when it comes to open-ended papers like this, and the idea of no sources and just writing about ourselves is definitely a first for me and I am quite nervous. Perhaps this is because, as you said in class, we are taught time and time again to crank out the standard research paper with sources and such that now I am terrible at choosing my own topics when I am given complete freedom to write something.

I'm not trying to make an excuse. I just want to touch base with you and I am trying to write my paper about my personal life and the effects/experience of violence in it. I am truly not a slacker or not taking the class seriously, but I am really struggling right now and since its gotten so late [1:50 am] I felt like I don't really have many options and since I'm pretty bad at this type of paper I would go with something that's a large part of my life. I will be honest with you and say that I want to try to write my paper about my parents and their divorce, which was a pretty intense and emotional experience for me. It was a violent experience and I think it has definitely affected and shaped the type of person I've grown to be.

I know the paper only has to be 1,000 words or more but as I said I'm pretty nervous about this kind of paper because I am not good at them and I'm not sure if this topic is "creative" enough and that I can produce something of great quality. Also I was hoping to write some of this in a very unconventional sense, almost as if in a visual narrative way like a story bring told. I will of course include a more "standard" essay in which I explain and discuss the effects on me to this day but I was not sure if my first idea would be OK with you? Because I'm not confident in this type of paper I don't know what's OK and what you're expecting. I know you said you want a paper that's "unique" and "unconventional," but I just want to check. It's a pretty personal topic for me so I want to be sure everything is OK before I actually put it all out there.

I apologize for the length and repetitiveness of this. I know it is a huge mouthful all at once but I wanted to touch base with you. Regardless, I appreciate your time and any response. I will try my best for this paper and hopefully it all works out. Thank you very much.

Sincerely,

Sam Roberts

Dear Sam,

No need to be nervous, especially if it comes from wondering whether your proposed paper meets my expectation. It will if you can rise to the occasion and move away from the conventional research paper based on scouring books, the internet, archives. Instead research your own life. I'm aware that students may see this kind of paper as a mountain too steep to scale, having been trained by too many high school teachers and college professors to remain safely below in the flatlands of ordinary prose girded with footnotes and end notes. Of course you are "terrible at choosing my own topics when I am given complete freedom to write something." It doesn't say much for American education when you are nearing the finish line—16 years of inching to it, eight in elementary and middle school, four in high school and four in college—and only now you are being offered the chance to be freed up and write from your heart and emotions.

As I mentioned in the opening class of the semester, when suggesting possible paper topics, I suffer from a serious and often life-threatening illness: MEGO, My Eyes Glaze Over. It infects me when I read conventional college papers. If after reading a half-dozen I leave the house for an errand, my glazed eyes put me at risk of falling off bridges, walking into high-speed traffic, tumbling down stairs. So far, I've survived all the close calls, luckily so because my health insurance doesn't cover MEGO injuries. The cure is MEOW: My Eyes Open Wide. These are papers that shine with self-reflection, often fearless with probings into the inner life.

I'm expecting a MEOW paper from you. Do indeed write about what you call the "violent experience" of your parent's divorce. Try to see the writing of it as a growth opportunity, not merely pounding out words to fulfill a course requirement. And please, no footnotes.

Be confident,

Colman McCarthy

JULY 25, 2005

Dear Professor,

I'm writing to you because I have a question about class tomorrow night. Some Washington Center students have been invited to attend a speech by the White House Chief of Staff Andrew Card on Monday. I want to attend this but it starts at 6 pm Monday night and that interferes with class. I don't want to miss class either so I'm kind of in a bind and I was wondering what you think I should do. I won't attend this event unless I get your okay. Let me know what you think if you get a chance.

Meredith Beardmore

JULY 25, 2005

Dear Meredith,

If you want to subject yourself to a governmental functionary working for a president who believes that violence is necessary and moral—the invasion of Iraq, executing people on death row, weakening environmental regulations—and who is likely to give a canned speech with a high boredom quotient, then go hear Andrew Card. I'd bet that halfway through his gab, you'll ask yourself, "Why am I wasting my time here?" Call me on your cell phone and I'll tell you: because you're an impressionable college student not yet knowing enough to resist the lures of getting close to Washington Big-Shotdom.

I'm hoping you are not impressionable, though this is one of a thousand hopes I have for my college students.

Can't guarantee it but I expect tomorrow's class will be worth your time: male-female relations and the interplay of violence and nonviolence. Plus a documentary about women who have freed themselves from violent husbands. I'm expecting a lively discussion, to which you could add a lot.

You are a valuable member of the class. You take the course to heart, and I'm always delighted when you speak—last week being no exception, on the abortion issue.

Kind regards,

Colman McCarthy

Dear Professor,

I'm coming to class. You reminded me of exactly what I don't want to subject myself to. Your class has changed me and thank you for your insight and suggestions. I just wish all the students that made me feel badly I was missing out if I skipped Card's speech could take your class. I enjoy it so much and I'm interested to see how the males in the class react/contribute to the discussion tonight. See you at 5:30.

    Meredith Beardmore

Dear Meredith,

So glad you came to class. See what an impact you had: inducing one of your classmates to write a paper about your questions to her. You helped make it one of our most relevant classes this summer.

    Yours,

    Colman McCarthy

Dear Colman,

This is Kirk Laubenstein. We met a while back when you spoke at Hobart and William Smith Colleges and when I came down to DC last Martin Luther King Day to go to the protest march at Lockheed Martin headquarters [in Bethesda, Maryland]. I am hoping that you can help me by giving me some guidance. I know we talked a bit about working in politics when I was in DC last, but I have now accepted a job as a councilperson's aide in the common council in Buffalo, NY. I think it will be interesting and I believe that I can do some good, but I have enjoyed being on the outside of government and being able to try and hold those in power accountable. Now I am one of the ones who needs to be accountable. I know I can be, I am just worried about it. I know that things in Buffalo are not the best, and that the political scene here is a bleak one, but I hope to do some good. I have also just finished reading your book

Involvements, which talks about war tax resistance, and now I am increasingly more a part of that system (even paid by those very same taxes). So what do you think about getting into the political game?

    Best,

      Kirk Laubenstein

JANUARY 23, 2008

Dear Kirk,

A treat to hear from you, though it's no treat to report that Lockheed Martin is still making cluster bombs as well as feasting off the Iraq War. But the protests go on at Lockheed's death bunker in Bethesda.

    Congratulations on landing a job with the city council. I'd suggest seeing it as a positive, starting with the chance to see the gears of government at work and with you able to oil them in a modest way. I've never thought it mattered much weather a person toils inside or outside government, so long as your conscience isn't numbed or compromised by your decisions. Remember Mother Teresa's line? "Few of us will ever be called on to do great things but all of us can do small things in a great way." If the council member you are working for, and on a good day working with, is a reflective person with an active ideal or two, then take advantage of it. Small things add up.

    You have the example of Mark Gearan, whose pathway to the presidency of Hobart and William Smith took him into government, both in the Clinton White House and then as head of the Peace Corps. There's no way to quantify all the lives he has effected for the good. You'll be interested to know that during Mark's time in the White House [as communications director, 1993–96] a group of gays and lesbians showed up one day at 1600 Pennsylvania to stage a demonstration. They were furious about Clinton's inept don't-ask-don't-tell military policy. Cops were called and a half-dozen protestors were cuffed and hauled off. The leader had been, like Mark Gearan, one of my students at Georgetown Law, a lad who evidently was listening hard the day we all discussed Thoreau's "On the Duty of Civil Disobedience" and unjust laws.

    So there I was, with two former students: one inside the White House cogitating and the other outside agitating. I was enormously proud of both, each involved in politics, however different the mechanics.

    Stick with your job for a couple of years, learn all you can. The

Letters   [63]

time may come when you realize, or fantasize, that you are as smart as your boss and YOU should be on the city council. Here in Washington, Congress has plenty of members who were once legislative assistants. They learned the ropes and then grabbed them to climb into the ring to win a seat in the House or Senate. One of them is Jim McGovern from Worcester, Massachusetts, who was Rep. Joseph Moakley's LA for more than ten years. Then he ran for Congress in 1996. He was trounced on the first try when he won only eight percent of the vote in the Democratic primary but came back two years later to defeat an incumbent. Now he has a safe seat and won in 2006 with no Republican opponent.

I had Jim as a student at American University in 1984, in the first class I taught there. When others would head to South Beach or Cancun for Spring Break, Jim would stay in town for another kind of excitement: sitting in the House gallery to watch and hear the floor debates— no doubt thinking, "one day I'll be down there." He has been one of the strongest supporters, by the way, of the Religious Freedom Peace Tax Fund Bill, proposed legislation to allow conscientious objectors to war the legal right not to pay taxes that go to military violence.*

If you do visit Washington, please come by. I have students who need to hear from a political pro like you.

Bring your best insider stories—

Colman

*The bill, first introduced in the House by California's Ronald Dellums in the early 1970s and proposed in every Congress since, has never made it out of the Ways and Means subcommittee. Over four decades, it received only one hearing, a half day. Every term, four or five senators and some forty House members co-sponsor the bill—all the rest stay clear. With half of the federal discretionary budget given to military and security programs, pacifists and other conscientious objectors to war would still pay their full share of federal taxes plus all other state and local taxes.

Dear Colman,

I've been thinking a lot about you lately, especially with all my new classes. I am really happy in Colorado for the most part. It is simply spectacular here and I am trying to get in as much skiing as possible. I feel privileged to be in such a beautiful and interesting place.

I think often about everything I learned in your class. Today in my philosophy and society class we discussed our government and my teacher posed a few different philosophical questions. What is just? What is a just government? Who should support the poor? I felt frustration because I feel that all of my supposed answers could so easily be argued down. Oh well. What really got me thinking about you was when my teacher asked how many of us voted. She proceeded to imply that those who didn't vote gave away their power and wasted that opportunity. I wanted to tell her that some people don't vote not because they are lazy or don't care, but because they don't want to just "choose the lesser of two evils." But then by not voting, are we not choosing an even worse evil, compliance? I am not sure. I voted this year but I wasn't initially planning on it. I eventually gave in and voted because I guess I thought maybe my vote could change things and I should not throw away the opportunity.

Did you vote, if you don't mind me asking? I don't think you did because you don't believe in voting. I remember this distinctly because I was at first outraged when you said that in class and then after hearing you support your beliefs, my views changed 180 degrees.

I find myself very confused at school. And very confused often. I suppose this is good. It means I am not too stubborn in my views and I am thinking. But it is also exhausting, never really knowing where I stand because there are so many different points of view and so many conflicting arguments for every conceivable topic.

Anyway, I won't write anymore because I know how many emails you get daily and how many you respond to. I really miss your class and think about all that I learned. I loved your class. I wish you would come to Boulder and speak. I think you would be a hit.

Bye,

Olivia Katz (I hope you remember me?)

Dear Olivia,

You hope I remember you? First off, save your hope and use it elsewhere. I can't see ever not remembering you, and for all the reasons that you well know. You came to my 8 pm college class at American University after being in your high school classes all day. You came not to get credits but because you had an open mind. You came out of pure desire. And, after all that, you fit in as if this was the most natural place for you to be. It was, especially the evening that you spoke up and gently suggested to one of your classmates—a second semester senior, no less—that she rethink her views on the death penalty.

Your professor who urged her students to vote is keeping alive the illusion that voting in elections can improve things. You have to wonder, then, when is all this betterment going to kick in? Two days ago, the Bush administration proposed a military budget over $700 billion—a 60% increase from 2001 when he was elected by the Supreme Court, 5 to 4. I've seen no evidence that voting has done much to help the 40,000 people around the world who die every day from hunger or the lack of preventive medicines. I've seen no evidence that voting makes the voter a kinder person or improves the character of the elected.

Those are the minor reasons I don't vote. The major one is constitutional. Every president, vice-president and member of Congress is sworn into office to "preserve, protect and defend" the Constitution. A noble and stirring thought, except that the Constitution sanctions violence: Article I Section 8 empowers Congress to raise money for the military, which it is currently doing to the point of bankrupting our economy. Article II Section 2 says the president is the commander-in-chief of the military. Put together, the Constitution calls for the elected to solve conflicts by killing people. Supported by voters, the elected—every president since Commander-in-Chief George Washington, every Congress since the first one in Philadelphia—have been reaching for the gun and the bomb.

People who vote are placing their faith in politicians who believe in violent solutions to conflicts. As a pacifist, it's only in political elections that I decline to vote. I vote every day to get up at 6 am to teach my high school classes, I vote every day to buy healthy and cruelty-free food. I vote every day to commute by bicycle. I vote every day to spend time with my family. I vote every day to buy products that do no harm to the environment. To my mind, that's true voting power—occurring every day—that has nothing to do with electoral politics, which involves passively pulling a lever once every four years.

And nothing to do with presidential elections that can be decided by a few swing counties in a few swing states.

I know that my non-voting views put me in the same holding pen reserved for heretics and deviants, but the heresy and deviancy we should be wary of is the belief that no alternatives to violence exist. It's also a matter of conscience. Every member of Congress, even those of the redoubtable Left, still believe in having a military. Pacifists reject that, even while knowing that large numbers in Congress are idealistic and have humane voting records. One of my former students, Jim McGovern, is certainly one of those. I think of members like Barbara Lee of Oakland, California, who was the only member to vote against the invasion of Afghanistan on September 14, 2001. To single out a current dozen senators and representatives who I've interviewed and would vote for were I not a pacifist: Jim McGovern, Marci Kaptur, Barbara Mikulski, Lynn Woolsey, Ron Wyden, Tom Harkin, Chuck Grassley, Bernie Sanders, Patrick Leahy, Ted Kennedy and Patrick Kennedy.

Don't be timid about speaking up in class. Do the opposite and speak as much as you can. Professors like it, at least the spirited ones. My favorite student last year was Jacob Cohen, a senior at Bethesda–Chevy Chase. Every class, he'd have his hand up—questioning, commenting, disagreeing, wondering, telling stories. He'd often skip his second period class to walk me to the parking lot and my bicycle, and we'd stay there for another hour talking.

No need to worry about where you stand on the issues. That's what college should be about: four or five years of shopping for ideas and ideals that help us make a difference by being different. And testing ourselves to do it.

This past semester I had a boy in one of my high school classes locked into self-testing. I asked the students to write a paper answering the most basic questions. Who am I? Why am I here? Where am I going? How do I get there? If I get there, what do I do?

The boy reached deep into himself. He wrote: "I am 16 and a junior in high school. Right now my mind is in a world of confusion. It is almost as if I have a devil and an angel on my shoulders but the devil seems to be more persuasive these days. My grades are poor, my attention deficit disorder is at its highest peak, and I struggle to make good choices about grades, drugs and alcohol.

"The amount of stress I endure every single day is unhealthy and overwhelming. I turn to nicotine to relieve my stress but all it really does is hurt me more. If I could just get my head on track, maybe, just maybe, I will be able to meet my parents' standards. Some days I just sit around all day, thinking how much better life is without work. And then reality strikes.

"At the beginning of every semester I tell myself you can do it, this is your time, but it never happens. I honestly believe I am mentally ill. I have the right intentions but I cannot get anything done. My priorities are all out of whack, and I am hanging on for dear life as I ride the roller-coaster of life. I have the work ethic and attention span of a goldfish.

"My relationship with God is probably my most confusing. I have always gone to church almost every Sunday since I was little. Yet I find it hard to get in touch with God. . . . I try hard to talk to God but I never feel his presence around me. I'm still waiting for that sign, that feeling when you know the Lord is watching over you. In my current situation I sure could use God's advice.

"Lately I haven't been to church that often, and when I do go, I don't really pay attention. I look around at my fellow parishioners and envy every last one of them. There could be an ugly, blind, deaf and autistic person, and I would envy them, just because they are one with the Holy Spirit. All I want is to be a person of faith, and right now I am lost in the world of Christianity.

"Even though I do a lot of lying around and doing nothing, I have never really thought too hard about what I want to be when I grow up. Partly because I need to get into college before I will be able to do the things I want to do. Hopefully I will mature enough in college so I will actually do some work. I intend on graduating from a four year university, and then see what happens after that. This may sound strange and kind of random but I am really interested in movies, the person who picks out the songs for different scenes. I don't know why but that job seems so awesome.

"Some other fields I am thinking about pursuing are real estate and architecture. Buildings and homes are so intriguing to me. I love watching the home and garden channel on TV. Being an architect would be amazing, but then again I don't really think I have the artistic ability to do well in that job. When I was little I always designed my fantasy house with little trap doors and cool staircases. I will hopefully choose a job that I love. My family is upper middle class, and I want the same for my children. I want them never to go hungry.

"Hopefully when I grow old I will be able to relax and ride my bike around town. I will play four games of golf every week, and sit and relax in my cozy Outer Banks cottage. At that point I will realize why we work so hard in life. We live life so we can get old, and ride our bicycles around town, like Mr. Colman McCarthy."

Not many high school papers like that come in. I read it several times, wondering whether this was another Holden Caulfield given over to excessive introspection or a cry from the heart for help. Four of my students in recent years have committed suicide, including a girl last year at Georgetown Law and a boy at B-CC who had been voted king for the homecoming dance. So when a student says he thinks he is mentally ill or is "hanging on for dear life," I take notice. I phoned his father and let him know about the paper. The father, who is well known in the community for his good works, said that he and his wife were doing all they could to offer emotional support for their child but were not sure if it were best to give the boy some space and distance or hover over him more closely.

So glad you like Boulder and the university. I haven't spoken there but was at Colorado College and Colorado State. I'm off to Oberlin next week, where students are pushing for a peace studies degree program, and schools in Missouri, Indiana and Ohio after that. If I remember, the University of Colorado has a peace studies major, though I'm not sure how well-funded it is or how many students enroll.

Do a favor for someone today. Tell someone you love them. And if you can't find anyone, look a little harder. I'm sure you are doing that all the time anyway. Otherwise you wouldn't be the special person you are.

With love,

Colman

Dear Colman,

This is not a letter that I anticipated having to write. I actually had the audacity to believe that [Virginia governor] Tim Kaine would do the right thing, and envisioned a different outcome. By now you will have heard that Kaine—to the disappointment and dismay of many, including his chief counsel, Mark Rubin—slid out the door without taking any action.* He simply left our petition [for clemency] for the next governor to deal with.

I received the news from [my lawyer] Steve Northrup on January 14 at 2:30 pm on the phone. The signs were so good that all was well that Tony Gray was in Bristol with plans to come pick me up.

Don't know what next moves, if any, will be made at this point. I expect that the lawyers will get back with me soon. This really knocked the wind out of me. I'm still reeling. Haven't slept, eaten or spoken, or left my cell since I received the call. I don't know how, or if, I'll bounce back. Don't know if I can muster the strength, will, courage, or discipline to do so. More frightening at this point is that I'm not sure that I even care to. It is truly madness. I'm alive but I don't have a clue as to where I stand in life, or any idea what life expects of me.

In truth/reality, injustice/evil cannot be redeemed. In a profound sense, whether we choose to acknowledge it or not, we are all—each one of us—responsible for the injustice in our world. Nonetheless, each one of us, without exception, is essentially a worthy being with a capacity for heroic action. Due to that, even though injustice can't be redeemed, we human beings can be. We may not be able to overthrow the injustice/evil but each one us can—must—refuse to cooperate with it. We must rebel against it, shout "no" to it. . . .

Tim Kaine was confronted with a real injustice. He supported my cause in the late 1980s, and cheered the sparing of my life and recommendation for a new trial of my case by former governor Doug Wilder in 1991. He cannot claim ignorance. He cannot claim that he did not possess the power to alleviate it. Nor can he claim that the injustice was not, is not—in fact and reality—a true injustice. For reasons that only he knows he simply passed on doing the right thing.

That failure of heart lies with him, and not with us. That is sad. And in doing so, Kaine, by his inaction, only compounds the injustice. For no legitimate reason or purpose, he has left me consigned to a completely totalitarian environment. An environment that he full well knows to be actively and progressively dehumanizing, an environment populated with broken, dysfunctional, mostly underdeveloped amoral souls (prisoners and guards alike) who are essentially left to fend for themselves; an environment that incubates, stimulates, breeds and distills mental dysfunction, amorality, immorality, dehumanization and predatory behavior; an environment that is measurably and verifiably detrimental to all of us (inside and outside); an environment that is self-defeating and self-destructive; an environment that is without redeeming value and one that only perpetuates the cycle of dehumanization and victimization. It's an environment that boasts of superficial orderliness, but in reality is nothing more than rationalized insanity.

It is an environment that I openly oppose and am at direct odds with; and it gives me no quarter. My rebellion against the negative status quo, my refusal to go along with the negative flow, my refusal to turn a blind eye to the injustice I see around me, my insistence on recognizing the innate humanity, dignity and subjective worthiness in all who surround me puts me at odds with the majority (though not all) I am confined with: and that places a target on my back. It makes my existence extremely complicated, often insane, and always dangerous. It surrounds me, constantly, mentally, spiritually and sometimes physically. It often leaves me feeling helpless, hopeless, alone, isolated and lost. It is constant and unremitting.

That is what Tim Kaine's inaction—his failure of heart—has wrought. Right now it is taking every ounce of energy, will and discipline I can muster to keep from coming among apart at the seams. Right now, all is darkness and madness for me. The constant urge for me is not simply to go on living but to grow, develop, to work out the meaning and purpose of my existence in this life; and to continue to seek out my own redemption.

The environment Kaine has left me consigned to actively seeks to drown that urge, to stamp the life out of it, to drown it of its vital force. Once again, it is men and the Darkness. I am neither saint nor devil. I am just a man, a fallible and bone weary man. Just me and the Darkness and, this time, I truly do not know which will prevail.

Kaine really knocked the wind out of me, old friend. I'm not in a good place right now, but am struggling with it. Thanks for being there.

For being a friend and mentor. You remain one of my heroes. Thanks for caring.

I'll try to write more. The gods are shooting craps for my soul.

Much love and peace,

Joe Giarratano

JANUARY 22, 2010

Dear Joe,

Don't give up. Don't give up. Don't give up.

Yes, it's cruel what Kaine did to you. Yes, it's cruel what the state does to you every day. Yes, it's cruel that this is a nation of laws but not a nation of justice. But despite all those yeses, as emotionally violent and as dispiriting as they are, the yes that you have been affirming all these years has moral force—a superior force—that has kept you unbroken and saying: yes, I refuse to be defeated, yes I am keeping faith with all my supporters, yes my life has a purpose.

Please draw strength from that. It's natural to feel wiped out by the hope-dashing reality of what just happened. And natural, too, to feel enraged and bitter. Who wouldn't be, when the prospect for your release seemed so favorable. Just try to stay afloat for now, getting through the next few days and weeks however you can. Your strength will return.

You may have had some letters from Joanne Kim. She is one of my students, not a conventional one. She is an Hawaiian, in her mid-50s, a former official in a national security agency, and has been coming to my classes for the past few years—not to get credit but just to keep learning and be aware that you don't know much until you know how much you don't know. When she heard the news about Kaine's turn-down, she phoned—speaking through her tears at the absurdity of the denial.

You know how I appreciate all you have done for my students—going back to our visits with you on death row in Mecklenburg, then the seminars at Augusta, and all the letters you have written to the classes. A new semester begins this week, and once more you will be part of the course—and as almost always happens, the part that touches them the most.

Peace, in the midst of it all—

Colman

*In the summer of 1988, Marie Deans, who ran a nonprofit in Charlottesville, Virginia, that specialized in investigating wrongful and malicious death penalty convictions, phoned and suggested I look into the case of Joseph Giarratano. She herself had done so and was convinced that he was innocent of killing Toni Kline and her daughter Michelle in February 1979 in a rooming house they shared in a low-income Norfolk neighborhood. Giarratano, in his early twenties, was a drug- and alcohol-abusing drifter doing menial labor on the Norfolk docks. Marie based her belief on several facts. Giarratano's trial took less than a day. He gave five confessions, all different, all coerced and all given in a confused drug-induced state of mind. His court-appointed lawyer, poorly paid, had little experience in capital cases.

Police work at the crime scene was sloppy. Evidence that would have been a help to Giarratano was not gathered. Toni Kline was knifed to death by a right-handed attacker. Giarratano, with a disabled right arm, was left-handed. He had no history of violence, other than harming himself with negative habits. On the night of the murders, he came to the apartment and, stoned, fell asleep on a living room sofa. He awoke in the morning, saw the two bodies in a bedroom and bathroom and panicked—assuming that he must have done it. He fled, caught a bus to Jacksonville, Florida. He found a cop, and thinking he was guilty of the homicides, turned himself in.

Deans, known in Virginia's prisons as the Angel of Death Row, was not the only one who examined the weak and discredited evidence and believed in Giarratano's innocence. Calls for either a new trial or exoneration came from Amnesty International, the Vatican, members of Congress, and the European Parliament.

After Marie sent documentation of her findings, I traveled to the Mecklenburg State Prison in southern Virginia near the North Carolina border to interview Giarratano. We spoke for several hours—about his case; his fellow prisoners, including one he believed was innocent; his postconviction lawyers; his gratitude to Deans; his efforts to overcome his past; his violent childhood in a dysfunctional family; and his work at self-education after being an eighth-grade dropout. On the last, he had more than succeeded in learning the art of writing literate sentences. He wrote a piece for *Yale Law Review* and an op-ed for the *Los Angeles Times*. Studying law, he became the only death row inmate ever to write a brief argued before the Supreme Court, one that had nothing to do with own case but was regarding the case of fellow inmate Earl Washington Jr., an illiterate, mentally disabled black inmate a few cells down the row. Weeks before Washington was to be electrocuted in Virginia's chair, Giarratano filed a civil suit arguing that the state was wrong not to provide lawyers for postconviction appeals by indigent prisoners. The state does provide lawyers but for only one appeal, even knowing that fresh evidence or new witnesses can show up on second and third appeals.

The case—Murray, director, Virginia Department of Corrections et al. v. Giarratano et al.—was argued in a two-day district court trial by Gerald Zerkin, a Richmond civil liberties attorney who by now was also Giarratano's appeals lawyer. Washington won. The state appealed to the US Fourth Circuit of Appeals, winning 2 to 1. Zerkin appealed to the full court and won 6 to 4. It was a surprise victory, the Fourth Circuit Court of Appeals having an entrenched record of conservative decisions. The state, however, wasn't finished. It went to the Supreme Court which heard arguments on March 22, 1989.

Giarratano described the corner in which Washington found himself: "Picture yourself in this situation. You've been convicted of capital murder and sentenced to death. You are indigent, functionally illiterate and mildly retarded. Your court-appointed lawyer tells you that you have the right to appeal your conviction and sentence but that he will no longer represent you. You have been moved to the death house. Your only choice is for you to represent yourself. You must file something with the court or be executed in less than 14 days. You have the right to file a petition for certiorari or a petition for habeas corpus and a motion for a stay of execution. But before you file you must learn to read, write, overcome your retardation, obtain your trial transcript, understand the science of law, learn how to conduct legal research, analyze vast amounts of case law, formulate your issues, learn all the rules, understand civil procedure, constitutional law, criminal law and acquire the art of legal writing. You must do this all of this and much more in less than 14 days in order to exercise your right to appeal."

In a 4 to 4 decision, with Virginian justice Lewis Powell recused, the Supreme Court ruled against Washington, arguing that both the Eighth and the Fourteenth Amendment guarantee indigent defendants legal counsel for a trial and one appeal—but after that, sorry. For Washington, it turned out not to matter anyway. Thanks to Deans and a team of pro bono defense lawyers uncovering DNA evidence, Washington would be fully exonerated. Freedom came on February 12, 2001, along with more than $700,000 in reparations. If it wasn't for the initial intervention of Giarratano, he would most likely have been a victim of state-sanctioned homicide.

After my first meeting in the Mecklenburg prison with Giarratano and writing several columns for the *Post* about his case, I made several more visits. Each time I brought groups of high school, college, and law school students to meet with him and his cellmates on death row. The warden, well aware that he was paid to do society's dirty work as the state's executioner, respected Giarratano for his intelligence and moral character. He also had a measure of sympathy for the men he was paid to cage and eventually kill. Bring students as often as you like, he told me. He arranged lunches for them with the prisoners. He allowed *People* magazine to report on the seminars on legal theory and death penalty law conducted for us by Giarratano.

For Giarratano, time was running out. In early 1991, twelve years after his conviction, a date with the electric chair had been set for mid-February. He invited me for a final visit the day before the scheduled execution. We met in the Spring Street prison in downtown Richmond, a facility built by Thomas Jefferson. He was the only inmate, the structure being on a prime piece of real estate and about to be razed by a developer. All other prisoners had been dispatched elsewhere. Our visit was in the cooling room, where the hot flesh of the electrocuted is carried to be cooled on a metal gurney before being laid into a coffin.

With time set for a midnight killing, which Giarratano asked me to attend, I said good-bye at noon after an hour of conversation and recalling the many times he had met with my students. That afternoon, Governor Wilder, a Democrat who had once opposed the death penalty when in the state legislature but then favored it when running for governor, called off the execution by commuting the death sentence. His decision, he said, was "complex but not difficult," largely based on his grave doubts about Giarratano's guilt. He commuted the sentence to life, with eligibility for parole in 2004.

It was a victory with a catch. A new trial with a competent lawyer would have been the fitting follow-up to the commutation—except for Virginia's twenty-one-day rule. A convicted felon has three weeks to file a claim of innocence. After that, it's over. Other states have three-year limits, others no limits. Since 1997, nearly 140 men have been freed from death row, the reasons ranging from prosecutorial misconduct to new evidence and recantings. About a thousand executions have occurred. The numbers represent a 14 percent error rate, one that would be considered intolerable if applied to other areas of life. Would passengers stay on the plane if the pilot announced a 14 percent chance the plane would crash on take-off? Would diners eat in restaurants that had a 14 percent chance of food poisoning?

From Richmond, Giarratano was sent west to a state prison in Augusta

County, about three hours south of Washington. My visits with students continued. For years I had been bringing Giarratano books on nonviolence, from Gandhi's autobiography to Dorothy Day's essays. I suggested to the warden that Giarratano be allowed to teach an academic course to fellow inmates on the literature of peace and nonviolent conflict resolution. I gave $5,000 to buy books to get the course started. Giarratano applied for and received an IRS tax exemption for the program. For the first class, eighteen inmates were enrolled, none of them getting parole points. I asked Giarratano whom he invited to take the course. The meanest of the mean, he said, men with three life sentences, 110-year sentences. On asking how he lined up the hard-core set, he explained that in the prison population he was seen as a demigod: one of the rare few who had left death row alive. To be selected to take a course from someone like that wasn't to be refused.

Each course ran for sixteen weeks and ended with a graduation ceremony. Its success—a marked decrease in the prison's violence and a waiting list of three hundred to take the course—was widely reported, with stories in Virginia newspapers and *Corrections Today*. In 1995, Brian Williams of *NBC Nightly News* sent Bob Abernethy to report the story. When handing diplomas to the graduates during the ceremony, I asked the students to say a few words about the course and what it meant to them. Almost all had the same thought: if I had known about the ideas of nonviolence and the practice of nonviolence when I was young, I might not be in prison today.

Several times I brought students to the graduations. One of them, a Bethesda–Chevy Chase senior girl, wrote to Giarratano and his class:

> Thank you so much for the lovely day. It was the first time I had gone to a prison, and I must admit that I felt a little apprehensive.
>
> But once I entered the visiting room and saw everyone mingling I felt more at ease. I'm so impressed by the commitment you men have made to find inner peace and deal with your violent environment. I can't imagine the struggles you must endure and the opposition you meet. You are deserving of my admiration and everyone else's. No matter what you may have done in your past, what you are doing now is what counts. One of the men who spoke when he received his certificate struck a chord with me—about looking within your own heart and how it's the hardest thing you can do. I agree and I understand. I recently looked within myself as well.

Deans, who did much of the research that led to the Wilder commutation, came to the graduations. In my anthology *Strength Through Peace*, one of the texts for the course, she writes: "I have yet to find a case where there hasn't been a red flag thrown up years ago—in grammar school or somewhere—where a kid said, 'I'm in trouble, help me.' He gave us the message loud and clear and we didn't pay any attention. And he ended up, years later, going down and down and killing someone. Let me tell you something. I resent the hell out of that as a member of a murder victim's family. These governors, these prosecutors, Ronald Reagan and George Bush all getting up and saying, 'I care about victims, I want the death penalty.' If they care about victims, they would have taken care of that victimized kid when he was six years old and prevented a homicide later."

The course lasted three years. Then someone in the state's Department of Corrections saw the *NBC Nightly News* story and ordered the Augusta warden to stop the program. The warden's objections—that the course was reducing violence—were overruled. It was seen as coddling inmates. You're running a prison, the warden was told, not a school.

Sometime after, Giarratano was shipped to a prison in Utah. States have exchange programs: if you have a troublemaker in your system and we have one in ours, let's swap and get them out of their environment. Giarratano was troublesome in a different way. He was seen as a celebrity prisoner: getting on television (NBC as well ABC's *20/20* with Lynn Sherr, Hugh Downs, and Barbara Walters in 1991), filing suits on behalf of other inmates and winning many of them, writing articles for law reviews and op-ed pages, working with human rights groups to expose violations in the state's prisons. Giarratano lasted less than a year in Utah. He went on a hunger strike to get publicity for reforms. He roused the state's ACLU to take action about prison conditions. He organized inmates. Utah packed him off to the state prison in Joliet, Illinois. I visited him there in 1997. We talked about setting up another peace studies course, which the chaplain thought well of. The warden said no. Months later, Giarratano was sent back to Virginia—this time to Red Onion, a supermax hellhole touted as fit for the worst of the worst. For four years, he was stashed in an eight-by-eleven-foot isolation cell, confined twenty-four hours a day except for three showers a week for five minutes each.

As a display of support, in the spring of 1999 the mayor of Charlottesville declared May 1 Joe Giarratano Day and issued a proclamation praising both his work on behalf of prisoners and his refusal to let the state beat him down. A dinner was held in his honor that evening at a Doubletree Hotel in

Charlottesville, with two hundred friends and allies on hand. One of them was retired judge Robert Merhige, who delivered a fifteen-minute speech in which he condemned the twenty-one-day rule and encouraged the audience to keep working to free Giarratano.

Giarratano is now held in the Wallens Ridge State Prison in Big Stone Gap, near the Tennessee and Kentucky borders in far southwest Virginia. At the time of the 1991 commutation, Governor Wilder said that Giarratano would be eligible for parole twenty-five years after his 1979 sentencing. He came up in 2004 and was denied. In 2007 he was denied. The next chance was 2010. Prospects were bright. The governor was Tim Kaine. Deans had organized a coalition of politicians, judges and former judges, psychiatrists, a Roman Catholic bishop, and a Washington law firm to make the case for clemency. He had been promised a job as a paralegal in a Charlottesville firm. If anyone would be open to the appeals, it was Kaine. In 1991 as a young lawyer who had been a defense lawyer in two capital cases, he was resolutely opposed to capital punishment. While running for governor in the fall of 2005, Kaine, a Roman Catholic who had once volunteered with a church mission in Honduras, told voters "My faith teaches that life is sacred. That's why I oppose the death penalty." In 1987, while awaiting the execution of a client, he had told the *Washington Post* that "murder is wrong in the gulag, in Afghanistan, in Soweto, in the mountains of Guatemala, in Fairfax County, . . . and even in the Spring Street prison."

It couldn't have looked better for Giarratano. By law, Virginia governors serve only one term. Kaine ran no risk of running for reelection as a turn-'em-loose governor. Kaine waited until his final day in office. His decision, spineless, was to not to make a decision: he would leave the appeal to the next governor. The new governor turned out to be a Republican, a Roman Catholic pro-lifer who opposes execution of fetuses but favors it for inmates in the womb of prison. Robert McDonnell took no action on the Giarratano appeal.

∽ ∽ ∽

Dear Colman,

I just arrived back in the US after finishing my two years as an HIV/ AIDS Peace Corps volunteer in Mali. I knew that the experience would change my life but could not have predicted the directions into which it would lead me. For years I was certain that I wanted to work for some nonprofit working in the sphere of international relations and conflict mediation. Seeing the needs of the developing world first-hand has led me to explore another field: medicine.

Superficially, the two are very different but I strongly believe they are closely related. Nomadic Peuhls in rural Mali, recent immigrants in the ghettos of DC or New York City and the urban poor of all races and ethnicities all face obstacles in receiving even minimal health care. As you frequently remind your classes, when thousands of children die every day of hunger or diseases which are easily treated, it is a form of "cold violence" that is too often overlooked.

Looking back at all of my work and volunteer experiences, I realize that each aspect I enjoyed and excelled in can all be found in the medical profession. Volunteering in Mali and working in schools and community health centers, I discovered a talent and interest in organizing events promoting healthy behavior, counseling individuals on health topics and working closely with health care professionals. As a counselor at the GI Rights Hotline, I worked with members of the military to help them discover solutions to bad situations. Whether their problem was medical, family related or an objection of conscience, I helped them to debate options and deal with challenging circumstances.

My undergraduate degree is in International Relations. To apply to medical schools I will first have to return to school to fulfill math and science requirements. I am applying to several post-baccalaureate premedical programs which start in the summer. I was hoping that you would write a recommendation for me. Before I left for the Peace Corps you had said you would but I realize you are very busy.

I have attached a copy of my description of Peace Corps service and a resume so you can review what I have been involved in the last few years. I will also be in DC next week so I may have an opportunity to sit in one of your classes at American or School Without Walls. I really enjoyed assisting with classes at Walls before I did Peace Corps. So it would be fun to visit again.

Thank you for your help

J Flament

Dear J,

Bless you which I'm sure the good Lord is doing all the time anyway.
What heartening news that you'll be giving med school a try. Just yes-
terday another of my former students, a senior I had at Stone Ridge, the
Catholic girl's school in Bethesda, and who went on to finish at Duke
with a magna cum, called to say she is being interviewed at Georgetown
Medical School—and like you is zoning in on poverty medicine.

Sure, a letter is automatic, as I said yes two years ago when I was lucky
to have you in my American U class. Don't forget my troublesome little
rule about recommendation letters: you'll have to bake something for
my wife and me. That's how I get all you intellectuals to work on your
kitchen skills and ease you out of the library and away from the books for
a while. It's not something I don't do myself, having been a cook during
one of the five years I lived in a Trappist monastery after college.

Can't wait to hear your stories about Mali. Like most world-ignorant
Americans, I'd be pressed to tell the differences between Mali and Malawi,
except that they are in Africa someplace. Get ready to spend the rest of
your days answering the question about Mali, "Where's that?"

No surprise that your two years in Mali were life-altering. I've
seen it up-close for the many dozens of my former students who were
shaken up and woken up by their Peace Corps experiences. Not sure if
I ever told you but I came to Washington in the mid-1960s to work for
Sargent Shriver, the first director, who hired me off the street when I
was a penniless freelance writer scouring the country for stories that the
establishment media were ignoring. Sarge Shriver happened to read one
of those stories, in the *National Catholic Reporter*, about one his poverty
programs in Harlem. If I hadn't written that piece and he hadn't read
it and called me—I was in the Midwest, having just covered Martin
Luther King's summer of 1966 campaign to integrate housing in white
Cicero, Illinois—who knows where I would be to now. Sarge Shriver
hired me to write speeches which meant traveling the country with him,
revising his lines up to the minute he walked to the microphone and
then spoke on his own because he definitely didn't need help from me.
A friendship grew, and he would become the person I've been closest to
outside my family. He is 89 now, physically robust but fading into the
early mists of Alzheimer's. Last week I had one of his children, Tim, who

has been running Special Olympics the past 10 years, speak to my high school classes.

My other connection with the Peace Corps is Mark Gearan, the agency's director during the second Clinton administration. Mark, who worked on the Clinton presidential campaign in 1991, was one of my students at Georgetown Law in the fall of 1989. It was a frenzied semester, what with two rightwing gunslingers in the class hot to shoot holes in any arguments I dared make on why nonviolence is more lastingly effective than violence. It was Mark who becalmed the class when the two lads were having at me. He is now at Hobart and William Smith Colleges as president.

I fear that Mark and I are on different sides of a current argument involving the Peace Corps. I wrote a column for the *Post* a few weeks ago supporting a proposed law that would allow people in the military to complete their tour of duty with two years in the Peace Corps. Mark thought differently, believing that soldiers should soldier and that warmaking and peacemaking are separate. I hated to break ranks by joining conservatives who supported the bill, but if I were a Senegalese farmer in a village 100 miles from Dakar and needed to have a bridge rebuilt after it was washed away by a flood, I think I'd prefer someone who spent a couple of years in the Army Corps of Engineers rather than an English major from Yale. I'd be interested in your views on that. I suspect you'll be on the keep-them-separate side.

I'll send the letter.

Let's catch up next week.

Colman

APRIL 10, 2005

Dear Professor McCarthy,

First of all, I would like to apologize for having to leave class early on Wednesday. I know I just slipped out of class. I am writing to you to express my sincere appreciation for you as not only a professor but as a human being. When I first heard you speak at NCS [National Cathedral School] many years ago, I was instantly amazed by your work and your chosen lifestyle. Then, being from DC, I had a couple of my friends either take your class at Wilson or during the summer course at Public Interest at Dupont Circle. Then I heard you speak during FOCI [Focus on Community Involvement, a Georgetown mentoring and service program], and it was then that I knew I had somehow to meet you and take your class. Thus far into the semester I feel that I have been the most intellectually stimulated in your classroom than most other places and certainly more than any other class I have taken. You have really opened my eyes and everyone else's to a totally different perspective here at Georgetown.

As a Culture and Politics major and a Peace Certificator, I find what the school is doing to you right now absolutely horrendous. I am sickened once again by our university and its policies. However, there is no use complaining. All we can do is act. I just wanted to let you know that I will do everything and anything I can do to keep you here at Georgetown. I know that much action has already been taken, but a little more won't hurt.

Keep your head high, as it will be, and know that you have touched the spirit of at least one of your students.

Peace and much love,

Lena Jackson

APRIL 14, 2005

Dear Lena,

Largest of thanks for your lovely and gracious words. I was moved by them. It's been a privilege to have you in class, since we go back a few years—my lecture at NCS and then the talk at FOCI. So I'm glad that we've had some contact, as less-than-ideal as it is with such a large class and not really that many chances for conversational education. I should tell you, though, that more than once I have looked at you and Kara in the back row and wondered to myself, hmmm, I wondered what they're thinking.

Now I know. Your thoughts about the course being dropped are the right blend of dismay and anger, ones that any half-sentient being would agree with. It's the nonsentient being, alas, who sometimes gets to make decisions at schools. Hard as I've tried, I'm without a clue, or even a scent of one, as to who at Georgetown first had the thought in his or her head, "let's get rid of McCarthy." It had to be someone. And then a second someone to agree, and the two locked their steps together and marched off to claim a victory on the academy's battlefield.

When told of the axing, I was of two minds: just get off the premises quietly, with no door slams, and say to myself that the expected happened. Or, as one world-weary and classroom-weary student told me, This is Georgetown, you didn't really think the school cares about peace issues, did you?

The second option, and the one I took, was to tell my students the facts as I knew them, since facts are one of the line items they or their parents are paying extravagantly for. I thought, also, it might be educational for students to be included in the process of how course offerings are chosen—the choices almost always not made by students. This time, you and other students are daring to say, What about our choice?

As all of this unfolds—I'm told *The Hoya* [the main student newspaper] is running a few supportive words on Friday*—the issue is getting the kind of oxygen that's needed, well beyond the airless defenses administrators blow at students. We saw this in the recent Living Wage Campaign: three years of The Big Stall when university officials arrogantly convinced themselves they could ignore the calls of the workers for a salary raise, not to mention the pleas of students standing with them. For all their many fine deeds, on this one the Jesuits acted as slimily as any corporate boardroom of greedy capitalists. Finally it took 26 hunger-striking students to shame the school's policy makers into coming across with the money to pay the school's lowest-of-the-low, impoverished janitors, maids, cooks, gardeners—and all the while the university loftily urging students [via the FOCI program] to fan out in the poverty neighborhoods of Washington to serve the poor.

My removal reflects the same attitude. This time, instead of stiffing the little guy, it's stiffing the peace guy. It wouldn't be irksome if Georgetown was a corporation and I was let go because of differences in thinking. The insufferable part is seeing the oceanic gap between what is postured—Georgetown stands for the Christian values of peace and justice—and the actual reality of having a peace and justice program that has always been minimally funded and is now being weakened still more.

On funding, you'll be heartened to know that one of my students—not an officially enrolled one, but a nurse at NIH who used to read me in the *Post* and who comes to class as my guest—offered the university $4,000 a semester to cover what it now pays me as the standard adjunct fee. The offer was declined.

Full thanks for coming up after class yesterday, on top of your letter. You were kind and generous, and a fine reflection on how you were raised. If I could give Moms and Dads grades on how their children turn out, yours would earn an A+.

Lotsa love,

Colman McCarthy

*On April 15, 2005, *The Hoya*, the Georgetown campus newspaper, ran a column by Chrissy Balz. It read, in part:

> On March 30, Professor Colman McCarthy was notified that his class Literature of Peace, would not be included in the fall course offerings. Wildly popular and filled quickly each semester, Literature of Peace is a course dedicated to pacifism and those who advocate it as a course of action. But more than that, it is a class that truly works to pursue all that this university claims to hold dear: a search for social justice, a better understanding of each individual's place in this world and the education of the whole person.
>
> Colman McCarthy is an anarchist-pacifist—one is hard-pressed to find a more diverse voice within the fall 2005 course offerings. The course is inarguably rigorous: each semester Professor McCarthy requires more than 30 Georgetown students to open their minds in ways they never have before, a proposition that daunts even the most eager overachiever. But more important than what Professor McCarthy brings to the Program for Justice and Peace Studies is what he brings to the students of this university. He is a true educator, one who goes far and beyond the dictates of any syllabus or core requirement.
>
> When he teaches, every student is moved. Some are moved to action. Some are moved to compassion. Others are moved to disagree. Whatever the reaction, no mind falls stagnant while Professor McCarthy teaches. Liberal or conservative, religious or agnostic, interested or disinterested, each and every student leaves Literature of Peace with the feeling that he has the power to make a change in the world.

And that's a feeling worth fighting for. How discouraging this decision is to prospective and future students.

⌐⌐⌐

Dear Mr. McCarthy,

Once again I have let time get the best of me and the summer is flying by quicker than I wanted and expected it to, so apologies for my late reply. As my time in Buenos Aires draws nearer, I have found myself busier and busier each day. I am excited about the trip [to study for a semester at the University of Buenos Aires] but also nervous. Being away from what I am accustomed to is going to be quite the challenge, but I think I would rather deal with the difficulties of a foreign country, culture and language than be at Georgetown. Every time I set foot on campus, I am reminded why I disliked that place so much; however, I know that it will eventually serve me well, so I try to keep my head up. But when a place is filled with people, both students and faculty, who consistently think that they are better than everyone else and acts like an institution that totally disregards the sense of community building, love, and peace, it breaks my heart to know that I am part of something like that. However, I know that I am a lot better off than most and someday I will eventually stop complaining and try to inflict some legitimate change.

Back to Argentina. I would love to meet your friend [Adolfo Pérez Esquivel, the 1980 Nobel Peace Prize winner]. He sounds fascinating and I would really be interested in seeing the work he is doing down there. Argentina has such a rich history and political background, I am really excited to study all of it. When I was choosing the place where I would go, I knew that I wanted to be in a Spanish-speaking country but not Spain. I have never been to South America. I have traveled to Cuba and Mexico and since there are only three countries that Georgetown offers students to study in (Ecuador, Chile and Argentina) I realized that Argentina would be the best fit for me. It has a good blend of Latin America and Europe but because of the economic collapse I think that the country and the people have both really become humbled by the experience.

It was really an honor this semester to be in your class. It really brings me to tears knowing that Georgetown ended your contract. It is such a sad thing to know that our world has come to this. To think that someone who is actually enlightening young people's minds about peace, and justice, and activism is not welcomed at an "intellectual" institution is ludicrous. I know and you know that they will never come out and say their real reasons, but they know that they are wrong; however, they have to follow the rules. No one makes exceptions anymore. No one is accepting of differences or uniqueness. Everything is so mainstream and by the book. You could actually take what they did as a compliment because it simply implies that they are not ready for you. They are not ready for your style of teaching and your "radical" views, but someday!

I saw Prof. Henry Schwarz two weekends ago. He was hosting the Marxist Literary Group and asked my Dad to be one of the speakers in a roundtable discussion with Selma James, the wife of the late C. L. R James, on the state of the Class Struggle in the Movement. Well, it was quite a sight. My Dad is very knowledgeable about Marxism and the "movement" because he was extraordinarily involved in the 70s and 80s. It turned out to be a battle between my Dad and James and her followers [the Marxist Literary Group]. She was extremely negative and pessimistic, and really just complained the whole time about the failure of the American Left without offering any pieces of advice. Well, the point of the story is that Schwarz just sat back and listened and catered to everyone's needs. He is a very inactive man to be the head of the Peace and Justice Department. His role and interaction during the event just proved how wrong he is for the job and why he probably did not stick up for you. I talked to him about you a little bit, because he knows my Dad and my Dad told him that I was in your class, and all he could say was, "Well, you know he is re-applying in the spring." I was in shock that those were the only words that could come out of his mouth. But once again, we are at Georgetown.

Of course I will keep in contact with you during the next year, but I would definitely be interested in helping my senior year. I know you don't plan ahead but I want to get it on paper so you won't turn me away when I ask! I would love to attend some of your summer classes and I will bring my friends so that they can form their own opinions about you and hopefully be touched.

I know that you meant no harm with your questioning [during class last week] of my friend RaMell. He loved it. I was just highly embarrassed. I embarrass quickly. He really loved your class and wished that he could have taken it, but he played basketball for Georgetown and it is really quite sad what they (or at least used to) make the players do. The administration kind of pushed them into all majoring in Sociology because they figured it would be the easiest subject with the least amount of work and it's hard to break away from the cycle. It wasn't until his sophomore or junior year that he really started to break away and delve into new subjects and try to expand his mind, but that's already too late. He always says that he has learned more during his short period of time with me (almost a year) than he did throughout his college experience (at least about what Georgetown has to offer). I suppose my NCS experience and of course the influence of my radical parents paid off. He actually liked you so much that he is going to send you a Georgetown basketball "thing" because all the seniors get to give a present to their favorite teacher during their time at Georgetown.

I hope to hear from you soon. I hope the summer is treating you well.

Stay out of trouble,

Lena Jackson

JULY 5, 2005

Dear Lena,

Another possible contact for you in Buenos Aires is Dante Furioso, quite an exotic a name but one that belongs to a person of stunning depth and kindness. By way of background, he is a third-year student at Wesleyan and will be, I believe, at the same Argentina university as you, specializing in Latin American studies. Dante was one of my most committed students at Wilson three years ago, an all-around delight in the classroom and a world-class agitator out of it. He led a student protest against the US invasion of Iraq, defying the principal's orders against leaving the campus during class time to demonstrate on Wisconsin Avenue. The repercussions were nil, because the principal, a troublemaker himself when in high school and college during the 60s, was actually heartened that Dante had taken to the streets.

I arranged for him to do an interview on C-SPAN, when I brought him and an Iraqi student at School Without Walls for a program on students against US militarism. It was an hour-long show, with me on hand as a teacher grateful to have two students who spoke persuasively and accurately about alternatives to violence. Dante's sister, Juliana, who was in my class this past year at Walls, turned down Smith and Brown to go to Evergreen State in Washington—the West Coast Hampshire. Should you want to contact Dante—he's leaving for Buenos Aires on the 19th—his phone is 202-882-1511. Both of you have much in common.

Yes, let's keep the ball rolling—uphill if necessary—to have you involved when you are back for your last year at Georgetown. Try to flush out any negative feelings you have about the university and its treatment of me. You're right, the real reasons for canceling my course are beyond knowing, at least for now. Henry Schwarz, I believe, had to be circumspect: the best way to keep his standing in the faculty lounge. I still consider him a friend, at least in the Mafia definition: a friend is someone who stabs you in the front.

The dust-up this past semester about my course is only the latest in a lengthy history of clashes between administration and students. It was in the mid-1980s that Georgetown gave an honorary degree to Ronald Reagan. Nothing unusual about that, if it's remembered that sucking at the roots of power is what any upstanding university will do when one Caesar or another is available to be hailed by clerics. Alas, there was one person at Georgetown who declined to join the hailers: a lad named Robert Johnson, the student body president, who not only blasted the decision but publicized that, on grounds of conscience, he would not attend the ceremony honoring Reagan. I remember writing about this for the *Post*, praising the student for taking a lonely stand.

I mention this because that dispute, plus all the others, including the school's being sued over its anti-gay policies, its past ties to the South African government, its chumminess with the Pentagon and its ROTC programs, might be a fit topic for your senior thesis in case you are shopping around for a topic. It would be fascinating to track down that student who staged the Reagan protest and interview him 20 years later for his reflections. The theme of the thesis would focus on the disconnectedness—and the grueling consistency of it in one issue after another—between the lofty preachments of the university and its shabby practices. No institution is perfect, obviously, but when one student grievance after another gets kissed off as trivial or a nuisance, then it isn't a matter of perfection but of defection—from the school's own stated, and often overstated, values. You aren't the first student to be angered by a university policy, nor the first to be dismissed by policy makers as a tad too idealistic for your own good. You're in the company of more right-minded people than you realize.

Enough heaviness. I heard a good one the other day [about private girls schools] Visitation, Holton Arms and National Cathedral. Visitation girls grow up to marry doctors, Holton Arms girls have affairs with doctors, and Cathedral girls BECOME doctors.

My summer class, at Public Citizen, 1600 20th Street, meets Thursdays at 5:45 pm. You'd be most welcomed.

Thanks for staying in touch.

Colman McCarthy

MARCH 28, 2006

Dear Professor McCarthy

I must begin this letter with a big I-have-been-a-bad-twenty-year-old, or rather, maybe I have just been a twenty-year-old: an irresponsible young person who was too caught up in her own life to step away for an hour or two and visit a friend. I sincerely apologize for not coming to visit you. My time was filled with work and personal problems, boyfriend problems rather, that I really should not get into nor would you want to hear about. But with that said, I have left the lovely District of Columbia and have since traveled around Brazil and am now back in Buenos Aires starting my second semester here.

Over break, as you know, I worked at Busboys and Poets. It's a great place, especially for DC to have. But a great place is always filled with its problems. Problems such as pretentious people who think that they are doing some justice by dining at the new hip radical chic joint on U Street, that is in fact adding to the gentrification of DC instead of countering it. (It appears that my Dad has had more of an effect on me than I ever thought he would). I walked into it very cool and casual, thinking that that was the kind of place it was or at least appeared to be. But by the second day of work, when my manager was telling me that I needed to dress, and I quote, "more fashionably," I realized I was in for an interesting ride. However, I survived and it wasn't bad. . . . I must say that the people they get to read/speak/hold workshops is a great selection and it is indeed something that is long overdue in DC.

In addition, I worked with my Dad at the Library of Congress. He is on sabbatical for the year as a Kluge Fellow (I'm bragging a little), trying to finish his book, which hopefully he will finish and if not, I am not sure if my Mom will let him live under our roof anymore. He is actually turning what he wrote his dissertation on into a book. A French Huguenot/Quaker named Anthony Benezet, who started the first school for freed slaves in Philadelphia, had some of the first positive things to say about both Africans and Africa, and also was highly influential to people such as Benjamin Franklin. So it is really quite fascinating and I got to work with him on his chapter on Africa. I am very into geography and maps, so he wanted me to read a number of Benezet's descriptions on Africa and go to the Geography and Map Division of the LOC (which is home to over 5 million maps) to find maps that appeared similar enough to the ones that Benezet used. So that was an extremely exciting project and I also did some organizing of files—you know, typical daughter stuff.

I left the states at the mid-end of February and arrived in Buenos Aires and dashed around this massive city trying to get my Brazil trip in order, making up for none of the preparations I had done at home. I ended up just traveling with one of my friends here, Dante and Nick ended up not being able to make it. But it was splendid. We started in Florianópolis, which is in the southern part of the country. Most of the city is actually on an island. We were there during Carnival, so our nights were spent admiring the craziness that was going on around us and our days were spent on lovely beaches. We traveled up to Rio which is as far as we got. It is an incredible city, surrounded by green mountains, the lovely Atlantic Ocean, lakes, a bay. It even has a legitimate forest within it. I was amazed.

The most exciting part of the trip was a tour we took through a favela, actually the largest favela in Latin America. It sat on a large hill between two well-off neighborhoods. So it was basically just squeezed between two areas where there really is not enough space but because of the way favelas are formed, with everything built on top of each other, it has somehow worked. Some 200,000 people live there. It is home to some of the largest drug-dealer gangs in Rio but also is completely self-sufficient. It has barbershops, grocery stores, places to get your sewing done. It was really quite fascinating, and being able to walk through the entire thing was quite eye-opening. I remember seeing shantytowns/slums in India which are in far worse condition.

Bur enough about me. How are you? My Dad sent me an article [in the *Washington Post*] a few weeks ago about the stuff going on at Bethesda–Chevy Chase. I read the article* and of course was in shock. What actually is happening? And how are classes at Wilson, Walls, AU? Any word from Georgetown? I have been in touch with Henry Schwarz about Justice and Peace stuff. I think he means well but isn't quite tough enough to stand up for anything that could be controversial, which is sad for someone who is head of the Peace and Justice department.

You will be happy to know that this past week an exhibit at the Georgetown University library opened showing all of the radical pamphlets my Dad donated a year ago. He had them in the basement for years and my Mom was on him about getting rid of all the "junk" in our basement. So after much thought he decided to give them to the GU library. There was as nice reception where he spoke, along with President DeGioia, a surprise. If you have a chance you should stop by the library. They will be on display through April and then be catalogued.

Well, that's all I have to report. I hope you are doing well and that I hear from you soon. Once again, I am very sorry for being such a flake.

Peace and much love,

　　　your friend Lena Jackson

*On Sunday, February 26, 2006, the *Washington Post* ran a story by staff writer Lori Aratani titled "Students Call for Banning of Peace Studies Class," with a subhead "Bethesda–Chevy Chase High Protestors Say That Teachings Are Skewed."

> For months, 17-year-old Andrew Saraf had been troubled by stories he was hearing about a Peace Studies course offered at his Bethesda high school. He wasn't enrolled in the class but had several friends and classmates who were.
>
> Last Saturday, he decided to act. He sat down at his computer and typed out his thoughts on why the course—offered for almost two decades as an elective to seniors at Bethesda–Chevy Chase High School—should be banned from the school.
>
> "I know I'm not the first to bring this up but why has there been no concerted effort to remove Peace Studies from the B-CC courses?" he wrote in his post to the school's group e-mail list. "The

'class' is headed by an individual with a political agenda, who wants to teach students the 'right' way of thinking by giving them facts that are skewed in one direction."

He hit send.

Within a few hours, the normally staid e-mail list BCCnet—a site for announcements, job postings and other housekeeping details in the life of the school—was ablaze with chatter. By the time Principal Sean Bulson checked his Blackberry on Sunday evening, there were more than 150 postings from parents and students—some ardently in support, some ardently against the course.

Since its launch at the school in 1988, Peace Studies has provoked a lively debate, but the attempt to have the course removed from the curriculum is a first, Bulson said. The challenge by two students comes as universities and even some high schools across the country are under close scrutiny by a growing number of critics who believe that the US education system is being hijacked by liberal activists.

At Bethesda–Chevy Chase, Peace Studies is taught by Colman McCarthy, a former *Washington Post* columnist and founder and president of the Center for Teaching Peace. Though the course is taught at seven other Montgomery County high schools, some say B-CC's is perhaps the most personal and ideological of the offerings because McCarthy makes no effort to disguise his opposition to war, violence and animal testing.

Saraf and Avishek Panth, also 17, acknowledge that with the exception of one lecture they sat in on this month, most of what they know about the course has come from friends and acquaintances who have taken the class. But, they said, those discussions coupled with research they have done on McCarthy's background, have convinced them that their school should not continue to offer Peace Studies unless significant changes are made. This is not an ideological debate, they said. Rather, what bothers them most is that McCarthy offers only one perspective.

"I do recognize that it is a fairly popular class," Saraf said. "But it's clear that the teacher is only giving one side of the story. He's only offering facts that fit his point of view."

For his part, McCarthy, 67, finds the students' objections a bit puzzling. He said that although the two sat in on a recent class, they have not talked to him in depth about their concerns.

"I've never said my views are right and theirs are wrong," he said about the students who take his course. "In fact, I cherish conservative dissenters. I wish we could get more of them in."

The course is offered at Montgomery Blair, James Hubert Blake, Albert Einstein, Walter Johnson, Northwest, Northwood and Rockville high schools, but the Peace Studies course at Bethesda–Chevy Chase is unique for a number of reasons. Although a staff teacher takes roll and issues grades, it is McCarthy as a volunteer, unpaid guest lecturer who does the bulk of the teaching. He does not work from lesson plans, although he does use a school system–approved textbook—a collection of essays on peace that he edited.

For McCarthy, it seems Peace Studies is not just a cause; it is a crusade.

"Unless we teach them peace, someone else will teach them violence," he said.

Students might spend one class period listening to a guest speaker who opposes the death penalty and another, if they choose, standing along East-West Highway protesting the war.

But that, students said, is part of the course's appeal.

"We're all mature enough to take it all in with a hint of skepticism," said Megan Andrews, 17. "We respect Mr. McCarthy's views, but we don't absorb them like sponges."

When they walk through the door of their fourth-floor classroom, students said, they never know what they might find. Once McCarthy brought in a live turkey [days before Thanksgiving] to illustrate a point about animal rights. Everything went well until the turkey escaped and urinated in the hallway.

And Friday, when students opened the door, they saw Mahatma Gandhi—or rather Bernard Meyer, a peace activist from Olympia, Wash., dressed as Gandhi. Meyer spent most of the class time taking questions from students about "life" as Gandhi. McCarthy, too, jumped in, quizzing Gandhi about his views on arranged marriage. At the end of the period, he jumped from his chair.

"Let's take a photo of us with Gandhi," he said, gathering the students.

Susie Doyle, 18, said she respects Saraf and Panth for having the courage to speak out on the school e-mail list about their concerns. She does not agree, but said: "It would be a little hypocritical to jump on them. I have a little trouble with them criticizing the course since they haven't taken it, but it's important that they speak up."

In the meantime, Saraf and Panth said, they plan to do more research and present their case for discontinuing the course to the administration. For now, however, the administration said it has no plan to do away with Peace Studies.

"Peace Studies is one of the things makes B-CC unique," Bulson said. "It's been an institution here, and kids from all across the spectrum have taken it. It's not about indoctrination. It's about debate and dialogue."

APRIL 7, 2006

Dear Lena,

Go easy on yourself. You're not a flake. You've just overscheduled yourself a bit. A common ailment for college students. Plus, you are certainly ready for a break from the academics and politics of Washington.

Your thoughts about your time at Busboys and Poets coincided with a long story in a local magazine—the *Washingtonian*—about Andy Shallal, the creator and owner. I've known him for some time, going back to when one of his sons was a student at Annandale High School in northern Virginia and Andy was pushing to start a peace studies program at the school. I spent a day trying to organize something. In the end, that's all it was—trying. Follow-up by the administrators didn't happen, which is often the case. Peace courses are mostly seen as a gourmet items, especially in schools caught in the testing frenzy that is demoralizing teachers ordered to get the test scores up.

By the way, that's one regret about my peace class at Georgetown. I should never have given that final exam, and did so only because of my strong suspicions that a couple of the deans were looking for an excuse— that I was "too soft" on the students—to give me the boot. So an exam would show I was a tough guy. In the end, it didn't matter. I did apologize to some of the students in that class for putting them through the pain of an exam, and I apologize to you now.

Andy Shallal, I believe, is to be admired. Not many idealistic people have either the self-confidence or acumen to run a business. Gandhi never gave anyone a job or met a payroll, nor did King. Whatever negatives may surrounded Busboys and Poets, jobs are provided, people are fed both physically and intellectually. It's a business that stands for something well beyond making profits. That's also true about Whole Foods, a company for which I have high regard. Its founder, John Mackey, is a vegan and supporter of animal rights groups. Of course, he is asked why then does Whole Foods sell meat. His answer is that if he didn't, the stores would go under and a few thousand workers in the 170 or so stores would be out of work.

So compromises are everything. All of us should be wary of pointing our well-manicured fingers at the next person and shouting "sell out."

You're a pal—

Colman

~ ~ ~

FEBRUARY 1, 2012

Dear Mr. McCarthy,

I am sitting in second period watching an extremely boring video about what defines a recession knowing that just a few classrooms down the hall real learning is taking place. When I asked my second period teacher if I could come hear the guest speaker in Peace Studies, he responded "Are you kidding? Of course NOT." So instead of listening to someone who is addressing a pressing issue facing us, the closing of the School of the Americas, I sit in the back of a classroom, not paying attention to something I really don't care about. There is something seriously wrong with our education system and I am seeing it more and more every day. I miss your class so much! Maybe my first period teacher will be more understanding and I can come to your class for the next speaker. Hope to see you soon.

Sincerely,

Hannah Levin

FEBRUARY 4, 2012

Dear Hannah,

So what prompted the teacher's denial? I'd guess fear. If your ticket was punched and the response was, "Sure, go ahead, enjoy it," and you left, you might be missing something about the recession that could have been worth 25 points on the final exam. You'd get a low grade, the teacher a poor evaluation, and Bethesda–Chevy Chase High School might not be winning President Obama's "Race to the Top"—the current educational solution to get America's children to keep up with all those Chinese and Japanese whizzes.

What prompted you to obey the teacher's order and stay put? I'm guessing fear again. If you did leave, extra homework might be dumped on you, your parents might be called about your disobedience, you might be dispatched to the principal's office, a recommendation letter for college might not be written—which you don't need because you've won early acceptance to Williams College.

You're right, something is seriously wrong with American education. It's fear, from the bottom up. Students who stray from the accepted way fret about the teacher's reaction. Teachers who deviate from academic probity—as in letting you take in the Peace Studies class a few rooms away—fear the principal's response. Principals fear school boards. School boards don't get out of line because they fear having funds cut off by the politicians. And politicians behave themselves in fear of the voters.

Everyone fears the Powerful One just above them. Conformity reigns. Like unruly puppies, students are being trained in obedience schools and after enough yanks on the leash know when and how to heel.

Grading, testing and homework represent teaching by fear. Scare children into learning. Score well on tests, goes the meritocratic message, and pathways to success widen. Do poorly and they narrow. Bow to a teacher's demand for test preparation, no matter how rote the drilling, or spend hours writing irrelevant papers, and the slavishness will pay off. So it is claimed. At the end of the course parents can ask their child, if they ask at all, not what did you learn, but "What did you get on the final exam?"

Maria Montessori, who opened her elementary school in a Roman slum in 1907, never afflicted her bambinos with tests or homework. Nor do Montessori schools today. Socrates never demeaned his agora students with those assaults. Two of history's supreme teachers believed in desire-based, not fear-based, learning. Evidently the grandees of American education are wiser.

A B-CC parent phoned a few years ago, wanting to know how her daughter was doing in my class. "How would I know," I answered, "I'm her teacher."

"What did you say?"

"I'm your daughter's teacher, I have no idea how she's doing."

"What's her grade?"

"I don't know, I'm a teacher not a grader. Grades are unimportant."

"I want her to get into a good college, so grades are important. Once more, how is my daughter doing in your class."

"Once more, dear sister, I don't know. But I have an easy way for you to find out: ask your daughter. She'll tell you."

In fact, the student was a joy to have in class. She had an open mind, strong ideals and relished the give-and-take of our class debates—none of which had a thing to do with grades or getting to the Ivies.

The illusion of grade-based excellence remains, reinforced by fear-based learning and fake academic rigor. In more than 30 years of teaching, I have seen no evidence that acing tests improves a student's character, leads them to be kinder or more loving or strengthens them to stand up against abusive power. A while back, the *Post* asked me to review a book by Noam Chomsky titled *Chomsky on Miseducation*. It was a collection of essays and interviews, stitched together by Chomsky's belief that education should be about freeing minds, not controlling them. "A good teacher," he argued, "knows that the best way to help students learn is to let them find the truth by themselves. Students don't learn by a mere transfer of knowledge, consumed through rote memorization and later re-gurgitated. True learning comes about through the discovery of truth. Not the imposition of an official truth. That never leads to the development of independent and critical thought. It is the obligation of any teacher to help students discover the truth and not to suppress information and insights that may be embarrassing to the wealthy and powerful people who create, design and make policies about schools."

Ten years ago, when B-CC was being renovated and students were sent to a building too far away for me to commute by my Raleigh 3-speed, I was invited to teach at the Stone Ridge girls school in Bethesda. My initial and main challenge was to help each girl to relax. Some of them came to school hauling 30-lb backpacks crammed with science books, math books, English books, notebooks. Thirty lbs. of books. All in the name of homework. Many of the girls looked to weigh less than 120 lbs. They were packing one-fourth their body weight.

To minimize back strain, I used no textbook for the course. Instead, I copied an essay by Gandhi or Tolstoy or Dorothy Day and got the discussion started by having a student read it aloud, paragraph by paragraph, stopping to get the class's reaction.

That morning you were a bored captive learning nothing useful about recessions, my guest speakers were two dissidents making the case for closing the School of the Americas, more accurately the School of the Assassins. Run by the US Army at Ft. Benning, Georgia, for more than three decades, it trained soldiers from Latin American countries—El Salvador, Colombia, Nicaragua, Honduras, Panama—who return to obey thuggish governments to kill or torture priests, nuns, trade unionists, journalists and others seen as threats to law and order, as defined by dictators and US companies selling them weapons. SOA graduates were responsible for the killing of Archbishop Oscar Romero as he said Mass the morning of March 24, 1980. Not long after, they killed six Jesuit priests, their housekeeper, and her daughter. They hacked to death four Catholic churchwomen. They directed the massacre of nearly the whole town of 800 in El Salvador's El Mozote, a slaughter that the State Department of Alexander Haig initially denied happening.

My two speakers, both recent college graduates and knowledgeable with facts that twin with their passion for justice, lobby Congress to cut off funding for the school. No student in either my first or second period class was aware that the Army had been training assassins and not aware, either, that a Roman Catholic priest, Fr. Roy Bourgeois, has been protesting for 25 years at the gates of Ft. Benning. They are aware now.

Thanks for your letter. I think you know how grateful I was to have you in class last semester. Your gentle ways of speaking your truth, of disagreeing with me when that was definitely needed, and your open-mindedness were gifts that I treasured. I spoke at Williams College two years ago and will pass on the names of a couple of professors whose courses you might want to take. If so, they'll be lucky to have you, as I was.

Do well,

Colman McCarthy

P.S. If you want to learn about the recession, you might start to read the twice weekly columns of Paul Krugman in the *New York Times*. He won the Nobel Prize for Economics three years ago. I'd suggest, too, *Small Is Beautiful*, the enduring book by E. F. Schumacher which offers solutions on the just distribution of wealth. Try it for summer reading.

Dear Professor,

How are you doing? Do you teach summer classes or do you get a chance to take a break? I hope you do.

I have a bit of a situation with a friend and I was wondering if I could ask you for some advice. I promised I wouldn't tell anyone about this but I also can't in good conscience be myself and not at least look for a way to help him. A good friend, who I have been dating on and off, recently told me that he can't see me anymore because he deals with intense depression that has been with him for the past four years. He said he thinks about killing himself every day, sometimes more than once in a day. He seems to have given up on any sort of therapy and refuses medication. He admitted that while a few people know that he has struggled with this, no one knows that he isn't cured. Except for me. Meaning he has been really good at hiding it.

Besides the initial shock of realizing how ignorant I was to his feelings and thoughts, I'm not really sure what my role in this is supposed to be. I stressed how he should really start talking to someone again, and he said I don't need to be too concerned. But I also know that I can't handle the responsibility of being the only one who knows he feels this way. How long is he able to hide this before something happens? Don't I hold a certain responsibility as one of his friends who knows he is struggling with this? He is an extremely intelligent and sensitive guy. I feel like he could be so happy but he just can't see that right now. He seems to be functioning on a daily basis just fine, and I feel like his logic in the end will prevent him from doing anything too rash anytime soon. Do you have any advice as to how I take this information?

He told me because he cares about me and he said I deserved to know why he couldn't be with me anymore, and while I know he isn't expecting anything else from me, I just really don't know what I am supposed to do now. He relates his situation best to David Foster Wallace, who wrote *Infinite Jest*. Maybe you've read it.

I thought you might have some insight as to what I should do. I appreciate your help, guidance and sensitivity in always offering to help your students.

>   *Hope all is well with you,*
>   Ariel F.

Dear Ariel,

You're right to be concerned about you friend, and right, too, to be perplexed on your role in his life now that he prefers that you don't have a role.

To start, I'd guess that his wish to not see you again is a symptom of the pain he is in. The intensity of the pain is the mystery you don't know, and can't know, at least experientially. My understanding of suicide is limited to the relationships I've had with students who took their lives: two in high school, two in college, one in law school. Each loss left me wondering whether I should have been alert to the signs of desperation. It's a hard call, not having a trained eye or ear to note the difference between a reactive depression—as in reacting to a negative experience that sends you stumbling but from which can regain your balance after a bit of time passes—or a clinical depression which is intense in its pain and despairing in its seeming hopelessness.

If your friend is rejecting talk therapy or medication therapy, or a combination of the two, it does leave you few merciful options that might help. If only for your own peace of mind, which you have a right to, I'd suggest sending a handwritten letter that offers him information. About what? Your feelings, whatever those might be. Will it help him, and by help I mean will it cure his illness? It's doubtful. But not totally. Will it comfort you? Odds on, yes. Should he take his life, you will have known that you weren't passive when he was moving in that direction.

I recall in class one evening speaking about suicide, making the point that if we know a friend who is in emotional crisis, we can take two actions: tell them to call someone for help and, second, tell them that however deep their suffering there is someone else who felt the same way and pulled through. Comebacks are possible. More of them happen than we realize. I have no empirical research on the effectiveness of those approaches but I don't know of any kind of research that's available to guide the lay untrained nonpsychiatric community.

The recent suicide of David Foster Wallace left much of the public, or at least the literate parts of it, baffled and saddened. It isn't an uplifting thought that your friend relates to Wallace's life and his choice to end it.

Right now I'd suggest you try a handwritten letter. In it, tell him you are a phone call away. Make it clear that you aren't trying to keep the relationship going. Say, too, that you are grateful for his honesty in explaining why he wanted to end it. I'm assuming when the off came in the off-and-on relationship that it was not a nasty screaming final scene but one that meant you would still be connected but in a different way.

Much praise to you for asking the right questions about you might do next. You might read William Styron, the American novelist best known for *Sophie's Choice* and *The Confessions of Nat Turner*. In 1990 he wrote *Darkness Visible: A Memoir of Madness*, a work considered a classic in the literature of suicidal depression. He did survive the darkness.

Yes, I am teaching this summer: one at the Washington Center, the other a six-week seminar at a Buddhist temple in town. I should take a break. Maybe it is, considering I have seven schools in the Fall and six in the Spring. Summer is cruising speed.

Keep on—

Colman McCarthy

⌒⌒⌒

Dear Professor McCarthy,

I'm the Japanese Canisius College student whom you met at Dr. DiCicco's class on March 8. There were two Japanese students, and I'm the one who wore black glasses and sat in the front. My name is Yurina Osumi.

I'm sorry that I could not respond to you when you politely apologized to all Japanese people [for the bombing of Hiroshima and Nagasaki in August 1945]. I was surprised and could not say how I thought and felt. Please let me speak about my thoughts and feelings now.

First of all, I would like to apologize to all Americans who died in the war and lost their family members in the war. As Americans killed many Japanese, Japanese killed many Americans. As a result, I'm not going to criticize the killings by Americans. Killing each other is war. Also I'm not going to criticize Americans because of the atomic bombs during World

Letters   [101]

War II. Of course, an atomic bomb is an inhuman weapon. I feel really sad when I think about people who suffered and died with unimaginable pain. My mother and her parents are from Hiroshima, and I was born in Hiroshima. My grandparents were luckily away from the hypocenter and were not affected by the bomb, but my mother was discriminated against when she tried to marry through an arranged marriage.

This is because the image of Hiroshima is being affected by radiation. But she met my father and gave birth to me, so my family's sufferings because of the atomic bomb was not as harsh as the other Hiroshima or Nagasaki citizens.'

As I said above, an atomic bomb is an inhuman weapon. But there are two reasons that I'm not angry about the United States. First, all wars are inhuman. There is no lawful, correct war. We don't need to focus on the use of nuclear weapons too much. All killings in war are wrong and brutal but that is what the Japanese also did during the war. Second, putting responsibilities on each other prevents future progress and learning from the past. It is impossible to revive nuclear bomb victims and people who died in the war. If so, what we should do is talk about the future, not blaming each other regarding what already happened.

There is one thing that I really want not only for Americans but for every nuclear weapons holder: never use them again. There is a sentence on the memorial stone at the hypocenter at Hiroshima: "Are not going to make the mistake." It is quite common in the Japanese language to leaving out a subject because the Japanese have a "guessing culture." Who should be put on this sentence as the subject? Right after the war, some Japanese insisted that the subject should be Americans. But I do not think so. The subject should be "We." We should learn that all wars and inhuman killings are unacceptable.

That's why I do not have any anger on Americans. I will only criticize those who think it is acceptable to begin wars and kill others. I hope that Hiroshima and Nagasaki will be the last places that were bombed by atomic weapons.

Thank you for your time. Have a good day!

Sincerely,

Yurina Osumi

Dear Yurina,

You are generous to take time from your studies to share your thoughts. I was delighted to visit your class at Canisius before my lecture in the evening. For as long as I can remember whenever I meet a Japanese citizen, I apologize for the bombing of Hiroshima and Nagasaki by the United States government. It was indiscriminate killing of men, women and children, few of whom had anything to do with the military policies of Japan's leaders. Harry Truman, the American president who ordered the bombings, lied when he said: "The world will note that the first atomic bomb was dropped on Hiroshima, a military base. That was because we wished in this first attack to avoid, insofar as possible, the killing of civilians." Hiroshima was a city, not a military base. An estimated 140,000 died. Even after August 6 and 9, the American military had plans to drop more atomic bombs on Japan. The historian Howard Zinn, who I am sure you have read, wrote in *Declarations of Independence*: "The terrible momentum of war continued even after the bombings of Hiroshima and Nagasaki. The end of the war was a few days away, yet B-29s continued their missions. On August 14, five days after the Nagasaki bombing and the day before the actual acceptance of surrender terms, 440 B-29s went out from the Marianas for a daylight strike and 372 more went out that night. Altogether, more than 1,000 planes were sent to bomb Japanese cities. There were no American losses."

In the years after the war, United States policy makers, seeking to build more destructive bombs that could kill greater numbers of people, began testing atomic weapons in the Marshall and Bikini islands in the Pacific Ocean. In time, the United States would stockpile thousands of nuclear weapons that are equal to a million Hiroshima-type bombs.

On November 1, 2007 Paul Tibbets Jr. died. He was the pilot of the Enola Gay, the plane that carried the bomb to Hiroshima. Tibbets was exceptionally proud of his killing so many Japanese and had no regrets. It was the opposite. He blustered to Studs Terkel, another American historian, that he would have no qualms about using nuclear bombs again against America's enemies: "I'd wipe 'em out. You're gonna kill innocent people at the same time, but we've never fought a damn war anywhere in the world where they didn't kill innocent people. If the newspapers would just cut out the [vulgar word], 'you've killed so many civilians.' That's their tough luck for being there."

You are correct that "there is no lawful, correct war." And that the Japanese government was also a killing machine. You are right to apologize to Americans. My own apologizing began in the mid-1980s when I met four Japanese survivors of Hiroshima and Nagasaki on their visit to Washington. They are called, as you probably know, hibakushas. I invited them to speak in one of my classes, including Tsutomu Yamaguchi who was a niju hibakusha—a survivor of both Hiroshima and Nagasaki. While in Washington they asked to speak to President Ronald Reagan in the White House. They were told no, he was too busy. The next day a newspaper picture showed Reagan in the White House hosting Japanese sumo wrestlers.

One person the hibakushas did meet was Concepcion Picciotto. She is the Spanish-born peacemaker who has camped across the street from the north side of the White House since June 1981. She has been there amid blizzards, heat waves, rainstorms, and lightning bolts. She has been arrested dozens of times by federal and local police, plus enduring denunciations by politicians and passersby. She usually sits in a folding chair surrounded by signs: "Ban All Nuclear Weapons or Have a Nice Doomsday." And: "Live By the Bomb, Die By the Bomb." Her site is known as the Peace Park Anti-Nuclear Vigil." I have taken my classes many times to visit Concepcion to learn from her. Many people in Washington, from media sophists to think-tank wheel-spinners, dismiss her as a crazy lady. Tourists see her as a curiosity. But not all tourists. The one group that most appreciates her, even to the point of calling her a saint and a prophet, are the Japanese. I have met many of them at the Vigil. And of course, I do my apologizing.

If you are ever in Washington, take time to meet Concepcion. She's right there at 1601 Pennsylvania Avenue, with President Obama at 1600 Pennsylvania. Five presidents have lived in the White House since Concepcion arrived but not one has had the neighborliness to walk over to say hello, much less had the grace to invite her one of the endless White House parties.

If you do come to Washington, I'd like you to meet my son John. He is a teacher and a baseball coach. He played baseball professionally, in the Baltimore Orioles organization, and two years ago went to Japan to visit Bobby Valentine, for six years the manager of the Chiba Marlins, one of the country's best teams. Valentine is back in the United States now, managing the Boston Red Sox. Bobby Valentine was enormously popular in Japan, not only because of his managerial skills but because he disciplined himself to learn to speak and write in Japanese. Not many Americans do that, regrettably.

It's springtime in Washington, which means the city is awash in the beauty of the hundreds and hundreds of Japanese cherry blossom trees— gifts from your country to ours long before we were enemies. During World War II, talk was heard that the trees should be chopped down. Calmer minds prevailed, for once.

I deeply appreciate your letter and the thoughtfulness behind it. Your English is excellent. I will show it to my students. They have much to learn from it.

My best to Professor DiCicco. I'm sure you are teaching him a lot, as you have me.

Sayonara,

Colman McCarthy

MARCH 19, 2012

Dear Professor McCarthy,

Thanks you very much for your response. I think all history classes all over the world are biased. A history class is not the only source of people's knowledge and feelings toward others. The media, opinions of parents, friends, politicians and neighbors are also important sources. In this situation, it is quite normal to believe "my country is great and correct." I personally think we should remember that the other people also have their beliefs and they believe they are right. We have to remember that what we are believing may not be correct from a different view.

From this, I may understand the feelings of Paul Tibbets Jr. Of course, "understand" does not mean "agree." If I were him I would have refused to drop the bomb. I would refuse to go to the war. But I believe that without understanding, it is impossible that two different people can learn from the past, agree on something and cooperate with each other. Mother Teresa said, "the opposite of love is not hatred but ignorance." I agree that ignorance is cruel and dangerous for our safety. You may wonder why I do not include myself with "the people." This is because I realized the ignorance in my heart and the realization it is still motivating me. When I was a child, I saw a TV program of Africans who were dying of extreme poverty. I felt sad, really sad, but I watched a funny movie the same day. I left food uneaten at dinner. At the time I realized my ignorance in my heart. It was quite easy to go back to my life by forgetting them or by making an excuse that I cannot do anything for them. After I realized my ignorance, I had my dream of becoming an aid worker and working for underprivileged people. It is easy to forget, so I always want to think about them by working for them.

As a result, I applied to the Japan International Cooperation Agency (JICA) to get a job. I wait to hear from them. JICA is an independent administrative agency. If I stay in until their 2nd step of the selection process, I will come to Washington for an interview at the beginning of April. If so I would like to meet you, your son and Ms. Picciotto. And the cherry blossom trees!

Thank you for your comments about my writing. I'm very glad to hear that. Have a good day.

Sincerely,

Yurina Osumi

MARCH 22, 2012

Dear Yurina,

You are right about bias in the world's history classes. Several years ago, Howard Zinn, the author of *A People's History of the United States* and a longtime professor of history at Spelman College and Boston University, came to one of my high school classes to speak. During the question and answer period a student asked Professor Zinn for his definition of history. He answered, "History is the winner's version of what happened."

During his talk, Professor Zinn spoke of enlisting in the US Air Force in World War II at 21. He was assigned to a crew whose mission was to fly from bases in England to bomb cities and towns in Germany. The young soldier believed, as did most Americans, that this was "a war of high principle" and "each was a mission of high principle."

Returning home from the war, and unable to suppress memories of saturation bombing, Howard Zinn began to have second thoughts. He writes in *Declarations of Independence*, published in 1990: "My doubts grew. I was reading history. Had the United States fought in World War II for the rights of nations to independence and self-determination? What of its own history of expansion through war and conquest? It had waged a hundred year war against the Native Americans, driving them off their ancestral lands. The United States had instigated a war with Mexico and taken almost all its land, had sent Marines at least 20 times into the countries of the Caribbean for power and profit, had seized Hawaii, had fought a brutal war to subjugate the Filipinos, and had sent 5,000 Marines to Nicaragua in 1926. Our nation could hardly claim it believed in the right of self-determination, unless it believed in it selectively."

This double standard was not limited to the war in Europe. Professor Zinn writes about the Japanese attack on Pearl Harbor: "The sudden indignation against Japan contained a good deal of hypocrisy. The United States, along with Japan and the great European posers, had participated in the exploitation of China. Our Open Door Policy of 1901 accepted that ganging up of the great powers on China. The United States had exchanged notes with Japan in 1917 saying, 'the Government of the United States recognizes that Japan had special interests in China,' and in 1918 American consuls in China supported the coming of Japanese troops."

With a few worthy exceptions now and again, most history teachers I know regard Howard Zinn as a rebel. For me, he is an icon—a pillar of honesty, a writer whose blade of a mind cuts through guff and cant. He analyzed history from the victim's point of view, not the winner's. And what exactly does winning a war mean? In your class the morning I was at Canisius, I mentioned the line of Jeannette Rankin, the pacifist member of Congress from Montana and the only person to vote against both the First and Second World Wars: "You can no more win a war than win an earthquake."

We all have our own beliefs, as you say. Real intellectual courage is to move beyond defending our beliefs to questioning them, and keeping the ones that are firm—and discarding ones that are flab.

I hope you are hired by the JICA. If the directors are wise, they will do so. And give you a big salary. Should you come to Washington for the interview, please call. I would like to invite you to speak in my high school classes. Perhaps we can take a field trip to visit Concepcion Picciotto.

Your letter combines both self-reflection and open-mindedness.

You write clear and creative English, better than some of my American students.

Good-bye for now,

Colman McCarthy

❧ ❧ ❧

Dear Mr. McCarthy

I hope everything is going well. I'm sorry I never had a chance to visit a class of yours when I was home for winter break.

I have a couple more months of freshman year at Oberlin and am searching for a job in DC for the summer. I was wondering, do you know of any jobs or paid internships that I might be right for? I would be happy to write articles, do research for an organization, work at a restaurant, or even be a bike messenger. Almost anything. I know you've lived in DC for a while and know a lot of people, so if there are any opportunities or if there's info you can give me that might help me out, that would be great. Maybe the Center for Teaching Peace has a summer internship? Let me know.

Also I would love to bring you out to Oberlin to speak, either for the end of this year or next fall. If you are interested, I will get working to try to set things up.

Best,

Peter Hartmann

APRIL 9, 2011

Dear Peter,

As you don't need to be told, Washington is packed every summer with interns. And as you DO need to be told, the word intern has French origins—meaning "slave." Internment camps.

I'd advise staying clear of a summer of slavery. But I do know of some well-paying jobs: outdoors, four or five hours a day, plenty of socializing, plus physical exercise. What job? Caddying.

Where? The top choices are the Chevy Chase Club, which is closest to your home, and a bit further away, Columbia Country Club, Burning Tree Golf Club and Congressional Country Club. The current rate for carrying two bags is around $80—in cash which means no taxes taken out, unless you want to be taxed to oil America's war machine. In caddying, sometimes you aren't even lugging clubs because the foursomes ride in golf carts that carry them. You just have to keep an eye on the ball—or balls as each player swings away. After that, it's mostly a matter of holding the pin on the greens, raking the sand traps, replacing divots, keeping quiet on backswings and calling out "great shot" when the duffers hit it anywhere straight or anywhere remotely close to the hole.

I know the pro at Chevy Chase, Jim Fitzgerald. He's friendly and is as gracious to caddies as he is to members. I had his daughter in class at Bethesda–Chevy Chase, where she was a star on the golf team: all boys except her. Of the four clubs, Chevy Chase would be the easiest on your legs and back. The course is fairly flat and, with only two par fives, not long.

Not to stereotype memberships at the clubs, or at least keep it somewhat under control for the moment, Chevy Chase is Old Wasp Money, Columbia is middle-class Catholic, Burning Tree is Old Boy Republicans and Congressional reeks with New Money. If you are going to join the servant class, you'd be better treated at Chevy Chase. The membership is sedate, mannered and accustomed to being civil toward the help. It's the opposite of Congressional. With upwards to a thousand members clawing to get tee times, it might as well be a public course. Lobbyists and assorted deal-makers invite members of Congress to freeload. Tip O'Neill, Dan Quayle, Sam Nunn, Dan Rostenkowski, Marty Russo and Tom DeLay were among the politicians who did the public's business at Congressional. In the 1990s Bill Clinton brought in his entourage so often that the club finally told him no more. Before he teed off, the course had to be cased by the Secret Service. Adjoining fairways had to be cleared of players and the woods searched for possible snipers. Burning Tree, where women are not allowed on the property except once a year at Christmas time when they can buy presents in the pro shop for their husbands, is where 16-year-old Pat Buchanan caddied for Richard Nixon in the 1950s. Like Nixon, few Burning Tree members play well. The high-handicappers dodder around the course and stagger into the grill for a 19th hole of gin rummy and shots of Johnnie Walker.

Looping at Chevy Chase would expose you to two worlds: the one of WASP high-breds and the one of nonpedigrees where caddies orbit, spinning around suns and moons of their own making: some as down-and-outs, a few as drifters who can't or won't hold regular jobs. Listen and learn from them. It will be far more than what you'd pick up shuffling papers with interns on K Street. You could ask Oberlin to give you three credits for your summer course in Advanced Sociology.

Give it a try. I'd be glad to say a word for you with Jim Fitzgerald.

From the back tees,

Colman McCarthy

P.S. It's not well-known, but one of the Chevy Chase members is Chief Justice John Roberts. Who knows—you might get to caddy for him. When handing him his putter, you can suggest that he stop supporting the death penalty. Another member is Alan Greenspan, who may get "irrationally exuberant" when he makes two pars in a row. Ask him if he has any regrets about all the mistakes he made as chairman of the Federal Reserve. Ask after he tips you, assuming he does. Could be that he doesn't. You know, fiscal restraint.

JUNE 16, 2011

Dear Mr. McCarthy,

I'm reporting back from my first day of caddying. One bag for 18 holes wasn't too bad, and I was paid well. I just have to keep getting there at 6:30 am, and I can expect to go out once or twice a day.

The exposure to the two very different worlds within our society is going to make the job a lot more interesting and eye opening than I could have known. I'm not really a part of either of the worlds but it's remarkable to realize that I am more familiar with the culture of the older black caddies than of the rich white men who send their sons to Georgetown Prep.

Those sociology credits would be useful considering I may major in that department.

There's a poster in the caddy shack: if a duffer asks you if you like his game, you answer "I like it alright but I prefer golf."

Peter Hartmann

Dear Peter,

Heart-tingling moment, isn't it, walking up that long uphill 18th hole to finish the round? It's never been officially sanctioned but caddies do have an anthem of their own—sort of. It's "Carry It On." Joan Baez sings it best. It's not about golf but some of the lyrics do fit, eerily.

Keep me posted. Don't hesitate to strike up conversations with your players. Harmless queries to get them talking, like when they took up the game. Do they take lessons. Inquire, too, about their working lives—discreetly of course. You might have a trust-funder on your hands, not overly eager to reveal that money works for him rather than he works for money. You'll know the trust-fund set by their names, ones like Scuffington Griswold III or Cadwallader Buckinghman Smith IV. As for the ladies of high lineage, nicknames prevail: Flossy, Pinky, Chessie, Hoopsie, Lulu.

Here's hoping the summer works out for you. I'd imagine the truths that prevailed in my caddying days remain so in yours. The worse the golfer, the heavier the bag. Golfers who stand paralyzed over the ball before hitting it score higher than those who miss it quick. The richer the golfer, the madder they get when losing a ball. The problem with most golfers is that they stand too close to the ball—after they hit it. If a player ever asks you for advice, like after four-putting for an 11, pass along the advice Sam Snead once imparted to a hopeless case: take three weeks off and then quit altogether.

Keep carrying,

Colman McCarthy

Dear Professor,

First, I wish to say thank you for helping me remember that I am a living human being, and that showing emotion is not a sign of weakness but of life. It has been many years since anyone has asked me to write something about my life, much less to write sincerely and from the heart. In college "writing from the heart" is considered unsubstantial and therefore unacceptable and utterly irrelevant. The American education system might be one of the best in the world when it comes to gaining skills like critical thinking, analysis, research or math. We can all do math and write an analysis of United States foreign policy. What we seem to have forgotten is how to write from our hearts. Research our own lives. It took more effort for me to write this kind of paper than any assignment I had to complete over the course of my college career. This is a sad fact, yet very much true. Somewhere over the course of my education, I forgot how to speak of emotions and learned to instead always search for facts.

I have found that humans are never really equipped to deal with difficult situations, no matter how well we think we prepare for life's unpredictable ways. It is within our nature to always assume that bad things will not happen to us. However, once they do, regardless of how difficult the task ahead of us may be, most of us find the strength within ourselves, strength we often did not even know we had, to face the pain, the fear, the hurt.

It was fall of 2008. Our relationship was just beginning to take shape and neither one of us knew exactly how we felt about each other, and even if we did, we did not know how to put it into words nor was it necessary to do so. For a few months we let ourselves be naïve and lost in our own little world of blissfulness, knowing full well that it will not last as such. There was a war in Iraq and he had to go "spread democracy" and teach Iraqis how to live their lives—for the third time. It was a first for me, though. First love, first war, first real pain of life. And just like that I went from being a self-involved, immature high school kid to an adult who's loved one was fighting a nasty, and in my strong opinion, unnecessary war. I grew up that winter.

I am not going to tell you about all the horrors that the loved ones of those in combat go through on a daily basis. It has been told many times, and I am no different or more special than a mother of two struggling to make ends meet and praying that her children's father comes home alive and in one piece, or the mother of a young soldier who just finished high school and left the family nest for the first time to go fight for his country. We all struggle, and it is never easy. Some of us get to see the moment when they come home, others are not so lucky.

Since Iraq, my Marine has served in Serbia, Jordan and Turkey while I have been studying at American University. It has been four long years of online conversations, long distance calls, emails, Christmas cards,

Valentine's Day flowers, and occasional visits. He was supposed to be discharged four times now due to having three surgeries for injuries sustained while in the service. Every time we let ourselves believe that this will be the time he finally comes home, the Marine Corps has come up with new rules, procedures or bureaucracy barriers that would delay his discharge date. So the original two-year test to our relationship has turned into three, and now four years. It took a long time for me to be able to discuss our situation without bursting into tears and feeling like my heart will break. But people get accustomed to anything, given enough time and effort. Such is life.

The main barrier to our relationship over the last few years was finally broken down, thanks to your class. Ever since he came back from Iraq the last time, he has never been the same. Whatever horrendous things he had done and seen had left a scar on him, one that was only visible to those who love him. I spend many nights trying to understand how to help him and what it is that has happened, that could forever change the man I love into a mere shadow of the person he used to be. It was not until I came to your class and we had a session on military members that I was given a better perspective of his situation. For the first time I understood the pain, the inability to cope, the feelings of guilt and shame. Thank you for that too. While his service is still ongoing, just yesterday he was informed that his new release date is June 16, 2012.

Sincerely,

Mika Lesevic

APRIL 7, 2012

Dear Mika,

So glad you broke free, to find strength in your emotions. All of us lead two lives, outer and inner, exterior and interior. I've been reading T. S. Eliot's *The Confidential Clerk,* about a musician who is changing careers. A friend tells him:

> It's only the outer world that you've lost.
> You've still got your inner world—a world that's more real.
> That's why you're different from the rest of us.
> You have your secret garden, to which you can retire
> And lock the gate behind you.

Garden is a perfect metaphor. Growth is implied. We tend to think, mistakenly, that the person who leads a full life is forever bustling and opening doors to personal enrichment—rushing in, organizing, making progress or making waves, so it's thought. Activity has come to mean fullness. Inwardness involves the opposite—moving into the secret garden, tied to no plans, expectations or other baggage except the fragile notion of connecting with one's private self, not the public one. The interior life is not about results and even less about production. What can happen is a feeling of contentment, one that might lead to self-acceptance. We hear about people, wearied by life's demands, who bolt for the hills "to find myself," but often enough they know fully who they are. They just can't stand it.

Fidelity to the interior life often has the ring of mysticism to it, of opening bottles of Zen and breathing in the ether of otherworldliness. This is why I ask my students to keep journals throughout the semester. Writing is a fruitful discipline, a quiet time cloistered from the noises of dailyness. A journal can become a haven, with the writing—even if only the jotting of a few paragraphs—being the place where our solitude is tended. Or as you said: "What we seem to have forgotten how to do is write from our hearts." It's likely fear-driven, a fear of standing exposed. An expression of this came from Florida Scott-Maxwell in *The Measure of My Days*, a book I've relied on for years: "The ordeal of being true to your own inner way must stand high in the list of ordeals. It is like being in the power of someone you cannot reach, or know more, but who never lets you go, who both insists that you accept yourself and who seems to know who you are. It is awful to have to be yourself. If you do reach this stage of life, you are to some extent free from your fellows. Many do have to endure a minute degree of uniqueness, just enough to make them slightly immune from the infection of the crowd, but natural people avoid it. They obey for comfort's sake the instinct that warns, 'Say yes, don't differ, it's not safe.' It's not easy to be sure that being yourself is worth the trouble but we do know it is our sacred duty."

If the Marine commanders are telling the truth to you and your boyfriend—as they haven't in the past—he will be released, as you say, in mid-June. There is no way of predicting how your relationship will be affected either by the negatives he has gone through as a soldier or the positives you've been through as a student. Safe to say, each of you is much different than when you first decided to share yourselves with each other. How different, is the question. I have known soldiers who returned from war zones, whether in Germany, Japan, Korea, Vietnam, Somalia, Iraq, Afghanistan or other lands where presidents and congressional warlords believe they must dispatch the young to preserve the American Empire, and they adjust to civilian life with little or no friction and much the better for having been in the military. Others come home with wounds to their bodies and spirits so severe that no healing can help, even assuming that healing is available which too often it isn't. No drugs, no medicines, no therapies and no comforting from loved ones can effectively restore what has been destroyed by the violence of war.

I once had a veteran who approached me at the end of the first class of the semester. Saying that he did three tours in Iraq and Afghanistan, he asked that I never inquire what he did there. I pledged I wouldn't.

The *Washington Post* ran a column, "The Last Thing We Need Is a Parade," on February 12, 2012, by an Army infantryman, Colby Buzzell, who was in Iraq in 2003–04. He wrote that "veterans are struggling. In this country an average of 18 veterans commit suicide every day. The jobless rate for Iraq and Afghanistan veterans is as high as 15 percent. They're trying to find work despite having been labeled ticking time bombs, unable to assimilate back into society, plagued with post-traumatic stress." On April 8, the *Post* ran another column, by George Masters, a veteran, titled "Just Bring Them Home." He wrote: "While the wars in Afghanistan and Iraq kill and maim, I think how they are shaping the future of returning veterans. Many of these men and women will come home and go missing, and you won't even know it. Returning from a war is more than getting off an airplane and putting on civvies. Combat changes a person. It changed me. . . . If you've never hunted a human, if you've never been hunted, if you haven't been shot at on a regular basis, just try to appreciate what this person has been through. Then get down on your knees and thank your lucky stars it wasn't you."

Curious, isn't it, that these two columns ran in the *Post*. For more than 20 years, beginning with the first invasion of Iraq in 1991, both its war-whooping editorial page and op-ed page were platforms for the Bush-Clinton-Bush-Obama militarized foreign policies. Self-duped and rabid, the *Post* was all but a secretarial service to the Pentagon and its pliant patrons in the Congress and the White House who expressed no reservations about sending our young to kill and be killed in Iraq and Afghanistan. Now that it's clear that these have been wars that couldn't be won, couldn't be explained and couldn't be afforded, the *Post* is perhaps now compensating by opening its pages to soldiers who did the dirty work that the paper once fantasized, as did Congress, as spreading democracy. What's needed from the *Post* and the rest of the war-cheering media, and likely never to happen, is a full apology to all the victims of the war: the hundreds of thousands, perhaps uncounted millions, of civilians in Iraq and Afghanistan and the American soldiers—the less than two percent of the population who risked their lives and sanity. And all for nothing.

With your boyfriend—"my Marine"—take whatever time you need to make a decision. Stable love needs three forces, the Three As: adjustment, acceptance and appreciation. Take time to judge whether adjustment to your new selves is possible. A few weeks, a few months. That should do it for clarity to set in. On acceptance, a question worth asking yourself is whether you are a better person—and is he a better person—when you are with each other. Accepting someone, as in the "for better, for worse, in sickness and in health" line in the wedding vows, demands a kind of maturity that comes with practice. Appreciation. Take a look at "Everyday Love," the Sidney Harris essay in *Strength Through Peace*, one of our course texts. The first lines: "What we commonly call 'love' is a lot of little things rather than one big thing. The big thing may bowl us over at first but it is the repetitive regularity of the little things that keeps love alive and afloat. Love begins as an emotion but unless it is steadily ratified by acts of the will, it becomes a dead letter as soon as the emotion subsides. This is why the great romantics often have the most tragic, disillusion or unfulfilled love lives, marked by the heroic gesture but deficient in the human touch."

I've enjoyed having you in the class. With your Serbian background and experiences, you've seen how raw life can be. Your presence in class has added depth to our many discussions.

Be brave,

Colman McCarthy

Dear Professor McCarthy,

I'm writing to tell you that I've left the Army ROTC program at the University of Maryland. As such, it's been a momentously stressful week. I've been called a hippie by an officer, told that my morals were "too high" by my parents, and still have to suffer through financial disownment. And still I cannot escape this military burden. I will either owe $80,000 to the government or be forcibly enlisted for three years. Though I hope to influence it, the choice is theirs. And though my decision is made, the die is cast. Those around me plead that I uncross this river, that I make some compromise for an easier life—a life of "honor." I've been offered alternative methods: a car upon graduation, a two-week trip to Europe. I've even been promised acceptance of my decision, should I attend further training. But it's all for naught, as my choice is simple, honest and true.

As a priest I recently spoke to reinforced, one must follow his heart. And though, as he in sighing admitted, some may live a disinterested lie of a life of "quiet desperation," as Thoreau said. I cannot.

For this reason, compounding all of my others, ranging from disagreement to the simple questions of what is right and how I want to spend my life, I had to cease to take the path I so recently tread.

I'm sending this letter to tell you this, and to thank you for the constant enlightenment I've found in your class. The simple and sad truth, however, is that the wisdom with which you teach is considered such lofty knowledge, reserved for the vain and excessively moral. This, however, is the fallacy of the dimwitted and depraved. But beyond this, it is a fallacy that penetrates all society. I only hope that one day the wisdom of your lessons might be common sense, and the brilliant men and women I know who chose to see with blinders in choosing their beliefs, might open their eyes to the greatness of the world, the atrocity of man's machinations, and the simple integrity which so plainly divides the two.

Again, thank you for everything. Also, if you have any extra credit opportunities, any opportunities to volunteer at the Center for Teaching Peace, or know of any job opportunities, I'd be more than happy to apply myself. Thanks again for being a true steward of simple goodness.

Sincerely,

J.

Dear J.,

First, be assured of my full admiration for your getting off the military
conveyor belt, even as it spins faster than ever now that the academic sen-
ates at Harvard, Yale and a couple other Ivies have welcomed back ROTC
in post–don't-ask-don't-tell fervor. Expect to be roughed up because of
your decision, as plenty of others before you have been treated like bricks
in rucksacks when they chose conscience over conformity. Counsel is
available from groups like the Center on Conscience and War in Washington and the War Resisters League in New York.

Counsel of another kind can be found in the literature of dissidence.
There's the story of the Buddhist spiritual master who went to the village
square every day. From sunrise to sunset he cried out against war and
injustice. It went on for years. His disciples began worrying about their
master. Taking action, they went to the village square to tell him he was
having no effect. None. No one in the village was listening, much less
heeding. Everyone's insane, they told him. It's time to stop. No, said
the master, I will keep crying out against war and injustice so I won't go
insane.

State schools like the University of Maryland are natural allies of the
ROTC. Research money has long flowed from the Pentagon to the giant
state schools in research for weapons contracts. So why not funds to train
soldiers to use the weapons. The chummy academic-military alliance is
perfumed with patriotic cant, a seductive scent that entices students to
believe recruiters that ROTC is a good deal.

One of my allies at Georgetown University was Fr. Richard McSorley,
who before his death in 1998 ran the peace studies program even though
administrators never seriously funded it. With the Pentagon less than
three miles from the Georgetown campus, the school's ROTC program
goes back to the 1920s. Like the Buddhist spiritual master, Fr. McSorley
fiercely opposed war. A pacifist and a survivor of the Bataan Death March
when he was a Jesuit seminarian in the Philippines in the early 1940s, he
believed the functional purpose of a military is to kill, maim and destroy
in the name of peace. At Georgetown, he was the sane man on campus.

He tells a story of a student who couldn't understand the priest's
opposition to ROTC: no one is forced to join, so what's the problem? Fr.

McSorley, who is in the Daniel Berrigan, Horace McKenna, John Dear and Steve Kelly prophetic wing of the Jesuit order, tried to explain with a parable: "An international prostitution ring has offered me $500,000 to help set up a Department of Prostitution at Georgetown. All the professors would be chosen by the International Prostitution Rings. Courses would be controlled by the Ring. Courses of academic excellence would be taught, such as 'The Psychology of Solicitation,' 'Comparative Prostitution and Its Relationship to Other Cultures,' 'Leadership in Prostitution.' These courses would be taught by duly certified national and international pimps. And what would you think of me if I chose that as a course offering for students on the grounds that Georgetown needed the money and, after all, no one was forced to take it?"

The student replied, "Oh, you consider it a moral question, don't you?" "I consider it both a moral and an academic question," the priest answered. "And if anyone thinks it is unfair to the military to compare it with prostitution, I reply that it may be unfair to prostitutes. Prostitution doesn't threaten the survival of the world. Prostitution isn't supported by taxpayers' money and the power of the Pentagon."

At Fr. McSorley's funeral at Georgetown's campus chapel, eulogists hailed him as a saint. Now that he was safely departed, let's haul out the finest of adjectives.

I have nothing against students who join ROTC. It's a way to get through college debt-free, plus get a monthly stipend as well as a guaranteed job after graduation. One of the nation's largest ROTC programs is at Notre Dame, the flagship of Catholic universities. When I interviewed its president, Rev. Theodore Hesburgh, in the late 1980s on how he reconciled the presence of ROTC on the campus of a school named after the mother of Jesus Christ—a supreme teacher of nonviolence—he replied that his goal was to "Christianize the military." I asked if he believed there was a Christian way to slaughter people. It was a brief interview, after that one.

One of Washington's flourishing ROTC programs is homed at Wilson High School, where I've been teaching since the mid-1980s. Nearly all the students in Junior ROTC are from low income African American or Hispanic families. Five elite private high schools are within three miles of Wilson: Sidwell Friends, Georgetown Day, St. Albans, Maret and Edmund Burke. None have JROTC. When leaving the Joint Chiefs of

Staff as its head, General Colin Powell boasted that he had helped place JROTC into more than 300 high schools. The militarizing of 14-years-olds is in the poverty schools, not the Choates, Grotons or Andovers.

You might take a look at *Hell, Healing and Resistance: Veterans Speak*, a compelling book by Daniel Hallock, a Cornell Navy ROTC graduate. His 1998 work is part oral history and part reporting. He tells of Jim Murphy, who was a founder of Vietnam Veterans Against the War and became dean of students at West Side High School in New York City, an alternative school of low-income children. "The kids I work with," Murphy told Hallock, "tend to come from the poorest neighborhoods in the city. So they're the easiest for [military] recruiters. I try to help them see what their options are, to help them understand that you don't have to sign up for four years and $40,000, that you don't have to give away four years of your life."

Some were disbelieving. Murphy recalled "a young man, Muslim, who was in the Persian Gulf War. He joined to get money for college, and he was sent to a Muslim country to kill Muslims. He says that 'they just blew people away. The Iraqis tried to give themselves up, but we just ran them down. There was no time to take prisoners on the front. So we killed them, ran them down, bulldozed them, buried them alive.' That was his 'be all you can be' story."

As I'm sure you know, I'm more than pleased you are in my class again this semester. I appreciate your generous words, but it was much more the course readings that affected you than I. And now your are putting the ideas of nonviolence into risk-taking action. I was heartened that you traveled the other Wednesday from College Park to American U when Peter Yarrow spoke and sung in our class. I'll be keeping for a long time the picture I took of you and Peter. Show it to your ROTC commandant on the way out, like sticking a flower in a gun barrel.

Take a look at World Learning, a DC nonprofit. It has paid internships. My center is a small operation—just my wife and me really—so the job opportunities are nil. If you need any legal help uncoupling from the ROTC, let me know. I can make some calls.

With large respect—

Colman McCarthy

$\sim \sim \sim$

Dear Mr. McCarthy

I'm sorry it's been a while since I wrote last. So much has happened and it's only now that I feel things are finally settling down. I'm almost done with school this year. Well, one paper and four exams away from being done, but close nonetheless.

I've had a wonderful semester here at Clark, probably the best so far. I think it's a combination of knowing which classes to take and finally feeling like I know this school inside and out. I took a great course on World Order and Globalization this semester which taught me about the pros (yes, there are pros, I found out) to globalization, as well as learning the usual cons. I found that this course was really interesting to me after my semester abroad in Namibia.

Namibia was AMAZING! I learned so much from being there, which was difficult to completely absorb at the time but now I realize how much it has changed me. First of all, I now realize that I can never be in the Peace Corps. Homestays for two weeks in Inkatatura (the black neighborhood of the capital city) were lonely enough. And I now know that I'm not going to save the world. I will be lucky if I touch one life in a positive way. And I realized that I don't have to go all the way to Africa. Many of the problems Namibia is facing can be found in the US (well maybe not in Bethesda).

I'll be working at the same summer camp I worked at last year in Darnestown, Maryland.

I would love to come to speak to your Bethesda–Chevy Chase class sometime in May. I can't wait to see you.

All the best,

Lori Chesla

Dear Lori,

If you are still the cheerful, patient and generous friend that you have always been, now's the time to rally all those graces to forgive me for being so far behind. I cherished your letter from last May, brimming as it was with your account of Namibia. Your line, "I will be lucky if I touch one life in a positive way" is what I've told the B-CC classes over and over. When I interviewed Mother Teresa, the saint of Calcutta and who by the way opened a house for girls only two miles from the high school at Chevy Chase Circle, she said at the end of our conversation that few us will ever be called to do great things but all of us can do small things in a great way.

Yes, please come to B-CC. Forty students are in each class, the first one at 7:25 am, the roughest of hours. Ever wonder how you managed to do that for four years? It was self-discipline. You have plenty to tell the class: about Namibia, your studies at Clark and how you were one of the most passionate agitators at B-CC. If I didn't tell you then let me say it now: I took delight in your fiery kind of idealism. You were something of an impatient colt, straining to break free and get running. Sure enough, you did.

If you are in town, let's talk and we can settle on a morning. I have classes at two other high schools, so you may have encores.

One recent visitor to B-CC was Vicki Schieber, who spoke on the death penalty. She is an ardent opponent. Nothing noteworthy about that, except that her daughter Shannon—B-CC '92 and class president— was raped and murdered in her apartment in Philadelphia in May 1998 when she was in graduate school at Penn. I've brought Mrs. Schieber often to my classes at B-CC and my other schools. She opens minds and stirs hearts. This is what one of my University of Maryland students wrote in a reflection paper: "I left class last week in a haze. I walked up the stairs mumbling things like 'oh my God' and 'that was moving,' but I felt a distinct emptiness in my laconic exchanges with my peers. I didn't really know how I felt. Vicki Schieber was, as many have called her, a saint. She was beautiful. When she spoke, my heart felt detached from other bodily sensations. I never gave much thought to the death penalty before I heard her story. The last time I ever considered it was in some nonsensi-cal 5th-grade social studies project. We had to debate one another. I was arbitrarily placed on the 'pro' side. No choice. Just assigned a position and told to support it. I am truly grateful that even at the age of 10, I already knew that most school related assignments were bullshit. Had I not, I probably would have been pro-death penalty today. Vicki Schieber moved me more than I can convey in words."*

I pass this along—dashed off at the beginning of class when I asked for everyone's reaction—because, first, Mrs. Schieber is part of the B-CC family, as you and I are, and, second, because the passion in the Maryland student's piece is much the same as you displayed in our class when you spoke up, debated, questioned, doubted and probed as if everything was riding on it.

And it was. Do try to come in some morning. My best to your family. I'm sure they are proud of you, as am I.

Peace, and lots of it—

Colman McCarthy

*After graduating from Bethesda–Chevy Chase High School in 1992, Shannon Schieber studied at Duke University. An academic rarity, she triple majored in math, economics, and philosophy. She graduated magna cum laude in three years while captaining the equestrian team. On May 7, 1998, while taking graduate studies at the Wharton School of Business in Philadelphia, Shannon, twenty-three, was murdered by a serial rapist who pried open a balcony door on her second floor apartment. It would take nearly four years of police bungling before the killer was captured and sentenced to prison for life without parole.

In the spring of 2006 Vicki Schieber testified before the Senate Judiciary Committee. Saying that both she and her husband were "raised in households where hatred was never condoned," she dispelled a prevailing myth "that families who suffered this kind of loss will support the death penalty. That assumption is so widespread and so unquestioned that a prosecutor will say to a grieving family, 'We will seek the death penalty in order to seek justice for your family.'"

As if they hadn't suffered enough already, the Schiebers were publicly criticized by a Philadelphia district attorney for daring to oppose the death penalty for their daughter's murderer. "Responding to one killing with another does not honor my daughter," Vicki Schieber told the Senate, "nor does it help create the kind of society I want to live in, where human life and human rights are valued. I know that an execution creates another grieving family, and causing pain to another family does not lessen my own pain."

Her expression of mercy and logic echoes the thought of Kerry Kennedy, a child of eight when her father, Senator Robert F. Kennedy, was assassinated in Los Angeles in June 1968: "I saw nothing that could be accomplished in the loss of one life being answered with the loss of another. And I knew, far too vividly, the anguish that would spread through another family—another set of parents, children, brothers and sisters thrown into grief."

At about the time she testified before the Senate, which was only one of many legislatures she attempted to educate, Schieber left her job as an executive director of a trade association to volunteer full-time for the nonprofit Murder Victims' Families for Human Rights. She is regularly invited to speak to civic, religious, political, and academic groups on capital punishment. As a Roman Catholic and a former nun, she is aware that large numbers within her church are pro–death penalty and that it was only in recent decades that the hierarchy—from local bishops to the pope—began inching away from its centuries-long endorsement of executions. Often ardently, the church went along with the thinking of Thomas Aquinas: "If any man is dangerous to the community and is subverting it by some sin," he wrote in the *Summa Theologica*, the "treatment to be commended is his execution in order to preserve the common good."

In 1994, eleven years after a majority of Catholic bishops opposed the death penalty—"precisely because life is sacred," as stated in the pastoral letter, "The Challenge of Peace"—Cardinal Joseph Bernardin told writer James Megivern, author of *The Death Penalty: An Historical and Theological Survey*: "We do not have a large percentage of our people with us. If it really is the case that 75 percent of our people do not agree, well then, that means we really have a job ahead of us to explain to them why we take this position."

$\sim \sim \sim$

AUGUST 2, 2007

Dear Mr. McCarthy,

My name is Melissa Smalley. Last week I had the pleasure of hearing you speak when you came to American University to talk to my friends and me participating in the National Student Leadership Conference's International Diplomacy program. Hearing you speak was one of the most enjoyable aspects of the program for me. I had become so used to people talking about corrupt politicians and proper political procedures that I had started to lose sight of why I am interested in international relations at all: to help people. I've always wanted to help others, not because it would benefit America or make me famous but because it was the right thing to do. To hear you talk about peace and morality was so refreshing. I wanted to write and say thank you for taking the time to visit with my group, and for signing the copy of your book that I purchased. I haven't started to read it yet, but it will be interesting to hear different world leaders' thoughts on peace and human rights.

My mother also has an interest in peace studies and conflict resolution. After talking to you on the phone yesterday (which totally took her by surprise!), we started discussing your lecture. It was amazing to find that we could both relate to the idea of peace studies despite the differences in our age and opinions.

Throughout your speech, you urged my fellow students and me to try to get our schools to create a peace studies and conflict resolution curriculum. I think it would be wonderful to have classes that teach students the peaceful history of the world. I plan on talking to the head of the Social Studies department when I return to school. Any suggestions as to how I can approach her to get this started for Manalapan High School would be greatly appreciated.

My mother told me that you had extended an invitation to sit in on your class at American. The university is currently my first (and only) choice and I hope that I will be attending your classes as an incoming freshman in 2008. Do you think you will still have the $100 bill by then?

Yours truly,

Melissa Smalley

AUGUST 19, 2007

Dear Melissa,

How strong are your nuisance skills? Your nagging skills? Your hanging in skills? If you want to get peace studies courses in Manalapan High, making a nuisance of yourself, plus being a world-class nag, plus refusing to get lost if you are told to by everyone from the know-it-alls on the school board to know-nothing politicians: all of that is the kind of grittiness you'll need. Just to get one course in place for 25 or 30 students a semester. And not for this coming school year but the next year, if we hurry.

The touchiest problem of all this is the reality that Manalapan High, like all public schools, is a government-run and government-funded school operated by government workers we call teachers. Governments tend to resist innovations; otherwise we would have had peace studies departments in every one of the nation's schools by now. It doesn't help that the United States government is, as Martin Luther King Jr. consistently argued, the "world's leading purveyor of violence."

State and local governments, including school boards, mostly go along with it. Which means that when you manage to get a few moments with the head of the Manalapan High social studies department trying to persuade her or him to create a peace studies class, what you are really doing is trying to change the government's ways. A government is a collection of people who themselves went to schools that had no peace department the way their schools had English, math or science departments. Flexuous, they think: I turned out well, I didn't study peace, so why change things? And that's making the large assumption that someone like you isn't dismissed as an unpatriotic and ungrateful malcontent: Who are you to think you know better than we do?

Schools ought to put a sign over the main entrance: "Students, you're here to learn how to think." In small print: "Just don't get any big ideas."

That's where your nuisance and nagging skills come in. Almost all social reforms—ones that brought about growth, not mere changes—have come from below. When the 40-hour work week was first proposed—by Eugene Debs, the five-time Socialist candidate for president from 1900 to 1920—the idea was dismissed as lunacy. Debs went further. He called for paid vacations for the workers. More lunacy. Then he went too far and urged people to oppose the US entry into the First World War. He praised opponents of the draft. For that, he was sentenced to 10 years in federal prison.

Debs never yielded. He was a nuisance and a nag, and he hung in. When you propose your peace studies idea to teachers in the Social Studies department, ask if they know about Eugene Debs. If they know a fair amount, suggest they pass along the information to their classes. In depth. If they don't know much, suggest that they aren't qualified to teach. Suggest politely, of course.

To be practical, and to go where most reforms begin—below—you might think of finding some first or second year students who can do the pushing for peace studies after you graduate. Drum up interest at the school. Write a column for the school newspaper. Do some reporting for the paper: interview the principal, some teachers, parents. Get your Mom in the story, first paragraph if necessary. Write an op-ed for your local newspaper on the need for peace education. Start an anti-war protest. Hit the streets with some peace signs. At one of my high schools, Bethesda–Chevy Chase, I gave my students the option of protesting the war every Friday morning first and second periods on the highway in front of the school. Students hold their signs. "Money for Books, Not Bombs." "Study Peace, Not War." "No Blood for Oil." "Honk for Peace." "Honk again for Peace."

The other morning, a woman emerged from a tall office building across the street from our protest. She looked angry. Here it comes, I thought: a right-wing crank telling us she's going to call the cops. She crosses the street. Students are watching.

"I have a little problem," she begins. "You aren't making enough noise. Back in the '60s when we were protesting the Vietnam War, we made plenty of noise." She takes out her wallet and writes a check for $50. "Go buy some bullhorns. Do it right. Make your voices heard. Really heard."*

The students gave her a round of applause. I invited her to my class the next morning to tell her story—which included, for sure, her arrest record. My students learned a lot.

So there's plenty you can do, both inward and outwardly. Go inward and ask yourself how close you are to living simply. There are the lines that Dorothy Day wrote: "As you come to know the seriousness of our situation—the war, the racism, the poverty of the world—you come to realize it is not going to be changed just by words or demonstrations. It's a question of risking your life. It's a question of living your life in drastically different ways."

So glad you are thinking about American University. I can't imagine you wouldn't thrive. The School of International Service has many of the university's most seasoned professors. I taught the first peace studies class in 1984, and now we have a degree program. If you do make a campus visit this Fall, please call ahead. I have a Wednesday afternoon class, The Principles and Practices of Peace—you'd be most welcome to join, plus a couple of morning high school classes. Press me a bit and I'll give you another chance for my $100 bill.

I enjoyed speaking with your Mom. She's a sweetheart.

Colman McCarthy

*On November 22, 2005, *The Tattler,* the B-CC student newspaper, carried a news story by senior Dan McCartney, "Teachers Protest Peace Studies Demonstration." It read:

Traffic along East-West Highway is usually heavy in the morning. But Fridays bring even more noise than usual—students shouting and horns honking, all in opposition to the war in Iraq. Excitedly waving signs, the students enrolled in Mr. McCarthy's Peace Studies course encourage cars to honk to show their opposition to the international conflict.

More locally, however, they are receiving a negative response from B-CC teachers who say the honks are disruptive to any first-period class on the outside of the A building. It's a constant distraction every Friday morning. "How am I supposed to teach over the noise?" asks Mrs. Kirk, who teaches in a classroom that faces East-West Highway. "It doesn't accomplish anything. . . . It's just a distraction." . . .

Mrs. Kirk also acts as the Faculty Representative on the Leadership Team, and has received several complaints from her colleagues.

Mr. McCarthy remains skeptical. "Those who choose to protest know that studying nonviolence should be backed by opposition to the US killing spree in Afghanistan and Iraq. Why aren't all B-CC students given the option of joining our protest?" he wonders.

Mr. McCarthy is a volunteer teacher and is thus exempt from restrictions placed on the MCPS [Montgomery County Public School] staff. There is currently no concerted effort to ban the protests aside from the objections some teachers have raised. The "Students Guide to Rights and Responsibilities," published by MCPS, states students "have the right to meet in groups to . . . demonstrate peacefully" and requires that such demonstrations be "orderly."

Mr. McCarthy's support for the protests remains unfaltering. "We should be making more noise, not less. We need some big bass drums, a half-dozen bullhorns and cowbells, and two or three tubas."

The same issue of *The Tattler* ran a column by Laura Swartz:

For the past 15 years, B-CC students have witnessed spirited Friday morning protests led by B-CC's popular Peace Studies class taught by Colman McCarthy. However, this practice has recently come under protests of a different sort from several teachers throughout school.

The Peace Studies protests, held weekly during the first period class, are meant to raise awareness of the United States' violent activities abroad. The protests also allow students to exercise their First Amendment rights to assembly and protest—a lesson well worth teaching in American public schools. That teachers would oppose the protests now, when there is more reason for protest than there has been in the last fifteen years, is astonishing. Students should be able to protest, especially when they believe their opinions should be expressed. The students protesting are protesting for peace in the world, an admirable goal. Why should teachers oppose such protests, especially in today's world of conflict and suffering?

The biggest complaint is the honking that protestors create on East-West Highway. Teacher complaints about the "Honk for Peace" signs protestors hold up are completely unjustified, especially when simply closing a window shuts out almost all of the noise. Many B-CC students have had the experience of looking out the window to see what all the honking is about, then turning back around and getting on with the lesson. Peace Studies only protests for a half an hour a week.

Teachers should not be infringing on a group of students' right to free speech, but should rather commend those students willing to stand out in the Friday morning cold to make sure their opinion is heard—by both those on East-West Highway and those in school.

The February 14, 2006, *The Tattler* ran a letter to the editor:

I am writing in response to an article in *The Tattler* by Dan McCartney on the subject of Mr. McCarthy's Friday morning protests on East-West Highway. When I read that the protests were "receiving a negative response from B-CC teachers," I was shocked. I took Mr. McCarthy's class during my senior year, and before then, I had never been involved in any type of political protest. I consider taking Mr. McCarthy's class among the most interesting, exciting and stimulating things I ever did at B-CC.

I would like to emphasize the importance of reminding B-CC students and staff that there is a war going on. Like many other B-CC students, I am ashamed to say that I had never even met someone who been to Iraq until after I graduated. I've moved away to a less affluent area [Idaho] where many students are forced to join the army to pay for college, and making friends that have served in Iraq has become a constant reminder to me of the violence that is taking place in the Middle East. However, as a high school student it was something I almost never thought about.

I am truly sorry for teachers . . . who find the protests to be "a distraction." To me, they meant much more. They were the one constant reminder of the tragic loss of life overseas. If students could be reminded, maybe just for 20 minutes once a week of what is going on, I think it would be a positive contribution to the Bethesda–Chevy Chase community.

Amanda Hunt
Class of '05

After B-CC, Amanda did undergraduate work at American University and took two of my courses. In May 2013 she graduated from Tulane University Law School.

✌ ✌ ✌

Dear Professor McCarthy,

I cannot emphasize how much meeting you has impacted my Washington, DC, experience but also my life. You taught me so much and I will never forget your class. You really are living your passion. It shows every day. Sociology is my passion and yet none of my professors answer the problems we face as a society. So many times I have felt overwhelmed by the social inequality we face. You gave me hope. You gave me strength. You gave me a tool to make change. The most important thing you have taught me is the power of individual choice. Now I feel like I have millions of choices to make every day. Second, you taught me about violence to animals. I no longer eat meat. Third, I believe you have changed my career path and educational aspirations. Now I want to be a peacemaker. I believe this has been a calling. I hope we keep in touch and I would love to have you speak at Hiram College.

Continue to be yourself because so many people are inspired. I really hope one day I can be like you.

Peace,

Sara T.

SEPTEMBER 28, 2008

Dear Sara,

I think you know how much I enjoyed having you in class, and your diligence in carrying out your official duties as Chief Digression Stopper. Add that to your resume in the grad school applications.

These are a few thoughts stirred by the questions you raised in your parting letter and essay, both of which, to your credit, were marked by innocence and honesty.

Of all those who enjoy peace of mind, it would be assumed that peacemakers came by it automatically as part of the package. They have peace of mind because they have minds for peace.

Were that true. Consider some of the greats. Gandhi of India was a domineering husband and a vindictive father. Tolstoy was emotionally cruel to his wife, as was Martin Luther King Jr. Albert Einstein, who wrote forcefully about nonviolence and pacifism—"I would teach peace rather than war, love rather than hate"—was coldhearted to both of his wives.

In their personal lives, at home with their families, these visionaries were nearsighted, their minds more in turmoil than at peace.

Based on several decades of observations and interviews, culling for truth in sites ranging from hospital burn wards where nurses and doctors were saving lives to death row cell blocks where wardens and guards were paid to take lives, I've met peacemakers who assuredly achieved peace of mind.

They traveled different paths, knowing that if your path has no obstacles it probably won't take you anywhere.

Harmony between mind, body and spirit. With lifestyles that are low on exercise and diets high on foods that come out of factories and not out of the ground—refined starches, processed meats, sugars, fried glop, fats and alcohol—bodies become war zones, with organs, bones and cells the inflamed, pained or diseased casualties. Peace of mind can co-exist with illnesses, but it is less likely when the illnesses are self-caused.

Paul Shapiro, an investigator for the Humane Society of the United States, earned a Peace Studies degree from George Washington University. I had Paul as a student, first at Georgetown Day and later at American University. He became a vegan as a teenager, a commitment that has remained firm for the past 15 years due to his belief that human rights and animals rights are equivalent: "The only morally relevant characteristic that is needed to warrant the granting of rights is capacity to feel pain and suffering."

Hitting bottom doesn't mean bottoming out. Who hasn't been bruised by life? Who hasn't been stuffed into a crawl space? Who hasn't fallen while racing—or diving, jumping or lifting—for the gold medals? Those who can sink to the depths and slowly ease back up—call them lazarists, odds-defiers, comeback kids—find peace of mind a treasure beyond description. They let go of competition and move toward cooperation, starting with cooperation with their own gifts.

In the late 1960s, Bobby Muller was a Marine Corps platoon leader in Vietnam. Killing people and doing unconscionable things, he found himself spiraling down a "path of darkness." Severely wounded in a firefight and suffering a spinal cord injury, Bobby returned home unable to walk. He helped found Vietnam Veterans against the War, where I came to know and admire his work. By rough estimate, and with Bobby's help, I wrote dozens of columns about Vietnam vets—about their being mistreated by politicians who started the war, and about men and women regaining their lives. At a peace conference at the University of Virginia a few years ago, Bobby said: "By coming back, getting love, getting nurturing, getting out of where the forces of darkness and the negative energy [that] evil can work on you, it allows you the opportunity to rehabilitate, to rejuvenate. I've seen it with literally hundreds of veterans that were exposed to the most horrific combat. . . . Provide love, and get a decent environment, and even with those that have been crushed, you can oftentimes bring them back to wholeness and good health."

Don't look up, don't look down, look around. Most of us go through life as sightseers, making tracks but rarely slowing to value what's in front of us. An exception is Wendell Berry, the down-on-the-farm

Kentuckian-agrarian-contrarian whose prose, poetry and prescience make him our era's Thoreau. You might look up "The Peace of Wild Things," a meditation on the importance of noticing, of resting in a woodland—of coming into "the peace of wild things who do not tax their lives with forethought of grief. . . . For a time I rest in the grace of the world, and am free."

Get your share of the grace. It's there, and you are ready for it.

With you,

Colman McCarthy

∽ ∽ ∽

MAY 19, 2012

Dear Colman McCarthy,

I have read and am very impressed with your book, *I'd Rather Teach Peace.* I am especially interested in your teaching style and success with students. Do you have an outline which I could get in preparation for discussions with our local Martha's Vineyard Regional High School teachers? I know you were here some years ago and spoke in their auditorium. Did any of our teachers then express interest in starting a course? I read many of your columns when we lived in the Washington area 1952–1996, then recently read your essay in *Peace Movements Worldwide,* on which I led a book discussion for the Unitarian-Universalist Society of Martha's Vineyard. Last year we had a discussion of *Living Beyond War,* and the author, Winslow Myers, came to our Chapel for a lecture. I'd appreciate any help if you have time to reply.

Thank you,

Roger Thayer

MAY 20, 2012

Dear Roger,

A treat to hear from you. Let me have your street address and I can send along a sundry or two that might give you a few ideas. I do remember my visit to the high school and was heartened by the positive reception from many teachers to get a peace studies course in place. Whether it ever happened, I'm not sure.

I would guess not. It rarely does, for two reasons. First, high school teachers are trapped in the current evaluation campaigns. Let's bounce the incompetents, time-servers and assorted academic layabouts. These deserve to go but caught in the net are quality teachers.

At Wilson High, one of the high schools where I've been teaching peace studies courses since the mid-1980s, evaluators have been swarming in of late. They slip into the classroom, take a back seat, open a notebook and start evaluating. They stay for half-an-hour, fill a page or two of comments and in a week send their findings to the teachers, with copies to the principal and assistant principals. Teachers have four possible ratings: very ineffective, ineffective, effective and very effective.

In the Fall semester at Wilson I had an evaluator—a "Master Teacher," 26, paid $90,000 a year, who herself taught for two years but who, by the lights of the city education chancellor, Michelle Rhee, is qualified to evaluate teachers because she has an MA in education. She rated me ineffective, just a notch above very ineffective. My class meets for 95 minutes on alternative days. During the 30 minutes that the $90,000 evaluator was in the room, one student, up late the night before, lay her head on the desk. I was marked down for lack of classroom management. Another student left to go the bathroom without getting my written permission. Another mark-down: for losing control.

Then it worsened. The San Francisco Giants happened to be in town, playing against our Washington Nationals. One of the Giants was Emmanuel Burriss, a second baseman who the year before helped his team win the World Series. Emmanuel, 24, was a Wilson graduate and had been in a class taught by my son John, who also runs Home Run Baseball Camp, where Emmanuel came as a 6-year-old and showed all the skills that 24 years later would win him a $1.2 million contract as a first-round draft pick by the Giants. John, who played in the minors with the Baltimore Orioles, had been his mentor.

For 15 minutes I told Emmanuel's story, inspirational as it was because he was the first ballplayer in 25 years to make it to the majors from the District of Columbia. The night before, the Wilson principal had arranged to have a ceremony at the stadium honoring Emmanuel.

I noticed in the back of the room the evaluator's hand was tearing across the page, in a fury of note taking. Maybe she's a baseball fan and really enjoying my storytelling, I thought. Hmmmmmmm. Not quite. When my written evaluation came in, I was scored for wasting time on irrelevant information, for not sticking to a lesson plan. That girl with her head on the desk was still sleeping and the boy in the bathroom had yet to come back after five minutes. Worst, I wasn't preparing the class for the upcoming final exams. Gulp. Except I never give exams in my high school classes.

Months later, another evaluator shows up. Clued by the last experience, I made the potential sleepers sit in the front row, allowed no one to leave for the bathroom—"hold it in, kids"—and definitely told no baseball tales. Now I was rated between effective and very effective.

The game goes on. I teach only one course, with my hourly pay less than what the janitors rightly earn. So I have no financial worries about being cut loose. But other teachers, hundreds in DC alone, have been sacked with little recourse and even less effect on raising the city's quality of education: 60 percent of high school students fail to graduate in four years, the nation's highest rate.

The second reason for peace education getting little footing is that school boards are suspicious: it's those "libruls"—the hate-America-firsters—always hot to propagandize impressionable children with leftist thinking. So we aren't overly welcomed. It's as if a lone peace studies course—for 25 or so students, one semester in the fall, another in the spring—is a virus that will contaminate the whole school.

The battle for peace education is being lost. Take comfort, though. I. F. Stone, long on barricades of causes seemingly going nowhere, gave us this: "The only kinds of fights worth having are those that you are going to lose, because somebody has to fight them and lose and lose and lose until someday, somebody who believes as you do, wins. In order for somebody to win an important major fight 100 years hence, a lot of other people have to be willing—for the sheer joy of it—to go right ahead and fight, knowing you are going to lose. You mustn't feel like a martyr. You've got to enjoy it."

My best to the Vineyard's Unitarians. Keep them united in these disunited times.

Yours,

Colman

Dear Colman,

Well, this was my last essay.* I'm not sure where to go from here. However I feel this course has taught me a lot and it's been absolutely wonderful to learn from you. Thank you so much.

I have a question, which is along the lines of the first lesson in the course. I live in a small town [Ojo Sarco, New Mexico] with a high incidence of crime and drug abuse. A few weeks ago a dear friend of mine since childhood disappeared, and he's assumed to have been murdered, probably in connection with drugs. While I'm not directly involved in these things, my town is small enough that it affects me. Recently I've been feeling frightened, especially at night. Today a friend suggested that I buy some pepper spray and keep it in my purse for emergencies. This started a discussion with my Mom where we talked about both sides of the issue. On one hand, I want to lead a truly nonviolent lifestyle. On the other, can I really put my trust in my ability to nonviolently protect myself. I can believe that it is better to die or be raped than to inflict temporary pain on my attacker but even as I state this I doubt my own words. I'd love your opinion on this.

Peace,

Aspen Meleski

P.S. In Lesson One there is a story of a man who had to gently restrain his wife [in Gerard Vanderhaar's essay "Dealing with Personal Attacks"]. I wonder: if she was going to harm their child and he didn't have the physical strength to gently hold her back, then what? With the options to reason with her or gently stop her gone, then what? Surely he shouldn't have allowed her to hurt his child?

*Aspen Meleski, fifteen, enrolled in the eight lesson home study correspondence course from my Center for Teaching Peace. The assignment involved writing eight essays reflecting on the eight chapters in the course text, *Alternatives to Violence*. I was Aspen's teacher, sending back each essay with my comments.

Dear Aspen,

Congratulations for finishing the course. It's the purest kind of education, based on desire, not fear. Tests, exams, homework and grades represent fear-based learning: if I don't ace the exam, something bad will happen to me. If I don't do my homework, I'll be in trouble. If I don't get an A, I'll fall behind. Students adapt. Many cheat. Whenever I speak at student assemblies, I ask halfway through the talk for a moment of absolute honesty: can anyone raise your hand and say truthfully that you have never cheated in school. Rarely does a hand go up. When I call on a couple of students to explain why they cheat, it's almost always the same reason: fear of the consequences if they don't score a high grade.

In Your Adolescent: An Owner's Manual, Carol Rinzler cannily explains it: "Little Kimberly asks her parents, 'If they tell you in nursery school that you have to work hard so you'll do well in kindergarten, and if they tell you in kindergarten that you have to work hard so you'll do well in high school, and if they tell you to work hard in high school you'll get into a good college, and assuming that they tell you in college that you have to work hard so you'll get into a good graduate school, what do they tell you in graduate school that you have to work hard for?' Kimberley's parent's answer: 'To get a good job so you can make enough money to send your children to a good nursery school.'"

We've moved away, stumbling really, from the kind of teaching and learning that Socrates believed in. He gave no tests, no homework and no grades. And went further: come to school however long you want and leave when you wish. I'm able to be Socratic at Bethesda–Chevy Chase High School, to which I bicycle every morning for a 7:25 am first period class. No tests, no homework and no exams. A few students see it as an educational paradise, the ultimate gut course. It's the opposite, I explain. No course will ever be as challenging: it requires self-discipline to write papers without being asked to, it takes energy to do the readings, it means prodding your conscience to use your gifts fully, it means giving total effort with that being the only reward, it means making demands on yourself rather than responding to the demands of a teacher. Sure, some students blow off the course and float through the semester, wasting not a calorie on pushing themselves. But many others seize the chance to do the opposite: study and learn because they want to, not because they have to. I'm sure you know the line: when you love to learn, you'll learn to love.

You asked about self-defense. A worthy question, one that we all think about, especially if we want to live nonviolently. As you wondered, "Can I really put my trust in my ability to nonviolently protect myself."

Some thoughts. Nonviolence offers no guarantees. Neither does violence. With about 22,000 homicides annually and a sexual assault every 17 minutes, it's clear that this part of the planet is a high-risk place to live, especially for women. I asked my American University students the other morning to take 10 minutes and write down everything they did in the past month to deal with their fears of sexual assault or sexual harassment. For 10 minutes, the men looked at me blankly. The women? They were busily writing away, some of them filling the page. I asked the women to read aloud what they'd written, so the men in the class could learn a bit about their sisters' lives, beginning with the reality that women are vulnerable in ways that men are not, that the sexes live in different worlds. The women wrote about never making eye contact with men on the sidewalk, carrying pepper spray in their purses and practicing on trees how to aim (one student told of spraying herself in the face the first time she tried), never crossing the campus alone even in daytime, never letting a boy get a drink for her because he might slip a drug into it, always locking the car door after getting in, phoning ahead when going somewhere, deciding what clothes to wear to a party. Men never think this way; women do every day.

In a crisis or panic situation, sometimes no attempt at self-defense will work—true for women and men. I remember taking my high school and college students to a Virginia state prison to spend time with prisoners on death row. The warden, a humane man, saw our visiting as a way to ease the numbing boredom endured by the prisoners. During the seminar, a student asked an inmate how best to defend himself if an attacker on the street threatened his life during a hold-up. First, the prisoner said, don't try to fight or flee. The attacker, who has probably held-up plenty of people before getting to you, is ready for that. Instead, defend yourself by saying something unexpected: try the Jesus defense.

Which is?

Look the attacker in the eye, the prisoner advised. Say Jesus loves you and so do I. And then reach out to hug him.

Everyone had a good laugh at that one. But the prisoner was serious:

short of giving over all your money, it's your best chance of coming out alive. You've defended yourself with an appeal to the attacker's humanity, not his evil. Will it work every time? Of course not. Will it work more often than a violent defense? Each of us has to decide.

For many years here in Washington I came to know William Proxmire, a five-term senator from Wisconsin and as passionate a person ever to serve in Congress. He was something of an athlete. Most days he ran from his home in the Cleveland Park neighborhood in northwest Washington to his office on Capitol Hill, showering and changing when he arrived, and then running back home in the evening. The inevitable happened late one night. Two thugs, one aiming a handgun, stopped him. Relating the story to me, Senator Proxmire said he had no money. They didn't believe him: hand it over or you're dead. Calmly, the senator said, "Go ahead and kill me. I have cancer and I'll be dead anyway in four weeks." Hearing that, the thug without a gun said to the other, "Let's leave this brother alone, he's a sick man, he's got cancer."

I told the senator his story is worthy of Gandhi. He smiled. I asked if he planned to keep running through that rough part of town. His little cancer tale probably wouldn't work again. "I have another plan," he said. I wished him luck.

Months passed and the senator was attacked again. Same story, except this time the two attackers were boys in their late teens. He asked them why they were robbing him. "We need money, why else would we rob you?" "If you really want to get money, I'll tell you where to get some, a lot of it." He told the two to come to his office the next day and he would give them jobs. Entry level work, answering phones, sorting mail, errands. The two did come. One turned out well, the other didn't and was soon in prison.

A footnote to these stories. Another senator, John Stennis, a Mississippi Democrat back when the South almost always sent segregation-minded Democrats to the Senate, was returning to his home near the National Cathedral. Two attackers jumped him on the walkway to his front door. Stennis, who served on the Senate Armed Services Committee and lavished money on military programs and thought that the violence of war was the proper defense for America, swung his fists at the pair. They shot him. Hospitalized, the senator survived—barely. His health never returned.

Those are the two options: nonviolent or violent defense. It's the same in our personal lives and our collective lives. I was visiting with my friend Joan Baez last month when she was in Washington for a concert. As she has done more than a dozen times over the years, she generously gave tickets for my students and passes for a get-together back stage after the concert. As much as anyone I know, Joan believes in and practices nonviolence. You might try to locate her autobiography, *And a Voice to Sing With*. In it are the lines: "Nonviolence offers no guarantees. But the curious thing is that people who do violence don't receive guarantees either. Statistics show that you have a better chance of coming out alive in a nonviolent battle."

It's been a pleasure to have you as a student. You have a caring heart, ample ideals, an open and searching mind, and plenty of energy to put those rare assets to full use. From time to time, let me know what you are doing and thinking. I'll do the same from this end.

Hello to your parents. Always show appreciation to them.

Colman McCarthy

∽ ∽ ∽

JANUARY 8, 2007

Dear Mr. McCarthy,

After a fantastic semester, I think it's only appropriate to say "thank you."

I am a very strong, forceful person—in case you hadn't picked that up already. I have strong convictions, and I tend to react strongly to people who disagree with me. Your class hasn't made me a 100% peacemaker, but you have given me a foundation and many ideas to refer to in the future. You've made me think more about nonviolence—not just on a global spectrum but also in my own life. The things I learned in your class will help me in conflict situations I face in the future. I will take what I've gotten from your class with me for the rest of my life, and for that, I say thank you.

My decision to be a vegetarian is mainly because of you and your class. Few other classes I have taken have prompted such a dramatic change in me. . . . Because of my decision, my family has stopped eating meat at dinner time. Your influence extends farther than you think! My new convictions about the death penalty also originated in your class. The many guest speakers we've had have been provocative and incredibly engaging. I've never been disappointed in your class, and I appreciate how much effort you put into getting guest speakers to come and share their experiences with your class.

Your commitment to teaching peace is astounding. I can't imagine bike riding around town every day and teaching difficult students a difficult subject in a unique way. Now I understand what you said about your class being a tough one—there is no homework or tests or requirements, self-discipline is the key. I like to think that at least a little bit I had read more in our book and spent more time researching the topics we've discussed. Even though the class was definitely not long enough, I have learned so much and my life has been changed—thank you.

Even if I forget everything I learned in your class, I think I'll remember the importance of gratitude. As a camp counselor, I always appreciated it when you recommended that we write thank you letters. I identified with that idea. I tried to send letters to all of our guest speakers. So thank you for teaching me the value of saying "thank you."

I hope to take a peace studies course in college. . . . I never plan on eating meat again. If I am able to, I hope to fight for the death penalty to be abolished. And I will never accept an explanation again without questioning it. I will never be swayed one way or the other without questioning and thinking myself. . . .

I can't express how grateful I am for your class, and I am very upset that it is over now. I hope to stop in often next semester, and I will be back next year to tell you that I've been a vegetarian for a year.

Sincerely,

Mitchell Crispell

JANUARY 15, 2007

Dear Mitchell,

It's true: if you want to make a difference, start to be different. That's what you've been doing this past semester, with me having a minor role that was little more than calling a few plays from the safe sidelines and you running with the ball. Pardon the wretched football metaphor—or maybe we can change it to field hockey since we had a couple of those all-stars sitting a few rows over to your left.

You brought plenty of energy to the class. You must have noticed how often I came to rely on it once I knew you were a singular doer among the talkers. And let's not forget the sleepers. You'd be surprised, or perhaps aghast, at how many of your classmates in their final self-evaluation papers confessed regret at sleeping so often. I imagine other teachers don't allow sleeping, for the usual reasons. Wake them so they'll learn the material and pass the next text. Wake them because I'm a gifted teacher, not a boring one. Wake them because they need to be disciplined. Wake them so they won't try that caper the next time.

I lean the other way, starting with the physiological: 17- and 18-year-old bodies, as study after study has shown, are severely taxed at 6, 7 and 8 am, and able to activate the brain cells and eyelids only by 9 and 10 am. With so many Bethesda–Chevy Chase students having lawyers as parents, I've often wondered why the county school board hasn't been sued for inflicting the pain of a 7:25 am opening bell. What pain, or as negligence lawyers like to say, what irreparable damage? Not getting into Harvard, what else! Here's Mom or Dad's lawyer telling the court that Mr. and Mrs. Smith's child would have graduated with a 4.0, not a 3.0, if the school day began at 9:00, not 7:25. With only a 3.0, Harvard was out. And now Billy Smith is at Mississippi State, and bleak future assured. We're asking $100 million in damages, the estimated loss in lifetime earnings compared to what he would have earned had he gone to Harvard.

Actually, and getting back to seriousness, Mississippi State is a worthy school. I've been there a couple of times, when I was on the golf team at Spring Hill College in Mobile, Alabama—a small Jesuit school not well known in the North or Northeast. It should be, having earned a deserved place in the history of civil rights. Spring Hill is praised by Martin Luther King Jr. in his "Letter from Birmingham Jail." Long before *Brown v. Board Education*, it was the first school in the South to integrate. King hailed the Jesuits for leading the way. It was a harsh, rocky way—as I learned when showing up as a freshman in the fall of 1956. Some 20 blacks were among the 800 white students. Caravans of the Ku Klux Klan drove through the campus in pick-up trucks, gun racks in the back windows and confederate flags waving from the front fenders. For four years, I was writing columns for the school newspaper, which meant I had a made-to-order civil rights beat directly in front of me.

A few years later, in the summer of 1966, I went to Chicago to write about King's efforts to integrate the all-white neighborhood of Marquette Park on Chicago's Southwest Side. King often said that integrating the North would be as dangerous, even more dangerous, than the struggle in the South. In the North, the racism was more hidden, a cancer eating away on the inside, rather than an open flesh wound visible on the outside—as it in the South. Leading a march in that neighborhood, King was hit by a rock thrown by someone in the bellowing racist mob on the side of the road. He said of that day: "I have never seen—even in Mississippi—mobs as hostile and hate-filled as I've seen in Chicago."

Look around in college for a course or two on the civil rights movement. It's not so long ago as to be ancient history, and the movement is anything but over. Check the newspapers for stories.

I'm as grateful for your letter's generous and gracious words as I am for having you in class. More than once I found myself thinking, if only everyone here was like Mitchell. Then I'd look around and check myself: stay real, only a few Mitchells ever come through.

Keep your heart on the Left. Anatomically, we're all liberals.

Colman McCarthy

◡ ◡ ◡

JUNE 5, 2012

Dear Mr. McCarthy,

To begin, thank you. Thank you for writing *I'd Rather Teach Peace* and *All of One Peace.* Thanks you for pushing peace education and for shedding light on the tremendous impact that this kind of education can provide to the lives of students. I am in my sixth year of teaching in inner-city schools in Baltimore and now Chicago and I can think of nothing I would like better than to give my kids the "seeds," as one of your students put it, of peace education.

In the fall I will begin teaching an elective research course for seniors at a charter school on the South Side of Chicago in a neighborhood that is both high poverty and high violence. Learning about justice issues as a college student, I experienced a major paradigm shift. When reading your books, I was forced to consider why I had not used authors like Dorothy Day, who is a personal favorite of mine, to inspire my kids.

And the answer was simply: I am afraid. I am afraid that I don't know enough about it to teach it, afraid maybe I don't "live" it enough and afraid that I will be preaching.

In the past when I have worked with nonviolence-related texts with my kids, their response was very often to tune it out and speak about the violence that they face every day, as if to tell me that I cannot understand and by presenting them with this information I am pretending that the world is a far different place than it is.

I suppose I am writing not only to say thank you but to ask a few questions.

- Does the Center for Teaching Peace offer any kind of professional development for teachers?
- How do I begin? What do I read? Where do I start?
- In your teaching experience you have taught in a variety of different schools. When teaching in an inner-city school, how did you tailor the curriculum? In what ways did it look different? What is your response to students' apathy? I know that kids are on different spectrums of understanding, but the apathy is disheartening.

I know you are an incredibly busy individual, but if you get this email and are able to respond, I would greatly appreciate it. Finally, and I think I cannot say this enough times, thank you. I felt terribly stuck in my teaching career. Burned out and a bit lost, I found your books and remembered why I became a teacher. Your words have meant a great deal to me.

Be well—

Maggie Hughes

JULY 29, 2012

Dear Maggie,

First off, let go of your fears and grab on, after relaxing a bit, to your strengths. You've been in the classrooms for six years, so it isn't as if you can't swim in the deep end—drowning as you may rightly feel. For your coming elective course, I'd suggest calling it "Is Peace Possible?" Right away, the title engages the students. Most will probably weigh in, either to themselves or out loud to you, with "hell no." From the first minutes of the first class, get them talking: about their experiences with violence, about their neighborhoods, their families. Another way to stoke things is, in the first minutes, to pass around to each student a sheet of paper—make it legal size—with questions.

These are a few I've used:

- I'm the one who . . .
- Why are you taking the course?
- What is your definition of peace? Of violence?
- What have you done recently to make someone's life easier?
- What do you most fear?
- What's best about your school?
- And the worst?
- Which person do you most admire?
- How did that person get that way?

The opening-day questionnaire sends a message that you care what is on their minds and maybe even what's in their hearts. Not many students, especially in large classes, ever think to themselves, my teacher cares about me, my teacher wants to learn about my life and me. When you collect the papers, ask the students if they'd mind if you read aloud some of the replies—anonymously. I've rarely had objections. The purpose is to let students know what their classmates are thinking. Sometimes the answers get people laughing, especially the one about fears. It's often spiders, bugs, slugs or shark attacks. Lighten things by asking "Has anyone ever been bitten by a spider?" or "Has anyone ever considered that spiders are probably just as afraid of us as we are of them?"

Another way to bond is to begin each class by randomly selecting a student—pick a name from the questionnaires—to come to the blackboard and write his or her name. Then ask a few questions: Where did your parents go to school? See if they know the names of their parents' elementary, high school and college, if they went. Ask about their parents' jobs or if they have lost their jobs. Ask about their favorite athlete. The last question: Tell us something about yourself that we would never have guessed or imagined. Some students are frightfully shy about getting up in from of everyone, so make it clear they can decline. I had a student last year whose mother had been murdered by her father and then the father killed himself. It was only toward the end of the semester that she was able to talk about it with the class.

The most effective way to tailor the curriculum is the way tailors do it with cloth: cut, sew and stitch according to the customer's size and shape. In many of the 25 years I was teaching at a low-income center-city school, I used no textbook. Instead I would copy newspaper or magazine articles—600 or 700 words—on an issue in the news. It might be on the death penalty. Have the piece read aloud paragraph by paragraph, stopping in between to get the students' reflections. Plenty of material is available on the internet. Check with the Death Penalty Information Center for facts. You might organize a class debate: three students to argue for the death penalty, three against. You can do this with almost anything in the news. Was it moral to kill Bin Laden? Has the war in Afghanistan been worth it? Are the "Stop and Frisk" laws a way to stop crime?

Another source of material, should it be a slow news day, are letters to the editor. Copy a couple, bring them in, have them read aloud and get the class talking. Give extra credit to any student who gets a letter published in the *Chicago Tribune*.

If the students remain unresponsive, don't take it personally. Some students have been so bruised by the hits of life that no educational effort of yours can ease the pain. For others, apathy is the only defense they know: I won't try because I've tried so many times before and lost. I'm out of the game.

Despite the breakdown, breakthrough can happen. When teaching in a juvenile prison—all minorities from 13 to 19—I had a boy who every time I passed out an essay to be read aloud and discussed would shred it and throw it at my feet. Class after class after class. One day he didn't shred it. That's progress, I thought. He still wouldn't read it. But the next class he did. Now I'm really getting somewhere. By the end of the semester, he asked if I could bring him a book. I wish I could report that the boy was eventually released from prison and is now a professor of philosophy at Harvard but, alas, he remains in prison on a homicide charge.

As much as possible, deemphasize homework. Do what you can to have students write in class, and read aloud what they write. Ask the class for its comments. And don't hurry it along. A guaranteed turn-off is when teachers announce "we have a lot of ground to cover." That means: open your minds, I'm about to tell you what you need to know. They gag. I do assign homework: Tell someone that you love them. If you can't find anyone, look a little harder. The world is filled with unloved people.

Much of this unconventional kind of teaching depends on what kind of support you get from the principal. If he or she is hard to work with, figure out how to work around them. It can be done.

I'd be glad to send along a textbook on which you could base the course: *Solutions to Violence*, which has about 80 essays in 16 chapters. Let me have your address at school. And by the way, what's your educational background? Start with elementary school, please.

Take care and care take—

Colman McCarthy

⌢ ⌢ ⌢

JULY 3, 2012

Dear Colman,

My name is Dan Anderson-Little. I graduated from Cultural Leadership Class Seven. About a year ago, on our "Transformational Journey," we met with you. You spoke to us about what you do and believe in. I read your *Strength through Peace* book. Between your talk with CL and the book I have been deeply inspired by you. I have become a vegetarian and a pacifist. I cannot thank you enough for this.

I understand if your busy schedule does not allow you to respond to emails such as this. However, if you can share some insight on this problem, I would greatly appreciate it.

I am currently in Pittsburgh at the General Assembly of the Presbyterian Church (USA). This is the meeting of the entire denomination which takes place every other year. I am participating as a Young Adult Advisory Delegate (YAAD). As a YAAD, I have a voice in the meeting sessions and an advisory vote.

There is a conflict facing the church which I've really been struggling with. I've been praying and thinking about this for a long time but cannot determine what the nonviolent solution is. The Presbyterian Church currently owns stock in Caterpillar, Motorola Solutions and Hewlett-Packard. In short (one could write pages about the situation), these companies support the Israeli occupation of Palestine, an injustice to the Palestinians. For example, Caterpillar bulldozers have been flattening Palestinian homes. As these companies continue to do business with the violent Israeli government, the Presbyterian Church is considering divesting from these companies. On the other hand, divestment could do serious damage to the Jewish community. First and foremost, it could affect significantly Presbyterian-Jewish relationships. The push for divestment has also been associated with some serious anti-Semitism. If we divest, the anti-Semitism could gain momentum.

Over the centuries, Jews have been persecuted and discriminated against, and Israel is a safe haven for Jews. With anti-Semitism alive and well, it seems to me that having a protected community of Jews is a good idea. I know "slippery slope" arguments are weaker arguments, but if the Presbyterian Church begins a secondary boycott of Israeli companies, the anti-Israel movement could certainly build momentum and Jews could potentially lose Israel.

Caterpillar doesn't do business directly with the Israelis either. It does less than one percent of its business with the US government. The US government then trades with its allies (including Israel), and that's how the Israeli government is supplied with the bulldozers. Caterpillar doesn't control the US government's actions, but they are still aware of them. Also, if divestment sparks a considerable boycott of Caterpillar and it goes out of business, the people who work for Caterpillar may lose their jobs. So divesting could cause many different consequences.

I cannot mindfully support the oppression of our Palestinian brothers and sisters, but on the other hand, the church has made a commitment to the Jewish community, and divestment could potentially risk the Jewish safe haven of Israel. The secondary boycott is also not focused and could have many other negative consequences. Is there another, more peaceful option that comes to mind? We have requested to talk with the companies but they will not talk to us.

Sorry about the limited description. It's obviously a more complicated issue; I hope it gives you enough information.

Again, I understand if your schedule does not allow you to respond. Thank you again for having such an impact on my life, you're truly a role model.

All the best,

Dan Anderson-Little
Class Seven, Cultural Leadership

[On June 20, 2014, the general assembly of the Presbyterian Church (USA) meeting in Detroit voted to divest its holdings in Caterpillar, Hewlett-Packard, and Motorola Solutions. The count was 310 to 303.]

JULY16, 2012

Dear Dan,

Welcome to the vegetarian and pacifist ranks. Without doubt, your body has become as strengthened by your nonviolent diet as has your conscience by your commitment to pacifism. Don't waver.

You deserve praise for getting involved, and in a nonsuperficial way, in the Presbyterian public policy issues. Thanks for sending your thoughts about the Pittsburgh general assembly, and for avoiding the simplicities that can strangle truth like kudzu choking flowers.

I take much of my guidance on the divestment campaign from Jewish Voice for Peace, the Oakland, California nonprofit that recently helped push TIAA-CREF to divest $72 million from Caterpillar. I'm also with Archbishop Desmond Tutu, who for the past decade has likened the Israeli occupation of the West Bank and Gaza to the apartheid of South Africa, which ended after divestment took effect. Economic power, whether exerted in well-publicized campaigns like the grape boycott led by Caesar Chavez in the 1970s or in individual decisions like yours and vegetarians or vegans to give no money to the meat, dairy and egg industry, has had its fair amount of successes. We'll see if it works with Israel.

When writing about the 45-year occupation, I am careful to criticize only the policies of the Israeli government—currently the Netanyahu conservative government and its ties to the hawkish Likud party—which do not necessarily reflect the views of Jews living in Jerusalem, Tel Aviv or the United States. You've seen it, I'm sure: criticize Israel and you'll catch it. As a senator running for the presidency, Barack Obama dared say it: "I think there is a certain strain within the pro-Israel community that says unless you adopt an unwavering pro-Likud approach to Israel that you're anti-Israel." Whether he's meeting with Netanyahu or Mahmoud Abbas, the Palestinian leader, Obama has been consistent. In his June 2009 Cairo speech, he laid it out: "Palestinians must abandon violence," including suicide terrorism and hate speech against Israel. "On the other hand, it is also undeniable that the Palestinian people—Muslims and Christians— have suffered in pursuit of a homeland. They endure daily humiliations, large and small, that come with occupation. . . . America will align our policies with those who pursue peace. And we will say in public what we say in private to Israelis and Palestinians and Arabs."

Three years later, conditions are worsening for the 2.5 million Palestinians and their drive for an independent state. On July 9, an Israeli government–created commission released a report arguing that the occupation is not an occupation but a legally entitled settlement. This disregarded the judgments of United Nations Security Council Resolution 242, the Fourth Geneva Convention and the US State Department. The latter renounced the commission's findings: "We do not accept the legitimacy of continued Israeli activity, and we oppose any effort to legalize settlement outposts."

What can you and I do, in our personal lives, while all this unfolds an ocean and a sea away? Stay as schooled in information as possible, for a start. Regarding that, I recommend a 2006 book, *Prisoners: a Muslim and Jew Across the Middle East Divide*. The author, Jeffrey Goldberg, lives in my neighborhood, and I came to know him when his boy enrolled in Home Run Baseball Camp run by my son John. Jeffrey wrote for the *New Yorker* magazine for ten years and is now with the *Atlantic*. In polished prose, he tells of being an American Jew who went to Israel while in college in 1991 to join its military. He served as a guard in Israel's prison, Ketziot, in the Negev Desert two miles from the Egyptian border, which held 6,000 Palestinians—bomb-makers, rock-throwers and suspected attackers.

Jeffrey met and befriended a prisoner, Rafiq Hijazi, starting with conversations between the prison's fences. "The feeling of connection I felt with him was not political," Jeffrey writes. "We were officially, as well as factually, each other's enemy. We were on opposing teams. I wore army green, he wore prisoner blue. He believed in the basic goodness of his tribe, as I did in mine, despite the perversities of Ketziot."

The friendship lasted. Hijazi, released from prison, traveled to the United States to earn a doctorate from American University and became a professor at a university in Abu Dhabi. "I have not stopped wanting what I have always wanted," Jeffrey writes in the final pages of *Prisoners*: "Security and justice for Israel and security and justice for the Palestinians. By the middle of 2006, though, the Middle East was a landscape of wasting sadness and obliterating furies, Hezbollah was at war with Israel, and despair was coming easily to me. Except when I recalled my last conversation with Rafiq in [Abu Dhabi]. We were having coffee. I had been thinking, in the most rational way, that if Rafiq and I could allow friendship to triumph over anger, then it wasn't impossible to believe that the rest of Isaac's children, and the rest of Ishmael's children, could stop their long and dismal war. Jews believe, of course, that Isaac is Abraham's chosen son; Islam came along and settled on Ishmael as Abraham's favorite. Without a direct statement from God, this is not a winnable argument. But what can be won is the recognition that both men came together as brothers to bury their father. The rest is commentary."

Try to find the book. If you can't, let me know. I'll loan you mine.

I enjoyed meeting you last summer at the Cultural Leadership program. You were generous to get *Strength Through Peace*.

Shalom—

Colman McCarthy

෴

Hello Mr. McCarthy-

I doubt you remember me. You came to St. John's College in Annapolis, Maryland, on September 11, 2011, to give a speech. I came up to you at the end of the speech and convinced you to give me one of your books, for free. You asked if I was a "freegan." I said "no, I just like free books." Well I wanted to share with you what I did with your book. When Occupy Wall Street began in NYC, I decided I had to check it out; the frustration of our sociopolitical situation led me to it. I took a Megabus from Annapolis to NYC and brought your book along with me. *Strength Through Peace* seemed appropriate. I must confess I was only able to read one of your entries in it. I was more infatuated with Gandhi's (but no hard feelings, right?).

I spent the nights sleeping on the cold, hard Wall Street concrete in Zuccotti Park, the skyscrapers' windows reflecting the stars I should have been sleeping under. During the days I marched with the poor, the rich, the middle class, the emaciated, the suffering, the burnt out, the "suits," the "hipsters," the right-wingers, the left, the anarchists, the communists, the Christians, the Muslims, the Jews and many others. "They got bailed, we got sold out!" "All day, all week, occupy Wall Street!" "We are the

99%" were some of the things we chanted. The experience touched my soul, it reinvigorated my desire for service.

You said in your speech "If you want to serve your country, don't join the military"—pretty ballsy considering our campus is a rock's throw from the Naval Academy. Let's throw the rock and get to the crux. I'm going into my senior year of undergrad. I plan on doing a yearlong graduate program at our sister camp in Santa Fe following my senior year. Two years from now, I'm free, plus I have my summers available.

What can I do to promote peace at a global level? I am a confident and eye catching public speaker, hard worker, big thinker and seeking to make a change in this world before the warmongers and greedy capitalists lead us all to the slaughter. "A man who was completely innocent, offered himself as a sacrifice for the good of others, including his enemies and became the ransom of the world. It was a perfect act." I hope I don't need to put the author down for you. I want to one day do the "perfect act." Help me get there.

By the way, I left your book in the free library at Zuccotti Park. I imagine the police threw it away when they took over the park. But maybe someone else picked it up and right now it's traveling around the world. I've attached a picture as proof (ignore the tear) and a few of my favorites from that weekend.

Best wishes,

John R.

P.S. I won't take "no" for answer.

JULY 10, 2012

Dear John,

You're a pushy lad. First, you won't take no for an answer, meaning, I suppose, that I should call an immediate halt to looking for answers to my own questions and throw one your way. For a moment, let me take refuge in the line of Walter Lippmann, who used to write syndicated columns: "Many a time I have wanted to stop talking and find out what I really believed."

Second, you managed to cadge a free book out of me and write to say that you hardly read it and then, unashamedly heaving salt on the open wound of my ego, announce that you left the book at Zuccotti Park. Next time someone comes up after a talk and tries grubbing a free book I'll have all I can do to not think of you. But no hard feelings, right?

I liked your letter, attracted to spunkiness as I am. One correction, if I may. It wasn't especially "ballsy" of me to say, with the Naval Academy nearby, "If you want to serve your country, don't join the military." I've said the same on the two times I was invited to speak at the academy. The midshipmen—women are called that too—handled it graciously while, of course, disagreeing.

I strain to make it clear that I am not anti-soldier. I'm opposed, as a pacifist, to military violence and the negative effects it can have on soldiers—the current epidemic of suicides, plus the PTSD—and does have on the victims of war. For the United States, the reckless funding of the military, as one Congress after another has been doing, has led to a wrecked and bankrupt economy to the dismal depth that last May's college graduates are struggling to find meaningful work.

Getting to your question about your promoting peace at a global level: for a start, replace the global with the personal. Think small, which is what you are and what I am and all of us are. Examine your life and ask are you being as loving a person as you can be and should be. Dorothy Day, the co-founder of the Catholic Worker movement in the 1930s, who served the poor of New York City a few blocks from Zuccotti Park before it was even named that, wrote in "Love Is the Measure": "What we would like to do is change the world—make it a little simpler for people to feed, clothe and shelter themselves as God intended them to do. And to a certain extent by fighting for better conditions, by crying out unceasingly for the right of the workers, of the poor, of the destitute—the rights of the worthy and the unworthy poor, in other words—we can to a certain extent change the world. We can work for the oasis, the little cell of joy and peace in a harried world. We can throw a pebble in the pond and be confident that it's ever-widening circle will reach around the world. We repeat, there is nothing that we can do but love, and dear God, please enlarge our hearts to love each other, to love our neighbor, to love our enemy as well as our friend."

If you focus your peacemaking on a global level, you run too great a risk of wearing out, giving out, running out and, worst, selling out. All of it leading to prolix philosophizing about the damage done by "the warmongers and greedy capitalists" and assorted nasties. Instead, take the next few years to acquire a skill that can possibly reduce someone's suffering, or lighten someone's load or lift someone's heart. You're in college, so it's too early to tell exactly what skill you'll be driven to hone—to "one day do the perfect act." You'll know when it's happening. Are baseball games won by the one perfect act of a home run or by a half dozen imperfect acts of scratch hits, well-placed bunts, sacrifice flies and hitting to the opposite field? Remember the line about Eddie Stanky of the Brooklyn Dodgers: "He can't run, he can't hit, he can't field. All he can do is beat you."

Keep in mind that as an American you won the birth lottery. If you had a room holding 100 people representing the nations of the world, only four would be Americans—one out of 25. As a lottery winner who beat the odds, you aren't cursed with the damnations that plague the lottery losers: the billions in the world who are jobless and friendless and who have little access to food, clean drinking water, medical or legal help and live in fear of abusive governments.

Enjoy your final year at St. John's. It's a quality school but on my last visit to speak there I saw only a slight movement to de-Westernize the Great Books reading list and to open it to the literature of peace along with writings by women. Do some agitating on the way, after that all Great Books cogitating.

I have a new book out, *Peace Is Possible*. I'd send you a free copy but. . . .

Keep plugging,

Colman McCarthy

〜〜〜

AUGUST 1, 2012

Dear Mr. McCarthy,

Thanks you so much for speaking to my class at American University (Community and Social Change with Professor Eleftherios Michael). Your words of wisdom were truly inspiring and opened my mind to many things. For example, I had been thinking about joining the military at some point in my life but you helped me see how many other avenues for change there are. To be honest, before this summer with Eleftherios, I wasn't sure if peace was possible or if people believed in it anymore, but after two months, and especially your lecture, I have hope. I have hope that working locally can bring larger change. I have hope that there are good people in the world. I have hope in myself for my future and my friends. I have no idea where will be in the future but I do know that I want to help people. If I am ever in DC again, I will definitely contact you. Thank you again for the inspiration and empowerment.

Sincerely,

Emily

Dear Emily,

Do remain in touch and do come by should your journey take you back to Washington. You had one of American University's wisest professors in Eleftherios Michael. And one of its most generous. You may have noticed that in gratitude for my speaking to the class, he gave me a bulging bag of fruit from Whole Foods: a pineapple, six bananas, three kiwis, five peaches and four apples. Now that's a real honorarium.

I'm glad you are having second thoughts, and maybe third and fourth ones, about joining the military. By coincidence, this summer I've been catching up on Tolstoy—less the fiction of his earlier life when he wrote *War and Peace* at 35 and *Anna Karenina* at 45 than the essays of the latter 1890s near the end of his days in 1910.

Two of those pieces, "Advice to a Draftee" and "Letter to a Corporal" might be relevant to your life as you come to the last months of your time at Loyola. The draftee was Ernst Schramm from Bavaria in southern Germany, who was faced with conscription into the Hessian military. "What should a man do who has been called upon for military service," Tolstoy asks, "that is, called upon to kill or to prepare himself to kill? And to this question, for a person who understands the true meaning of military service and who wants to be moral, there is only one clear and incontrovertible answer: such a person must refuse to take part in military service no matter what consequences this refusal may have." In the military, he argued, "is one not required to agree to the deaths of all those one is commanded to kill?"

The same theme is in "Letter to a Corporal." "Why do these men [soldiers] shoot at their brothers?" Tolstoy writes. "Because it has been impressed upon them that the oath which they are compelled to take upon entering military service is obligatory for them, and that they may not kill men in general but may kill them by command of the authorities. . . . But here arises the question: how can people of sound mind who frequently know the rudiments and are even educated, believe in such a palpable lie? No matter how little educated a man may be, he nonetheless cannot help knowing that Christ did not permit any murder but taught meekness, humility, forgiveness of offenses, love of enemies; he cannot help but see that, on the basis of the Christian teaching, he cannot make a promise in advance that he will kill all those whom he is commanded to kill."

In one of my recent classes at American, one of my students was Brandon Frazier. In his mid-20s, Brandon was a country boy from a small town in Michigan. After high school and seeing few job opportunities in his town, he joined the Marines. A paper he wrote for class, "I Should Have Questioned My Orders," was of one mind with Tolstoy. It begins: "No act is more violent than taking another's life. Four years of my life were defined by training to commit, attempting to commit or committing these very acts of violence. During this period I was one of the unfortunate Marines put into situations where murder seemed to be my only option. For me, this taking of lives was half the sad and violent story that was my life from ages 18 to 21. The other half of the story is one that most people do not consider when they sign the military contract that gives away the right to their own lives."

As a Marine, Brandon's work included tracking down suspected enemies, often breaking into homes to start firefights: "The act of killing, in these years, was as simple as three pounds of pressure on a trigger, and that's how we were trained. What I realize now, astonishingly for the first time, is that I should have questioned my orders at every instance when I was told to go somewhere to take another's life, and that killing another human being is far more complicated than three pounds of pressure on a trigger. There is no contract with any government in any country that can justify murder of any kind. . . . Today I feel terrible for what I have done and I have been haunted by nightmares every night since my return home."

Brandon graduated from American in May 2011, an achievement that brought a measure of stability to his life as he recovers from military life. With his permission, I had his valuable paper published in the *National Catholic Reporter*.

You mentioned in your letter, "I have hope that working locally can bring larger change." Here, too, Tolstoy might be instructive—this time less as a model for clearsightedness about the military than as an example on how not to work locally. In this instance, local means in your home with your family. While in his study writing about peace, justice and nonviolence, Tolstoy was at the height of his power. It's when he left the study that he sank to the depths. He was emotionally cruel to his wife. He forced her to bear 13 children. She was clinically depressed, suicidal and spiritually suffocated by living with a self-consumed genius. "He is indifferent to everyone around him," she wrote in her diary in June 1897, "and lives only for himself." A later entry: "I do not believe in his goodness and love for humanity. I know the source of all his actions: glory and glory, insatiable, unlimited, feverish. . . . He has no love for his own children and grandchildren." When one of his daughters, Masha, died, he felt little grief and confessed to not feeling unhappy. His son Ilya wrote of life with the 19th century's greatest writer: "As a boy of 12, I felt that my father was getting more and more estranged from us . . . gloomy and irritable . . . we all found him tiresome and uninteresting."

Tolstoy was not the only one who loved humanity but showed little love to the humans underfoot at home. Gandhi, married at 13 to a 12-year-old, was a domineering husband intent on controlling his wife. Gandhi's oldest son, Harilal, was so hurt by his father's coldness and absenteeism that he took to a life of dissolution—becoming a prostitute and contracting the disease of alcoholism. Gandhi all but disowned the boy and never reconciled. Martin Luther King Jr. failed as a husband, locked as he was in multiple sexual liaisons. Albert Einstein, who wrote passionately about pacifism, was emotionally cruel to both his wives.

Oddly enough, people who are generous in showing love to their spouses and children can be monstrously cruel outside the home. There was President Harry Truman. I came to know his daughter Margaret and her husband Clifton Daniel, the latter when he was the Washington bureau chief of the *New York Times*. Both told stories of Truman's enduring love of his wife and daughter. Yet here was the grand family man who ordered the dropping of two atomic bombs that killed tens of thousands of Japanese families in Hiroshima and Nagasaki—today, by the way, being the 67th anniversary of the Nagasaki murders August 9, 1945.

All of which, I'd say, bolsters our belief in the power of working locally—those at home, first off, and then extending it. Love those we know before those we don't know.

No doubt, the library of your hometown, Kennebunk, has all of

Tolstoy's writings. In case not, I'm including copies of his essays to the draftee and corporal.

Thanks for writing and for your overly generous words—

Colman McCarthy

∽ ∽ ∽

Dear Mr. McCarthy,

Football may contain some negative, violent aspects but by the end of this letter, hopefully my points will at least be understood.

I'll start with my worst argument: football is fun. It's fun to catch passes, block other players, kick the ball, and make tackles. If you're on the field you're always doing something. The game is never boring to play, and for most, to watch as well.

Even though America has a few serious problems, or as you would perhaps prefer the phrase "odd little country," in just about every category (social, economic, political, etc.), football is connected with our positives. It echoes our values: sacrifice, desire, effort and toughness. These qualities may be used in the wrong fashion by political leaders, but a lot of Americans are in favor of an aggressive attitude to "be the best" at just about everything.

I'm just getting started, however. Now to get to the real deal, the reason why I (like the previous paragraph) enjoy football so much and recognize it as the best sport in the world. [In our Bethesda–Chevy Chase class discussion] Nik Small touched on the whole family part of playing on the school football team but I'm going to go more in depth.

Without football, I would not be the person I am today. I would be a little undisciplined punk. That's what football does; it teaches you discipline and the most basic forms of it. It teaches you how to overcome adversity when times get rough. It teaches you teamwork and how to work with people of different races, religions and interests to achieve the mutual goal of success. It teaches you accountability. Responsibility. Determination. It teaches you how to work hard. Overall, football prepares you for life. You receive what you put in. I give it my all every play and it does pay off. It WILL pay off when I get a job and I'm working my tail off to impress my boss.

Football alters your outlook on life. You learn to see where people are coming from by listening to them. Your mind opens up. Why? Because if your coach is good enough, you learn how people think. It may be hard to believe but you really do learn how each individual perceives various obstacles. The weight training and workouts only complement the ability to understand people. I'm able to help people, not because I'll feel good about it, but because the people I'm helping will. It's one of those feel-good do-good type of deals. Now all of this may be difficult to believe or fully comprehend and that's fine. It's easier to understand if you're part of it. The relationships you form are unbelievable. Brotherhood is outstanding. The relationships will last me a lifetime.

If none of this has really spoken to you then maybe my next point will.

We're playing for a city. In my case, I'm playing for the city of Bethesda. I take great pride in playing for a team that represents the city I live in. I want us to be known for something.

Perhaps a better point is that football provides little boys with dreams and aspirations, as well as ambition. Football is one of the best sports for this—unlike baseball which is patient and boring. But I have nothing against baseball. I played it for nine years, it's just a different game. Honestly, football builds character and makes our lives more stable. Yes it is violent. Yes, one could argue that it's sexist or that females can't keep up with the physical demands. But my intentions are good. I'm not asking you change your perspective on football or change anything in any way. I just want you to know where we football players are coming from. Football is more than a game. It's a lifestyle.

Sincerely,

Michael Sullivan

OCTOBER 7, 2012

Dear Michael,

It goes without saying, but I'll say it anyway. I appreciate the time you took to offer your thoughts on your enjoyment of playing football and what it has done for you. Nothing you wrote makes me doubt this. At the same time, though, everything you say—football "teaches you accountability. Responsibility. Determination. It teaches you how to work hard," it "prepares you for life," "you receive what you put in"—could as easily be said about playing on the high school soccer team or baseball team. True, those are different games but it's certainly plausible that just as many high school soccer or baseball players could make the same claims for their sports as you do for yours.

Taking the argument further, all the personal benefits you attribute to football would still be present if you were playing touch football rather than conventional high-injury, collision-based, concussion-prone and necessarily violent football. It can be credibly be argued that touch football requires more agility, imagination and skill than regular football—minus the violence, minus the hitting and bashing, minus the dancing in the end zones and minus the expense.

Speaking of dollars, the September/October issue of *Bethesda* magazine reports in its cover story, "The High Cost of High School Sports," that laying out money to pay coaches and assistant coaches, plus the cost of referees, equipment (jerseys $50, pants $35–$45, hip pads $20, thigh pads and knee pads $15, reconditioning helmets $4,000–$10,000 a year, socks $5), field maintenance (B-CC spent about $44,000 in 2009–10, Churchill High nearly $107,000), and transportation to games means "tens of thousands of dollars more for football" than other sports. Left out are the medical expenses of treating injuries.

The extravagance of football is in keeping with the nation's other financially wasteful and violent pastime, war-making. Money squandered on football teams could as well be used for art or music programs—or to really get carried away, for Peace Studies classes.

It's not accidental that football is the country's most favored sport, and invading other nations to maim or kill people is our most favored way of settling disputes. It's no accident either that veterans of the National Football League are now filing negligence suits against the owners of their former teams for injuries the way veterans of wars in Iraq and Afghanistan are seeking legal relief for their injuries. The battlefields of football and the battlefields of wars zones lead to similar Post-Traumatic Stress Disorders. It can be argued that no one is forced to play football and no one is forced to join the military. Perhaps, but it has to be wondered why so few players in the NFL come from Ivy League or Little Ivy colleges and why so few soldiers in Iraq and Afghanistan are from those schools.

I'm hoping that your enthusiasm for the brain-rattling and brutish game of football is a passing phase and that soon enough you'll get the same satisfactions from playing the lifetime family sports of tennis, golf, swimming, running, bowling or quoits (yes, quoits, try it, you'll like it!).

Attached is a piece I wrote two years ago on sending high school football to the showers.*

I'm delighted you are in my Peace Studies class. You have a gentle and gracious manner. You may remember that on the first day of class you wrote on the questionnaire I passed out on "Why are you taking the course and what do you want to get out of it?": "I'd like to be a more peaceful person and I want to learn ways to spread peace."

Yours on 4th down and long—

Colman McCarthy

*Article from *National Catholic Reporter*, October 1, 2010:

In these pinched times of teacher layoffs, budget cuts and outright school closings, a prime way for school boards to economize is high school football teams. As the season opens, send them to the showers—permanently. No sport is more expensive, with uncounted dollars being squandered on field maintenance, helmets, pads, cleats, uniforms for players and cheerleaders, payments for refs, bus trips for away games, salaries for coaches—and not counting the health care costs for inevitable injuries to limbs, muscles and craniums.

Depending on the size of a school system, the annual savings could range from a few thousand dollars to millions. Instead of football, direct the money where it's needed: everywhere from teachers' salaries to a school's music, drama or arts programs. Get those grunting hunks of male flesh into the glee club or teach them the manly art of playing the violin or cello. If they aren't up for that, and they probably won't be, considering how football-crazed the country has become, involve them in lifetime family sports: running, golf, tennis or swimming.

How many high school football players 20 years from now, and in full brawniness, will be suiting up their wives in pads and helmets for an hour of hard hits on the front lawn? Instead, for recreation they are likely to be on the golf course or tennis court—and probably inept because they didn't play those sports in high school when they might have.

In his Senate days, Minnesotan Gene McCarthy had it right when he said that "being in politics is like being a football coach: You have to be smart enough to understand the game and dumb enough to think it's important."

Right now, some of the dumbest people are in Texas where the high holy days are the upcoming fall weekends when football is worshipped and the unwritten state law—"Leave No Football Player Behind"—is religiously obeyed.

A few years back, two high school districts in Texas spent $20 million each on stadiums. *The Dallas Morning News* reported that building 15 new high school stadiums in the Dallas area has or will cost $179 million. At Allen High School, football players scoring touchdowns will soon be dancing in the end zones of a $60 million, 18,000-seat stadium, cheered on by citizens who took lunacy to new levels by voting to tax themselves for the colossus.

This profligacy raises a question: what is so intellectually or culturally empty in these scatterbrain Texas towns that watching male teenagers violently hitting and mauling each other fills the void? Why are the values of school boards so off the rails that, by last count, the average salary of a football coach was $73,000 while the average teacher got $42,000?

One possible answer is that Texas is ground zero for academic stagnation: It ranks last in the nation in the percentage of adults with high school diplomas. At the same time that pampered high school students are entertaining fans beneath the Friday night lights, Texas students lead the way in underachieving: the state ranks 49th in verbal SAT scores and 46th in math.

Football, a collision sport that should be called bashball, is brutish and bloody. Among high school sports, it has the highest injury rate, double that of basketball and baseball. An estimated one in 100,000 players suffers serious spinal cord injuries. Except for enriching orthopedists and keeping ambulance drivers and emergency room doctors busy, and satisfying the gladiatorial cravings of beer-drinking fans, of what value is football?

The answer is none, if the stand of a few educators means anything. Since 1990 more than 40 colleges and universities have dumped football programs. Last November it was Northeastern

University in Boston, followed in December by Hofstra University in Long Island, NY.

Stuart Rabinowitz, Hofstra president, said it was time to "re-invest those resources [$4.5 million a year] into new academic programs and need-based scholarships." Other schools that have punted include Siena College in Loudonville, NY; Fairfield University in Connecticut; St. John's University in New York City; and Canisius College in Buffalo, NY.

The good news is that higher education is slowly seeing the light. The bad news: secondary schools remain clueless. A favorite pre-game pep talk of high school coaches is to send the boys from the locker room with the bellow: "Go out there and go for broke." A fitting line for financially broke is now the state of most school systems.

∽ ∽ ∽

Dearest Colman,

I received such a pleasant surprise yesterday, in the form of a picture text message from my Mom. To tell the truth, I tend to not be as excited as I should be about receiving such pictures because I tend to think that the amount of technology in my life is excessive and am frustrated by messages being sent thoughtlessly, but for this one in particular I was about to put those thoughts aside as a smile lit up my face: it was a picture of her with you in Minneapolis! What a treat. I hope you enjoyed your visit to the Midwest and found some warm company among the nice Minnesotans out there.

I've been meaning to write to you for the past week, as I've recently begun reading *The Kingdom of God Is within You*, by Tolstoy, after a friend recommended it to me. Have you read it? I expect that you have. Here's a quote from the book: "The Anarchists are right in everything; in the negation of the existing order, and in the assertion that, without authority, there could not be worse violence than that of Authority under existing conditions. They are mistaken only in thinking that Anarchy can be instituted by a revolution. But it will be instituted only by there being more and more people who do not require the protection of governmental power. . . . There can be only one permanent revolution—a moral one: the regeneration of the inner man."

My lack of interest in staging protests, and my penchant for finding commonalities between people, made me like this philosophy immediately.

I found the book informative (I hadn't seen as many connections between government and violence as Tolstoy did), affirming (it's nice to hear smart people explain why your beliefs are legitimate), and somewhat simplistic (he reduces Christianity to a set of straight-forward rules, losing the concepts of the mystery of faith as a result). That being said, I've really only read the first 100 pages or so, and there's much more to come! I'll update you once the task is complete, but I've also embarked upon another lengthy journey (no, not medical school—that will start in the fall), the reading of Proust, so my time is limited. I say that mostly to make you not too disappointed by the slow speed at which I've been reading of late. Somehow the majority of my time seems to be taken up with the daily activities that are meant to take very little time, like cooking and touching base with my housemates and friends.

I recently looked into the Cherry Blossom race, thinking I could bounce on down to DC for the occasion [April 7], but as it turns out it's the same day that I'm taking a CPR class: a commitment that cannot be rescheduled and that is required for me to lead a backpacking trip for some teens through Alaska this summer. I'm not at all pleased with the timing of this, but I'd still like to meet you in DC at some point this spring. Maybe we can go on a little jaunt of our own. Who needs a formal race anyway?

Sending lots of love your way,

Laura Christianson

MARCH 23, 2013

Dear and Special Laura,

Finally, a moment. Which is what Saturdays must have been invented for.

As expected, my visit to Minneapolis was a delight, as fleeting as it was. That your Mom came to my talk at Augsburg [College] was a treat. I acknowledged her presence when I started speaking, right after I thanked the Minnesotans for sending so many titans to the Senate all these years:

Gene McCarthy, Hubert Humphrey, Fritz Mondale, Paul Wellstone. That does make up a bit for inflicting Michele Bachmann on us. Another one I mentioned was Nicole Kast, whom I met 10 years ago when speaking in Wausau, Wisconsin, where her father, David Kast, a professor at the local community college, was my host. After high school in Wausau, Nicole went to Swarthmore: you know, arch rivals to your Williams for the top ranked liberal arts college, though Williams does seem to keep holding on. She did some agitating, and following graduation went to Chiapas in southern Mexico for more agitations. She's now at the University of Minnesota getting an MA in public health, and hot to get back to Chiapas. A few of the Augsburg professors who came to the talk told me, with some alarm, that the school's finances are shaky, which is why its poorly funded peace studies program will become even more reduced to beggary.

I do know the Tolstoy book, having found it in a used bookstore some time ago. There's the anarchism part, which you picked up on and which is surely getting you closer and closer to joining the anarchist ranks. Welcome. And then there are lines which I kept thinking of when beholding the orgiastic pageantry that the Vatican put on when picking a new pope the other day: "But Christ could certainly not have established the Church. That is, the institution we now call by that name, for nothing resembling our present conception of the Church—with its sacraments, its hierarchy, and especially its claim to infallibility—is to be found in Christ's words or in the conception of the men of his time."

I have scant expectations that the Vatican's Francis will come anywhere close to moving Catholicism to being a peace church or an animal rights church—to name just a couple of the bents of the Assisi Francis. When the new pope—and let's wish him well, of course—announces that the church is now a pacifist church and no longer blesses the Just War approach to settling conflicts, and that it's not moral to kill animals for food or any other reason, then it might be time for me to get back to the pews.

I wish I'd had more time to speak with your Mom about your doings in Boston. She gave me an overview—that you are happy, no surprise there—but that you hadn't yet picked a medical school. Praise to you for sticking to it, going back after majoring in English at Williams, to take the needed science courses and then bracing yourself for more years in the classroom.

My own classes are going well. One of my star students at Bethesda–

Chevy Chase, Hannah Levin, is a first-year at Williams, recruited for the soccer team. Her older brother, Jacob, whom I had in class six years ago, also went to Williams and was headed to hedge funds on Wall Street until he, as did you, studied in Oxford. It woke him up, joltingly so, and he's now an organic farmer in a North Carolina rural commune.

Sorry you won't be in the field for the Cherry Blossom. I'd get you a place in the front row with the Kenyans. A friend is one of the race officials, a true friend who last year made sure I was given a finisher's medal—though he knows I always run as a bandit, and though I limp in in just under two hours. My pal overlooks a lot.

Lots of love, and one favor please: stay special—

Colman

MARCH 25, 2013

Dearest Colman,

I'm so glad you brought up the other thought-provoking message from "The Kingdom of God Is within You," about the church. Reading those lines, and now your reflections on them, I was struck by the truth in them, and then by how radical the truth can be. I'm drawn to tradition—the feeling that my footsteps are somehow aligned with those who have come before me and those who will come after me, and to the idea that certain things remain constant over time—and am therefore susceptible to liking the idea of the Catholic Church, with its ancient rituals and hierarchy. But in practice the Church behaves as though it's only role is to maintain the status quo, rather than to think carefully about what the Bible teaches and how to best enact God's will.

The Episcopal church I have attended over the past several years has encouraged me to pause, listen, and reflect in community, and for that I am so grateful. And yet none have strengthened my convictions as much as I'd wish—somehow the thoughtfulness instilled by church services breeds kindness and warmth without generating the higher frequency energy of social reformers who are more willing to stir things up a bit.

I recently thought of you while reading a *New Yorker* article from January 28. In "The Force: How Much Military Is Enough?" Jill Lepore underlines just how massive our defense spending is (more than that of all other countries combined) and describes the evolution of the military in the US I was pleased to learn that early Americans "considered a standing army—a permanent army kept even in times of peace—to be a form of tyranny," favoring militias instead. She also quotes Eisenhower: "Every gun that is made, every warship launched, every rocket fired signifies in the final sense a theft from those who hunger and are not fed, those who are cold and not clothed. This is a world in arms. The world in arms is not spending money alone; it is spending the sweat of its laborers, the genius of its scientists, the hopes of its children. . . . This is not a way of life at all in any true sense. Under the clouds of threatening war, it is humanity hanging from a cross of iron."

Colman, I am increasingly upset that being a law-abiding citizen of this country requires me to fund and support acts of violence—administered through the prison system, war, a tit-for-tat legal system. The government's approach to solving disputes directly conflicts with my personal values and I can no longer rationalize my financial support of such a system. Could you please send along information on how to ethically evade taxes? Ideally I'd be able to write off all my taxes through charitable donations, but I believe you're only allowed to write off 50% of your gross adjusted income. I remember watching a video you gave me [*An Act of Conscience*] about a couple who refused to pay war taxes and had their house taken away from them. I'm not sure what the government would be able to take away from me that's of any value—although I would be devastated if they took my one-speed Schwinn.

As for my path toward medicine, I continue to plug along happily, though many related questions remain unanswered. Beyond deciding where to attend medical school, which is mostly a question of family and finances versus seeking an institution wherein pursuit of excellence is of the utmost importance—though excellence should be consistently sought by all institutions, some are far more successful at this than others. I also will have to eventually decide how I plan on using my medical degree to promote health and healing. I'm excited about all the learning that lies ahead, and even more so about the people I am to meet and the many possible directions I could go.

Sending lots of love your way, this day and always,

    Laura

Dear and Special Laura,

Another moment. I remember reading the *New Yorker* piece and, hesitant as I am to dare dispute a Harvard professor—yes, this is sarcasm because I'm not hesitating at all—Jill Lepore's next to last line was an example of calcified thinking: "Force requires bounds. Between militarism and pacifism lie diplomacy, accountability and restraint." This is an old oxymoronic game, equating pacifism with extremism, the irrational, the well-intentioned—but let's be practical, let's not take it seriously. Diplomacy, accountability and restraint. Let's have a think-tank sponsored conference to do some probing. US diplomacy and restraint are always touted and tooted. But when Congress gives the Pentagon nearly 60 percent of the discretionary federal budget and the State Department 4 percent, invading Iraq and Afghanistan are inevitable. The *Washington Post* reported on March 29 a study that the cost of the two wars will come to nearly $6 trillion Where is the accountability in that? Or the restraint?

The Lepore article had another weakness: bemoaning the excesses in military spending but not stating how much taxes are paid by individual citizens—topical right now with April 15 looming. What's needed, and it won't be happening soon, is for the IRS to send receipts to each taxpayer stating how of his or her money will go the military, how much to the Department of Education, the Department of Transportation, the Peace Corps, Americorps. With a public kept in the budgetary dark, somnambulating follows—along with the lavishly funded expansionist wars.

Which gets to your totally justified uneasiness about paying war taxes. Lots of options are available. Starting with the least likely: get your medical degree, leave the country, renounce your US citizenship, head for Costa Rica (no war taxes there; it has no army), open a clinic and take care of poor people. Look into the life of Albert Schweitzer and his medical practice in Gabon. Second, become a conscientious tax refuser. This isn't evasion, loopholing or cheating. Refusers tell the IRS what they are up to. They are willing to pay all that's due but on grounds of conscience refuse to pay for military killing. Refusers risk penalties and jail. The chances of the latter, by the way, are slim. The IRS is perennially understaffed and ever under pressure to go after the whales and assorted big fish, with fines. Tax cheats like Willie Nelson and Marion Barry were fined but never jailed. A third option is to keep your income too low to be taxed, which might not be hard considering what your medical school debt may be as well as the falling salaries of many doctors, not including plastic surgeons, which I suspect isn't your dream job.

For a few thoughts slightly more grounded than my Costa Rica counsel, you might check with some of the experts on conscientious tax refusal: The American Friends Service Committee and the War Resisters League. Both have ample literature and practical advice on war tax refusal.

Thanks for the Eisenhower quote. It's a staple in a film one of my students made, a documentary called *New Shoots for Peace*. Not sure if you saw it when you were helping with my classes during your winter break, but I have some copies. Eisenhower, a dim bulb at best, didn't write those lines. He had a literate speechwriter—Emmet John Hughes, who many believe, me included, was the most graceful writer ever to work for a president.

A couple of Minnesotans came through town recently, and with whom I spent some time. It was Julie McCarthy Napoleon and her daughter Murielle. Julie is the daughter of Austin McCarthy, whose brother was Gene McCarthy, the most gifted and far-seeing senator ever from Minnesota and whom I came to know both during his senate and post-senate days. Murielle, a junior in high school, Marlborough, a private girl's school in Los Angeles, came east with her mother for some college shopping. I showed them the sights of American University and its School of International Service which has far greater heft than the foreign service program at Georgetown, which is little more than a feeder for the CIA and FBI. Georgetown hires hawks like Madeleine Albright, George (Slam Dunk) Tenet and Douglas Feith. I told Murielle that if she comes to AU and takes my class, she's all but a sure shot for an A. She brightened at that one. Anyone whose great-uncle is Clean Gene most probably has an edge.

What good news that you'll be in these parts soon. Yes, we can catch up—perhaps a run at the American U track.

Always an upper to have your latest thoughts.

Bless you and all your loving ways—

Colman

෴෴෴

Dearest Colman,

You'll have to forgive me for this stationery, quite contrived and gaudy, but nevertheless, a gift from my dear aunt.

I am thinking of you always. I am inspired! I am writing 50 pages a week for my class [at Middlebury]: autobiographical writing. It's wonderful—I have found a true soul mate in my professor, Susan Wanner. She has been involved in several Quaker organizations, and she is currently getting me involved as well.

If it is still all right with you, may I send you a guideline/form for a letter of recommendation for me? To remind you, this would be a letter recommending my approval for a program (study abroad) in Nepal. I am so excited to go. I'll be studying the culture of Nepal, but I will also be practicing Buddhism. First-hand experience is the best way to learn, I think.

I am beginning the application process right now—getting a little excited and perhaps overwhelmed at the thought of studying abroad.

I think it will be good for my soul!

So I will send those materials to you unless I hear otherwise.

I hope you are still making gradual but important changes in the lives of high school students.

You're in my heart and mind—

Love,

Samantha Hubbard Shanley

FEBRUARY 1, 1997

Dear and Special Samantha,

This first: I should have told you before, but I was moved—not quite to tears but almost—when you introduced me to the audience that evening last fall in the Middlebury chapel. You were poised, well-collected and so void of any college-kid goofiness—I see it sometimes—that I said to myself, "my whole trip up here is totally worth this rare moment." We won't know for a while exactly what graces and talents are now developing within you but just the way you handled those couple of minutes in front of your schoolmates was an obvious sign that you are well on schedule to becoming what and who you are meant to be.

And now on to Nepal. Sounds exciting. You'll do well. Getting out of the US for a spell is a strong way to de-Westernize the soul, a task few undertake or even see the need to. Buddhists are about as far away from the graspingness on display daily at Crate & Barrel for anyone can get, so you can look back on your sales job there with some relief that you did escape. You have tons of books to read for your classes, but you might check the library for some writing by Thich Nhat Hanh—I think that spelling is right—and *The Asian Journal*, by Thomas Merton. In fact, in that Merton tape I passed on to you, the opening scene shows Merton speaking at a conference with Buddhists in Bangkok.

Nothing at Bethesda–Chevy Chase this week. First classes of spring semester start next week. My students in the fall were a joy. Three or four are already spiritually grounded. We had a decent turnout of parents coming to the class for a morning look-in. One of them was so astonished to hear her son speaking out in class in favor of the death penalty that she wrote a heartfelt letter to me a few days later expressing her amazement and grief over her boy's viewpoint, which was totally opposite hers. Mine, for sure, as well. I wrote back and said she had no cause to fret but might, in fact, rejoice: intellectual rebellion had overtaken the lad, and it was much to the good that he felt comfortable enough with himself to stand up to his teacher and the fine liberal folk at home.

Speaking of those who stand, I ran into Nick Bailey a few days back when I was at Colorado College for a talk. Nick mentioned that he saw you and the gang at the Birchmere over the holidays. I remember him at B-CC, and that notorious T-shirt incident which all but brought the free-speechers from the ACLU pouring into the school to defend Nick and his First Amendment rights. He made wretched grades, for which I frequently congratulated him because it showed he saw all to too clearly the absurdity of tests, grades and homework. He wound up going to a third-rate state school in Colorado but came alive academically, well enough to transfer into Colorado College, where he is now thriving in the final months of his senior year. A number of B-CC alums are also at CC: Amy Allen, Michelle Henderson and Emily Tatel, and a couple also from Wilson. I spent two days speaking to classes and then a student assembly. One of the deans has invited me to teach a course there in the fall—a three-week stint, class every day for three hours, which is what they label a block schedule. In two weeks, I'll be doing a similar hitch at Maret in the District: a week of teaching all day, from nine to three, in what the school calls Intensive Study Week.

Some readings are enclosed. I've taken on another class at School without Walls—mostly minority children who have little contact with whites.

Good going with your writing: 50 pages a week! That's more than Gandhi ever did. He wrote 500 words a day, every day of his life, from about age 20. It's all collected in more than 90 volumes, should you need a winter reading program.

I'm glad to write a letter for you, that's automatic.

Many blessings to you. When I tell my B-CC classes of former students who are using their gifts well, you can be sure that you are mentioned.

Much love,

Colman

∽ ∽ ∽

MARCH 6, 2012

Hi dear Colman,

How are you? I hope you are well.

How can I contact you about a freshman in college, who is looking for an internship this summer.

Most grateful,

Luby Ismail

MARCH 8, 2012

Dear Luby,

Always a joy to hear from a long-ago student. I'd be glad to talk with you but I am hesitant. The student him or herself should be calling me. That shows initiative. No doubt your maternal intercessional instincts are vibrant and strong but by the time children are in college it's time to ease them into poking around on their own for internships.

You agree?

Always yours,

Colman

Dear Professor McCarthy,

I hope this email finds you doing so well. I'm not sure if you'll remember me, I was a student of yours two falls ago in Law, Conscience and Nonviolence at Georgetown Law.

I was reading *Harper's* magazine the other day, a lovely article about not torturing children with Algebra, and your name was in it as one of the prescient few who saw that we were squelching a love of learning by rote math work. I figured it was a little cosmic signal to reach out and say hello.

Not just that, but also to ask if you had any kind of advice. I graduated from Georgetown in May and have taken the New York Bar, and I find myself being one of the few that is jobless and, I fear, directionless (and as I said in my paper for you) wondering whether this was a terrible idea to go to law school at all, fearing I'm going to be useless, and feeling not a little useless (and sad).

In the midst of the hustle of writing for contacts and seeking recommendations and otherwise feeling like a slightly less useful cog in the bureaucratic machine of former tuition payers, I figured I'd write and see if you had any words of wisdom for keeping on the path, and hoping against hope that we (or I) can be useful to the world as public interest lawyers, even as I feel like a puppy in a shelter window pleading to be taken to a home where I might bring a little joy or succor to someone.

So, I'm trying not to wait for my epiphany while prostrate, but if anyone can write away malaise about doing good in the world, I figured it would be you.

No need to reply if you're too busy, but suffice it to say this is a "Hello!" and a sincere thank you for being you.

All best.

Elizabeth

Dear Elizabeth,

If it's any comfort, and it probably won't be, you are far from the only newly minted lawyer hoping for the sun to break through the dark unemployment clouds. A while back, the *New York Times* ran a letter to the editor that was responding to a column titled "Law School Is Worth the Money." Included in the letter was this bit of gloom: "The job market for new lawyers remains abysmal, and that will not change for several years. There are far too many lawyers chasing too few jobs."

Not long after, the *Times* ran a story headlined "The Plight of the Young and Jobless."

I have former students despairing that they can't even find unpaid internships.

One suggestion, maybe a long shot, but worth a try. Write a note to Ralph Nader, PO Box 19312, Washington, DC, 20036, and, along with your resume, ask if he has openings in any of his public interest organizations. Mention that you were one of my law students. I've known Ralph for a long time, and I've found him always to be approachable and generous with his counsel.

I'm running a bit low right now on words of wisdom, but, believing that wise advice can sometimes be found anywhere, I passed around copies of your letter to the students at the beginning of my Thursday afternoon class two days ago at the law school and asked them to write down their thoughts for you.

These are among the replies:

• I can truly feel your pain as a person who always questions my decision to go to law school. This is my second time doing this to myself, the first being when I was a pre-med student at NYU. Both experiences were very different. At NYU I found myself lost and just sort of gave up. It was horrible. But at Georgetown, even though I still feel "lost," I am extremely driven, even if I don't know where I'm driving to. The experience has been amazing. Even though I am not sure if the law is right for me, I am still happy and this is simply because I have hope. My point is, don't give up, don't think too much, just "do" and do it the best you can. It is that way in which I believe you will find your way.

- I would recommend traveling if you have the money/time and just going outside, people-watching and engaging if you see an opportunity. Sometimes just watching people can open up a space to talk to them. Sharing simple kindness is underrated in its importance to the recipient. So that might be a good way to start not feeling useless. Perhaps you could volunteer in an area that is of interest to you that is not necessarily law-related.
- Defer your concerns to the universe. Uncertainty is a part of life. It is actually what separates reality from fiction. The "director" of your screenplay is a high power. Leave it to that power to sort it out. For now, focus on other things, small things, and have faith that the dots will be connected in due time.
- I can relate to the way you're feeling. I can easily see myself writing this letter in two years. There are many ways of moving through life and helping people and I'm sure you will find something to do. And you can always change directions. I'm sorry this is not much help. I'm struggling with this myself.
- New York is not the only place you can do good. Maybe your legacy is meant to be started elsewhere. A place where your talents, ambition and education will be appreciated. You might try expanding your search to include the type of work that you want in places you hadn't considered. You are not a puppy, you are a lawyer. Ten years from now, this will be only a blip. Stay on the path and you'll do fine.
- Don't lose momentum. Commit to sending applications each day. Set up informational interviews and send out your resume. Walk into each opportunity and say, ok, if these people don't hire me, someone will. Try volunteering at a legal aid location, get experience and feel productive. You are not alone. You are lucky to have a JD as a credential in order to get a job. The search takes time. Apply to jobs in places outside NY City, maybe a less popular place to be.
- I think any important starting point in a reply to [Elizabeth] is to assure her that she is not alone. Not just in her joblessness, which I'm sure she already knows but also regarding her fears of being useless or directionless and just wanting to bring joy to others. Our education system is designed to churn out workers to prepare us all to be cogs in the machine, to perform a handful

of boring and soul-sucking jobs that help no one or more often those in power. These jobs tire us out so we have no time or energy to pursue the things that make us happy, to learn who we are, to enrich our lives and relationships, or reflect meaningfully on what it means to help others and strive for a better society. I think many people—the employed and unemployed—struggle with feelings of uselessness and fear. It is natural to do so.

- But don't despair. If possible, try to look on this lapse in employment as an opportunity to resist, to think outside the box and explore "career" alternatives you may never have considered. I put career in quotation marks because I think it can be harmful to even look at your life as a career path. Take this opportunity to step back and find out what makes you feel happy and fulfilled, what makes you feel useful and what you think needs to be done to make the world a better place. Think of this totally independent of a job or a career path because that will only clog your mind.

- As for law school, regardless of whether you use it directly in your life, the knowledge you gain will be useful in your life.

Elizabeth: I was moved by my students' sincerity and willingness to relate. If their words are any kind of balm for you, then I'm glad I asked for their thoughts. One positive speculation, perhaps unfounded, is that the current downturn in legal work is cyclical and a comeback is ahead.

I remember you well in class, and often found myself admiring your intellectual and spiritual gifts—ones that turned up in your paper and always in our class discussions.

Please keep in touch, and may the angels always be with you—

Colman McCarthy

∽ ∽ ∽

Dear Professor McCarthy

Your letter of recommendation was, once again, beyond anything I could have asked for. I thank you from the bottom of my heart. Throughout the summer I have been working with a young girl who I've known since she was a child. Her name is Mary Fay. We worked on language and reading skills in practical life circumstances and environments. Additionally I spend much of my time (as I have for the past 3 summers) with one of my dear friends who has ALS. Her name is Claire Collier. Claire and her 3 children are teaching me more than any class (besides yours) at Georgetown ever did. In the meantime, I received the third and fourth surgery on my right arm: left over wounds [from field hockey] at Georgetown, over 100 stitches up my arm.

I have been using a lot of my free time to work on my dissertation. Since I decided to get two Master's, I have two dissertations to do. I am privileged to receive these degrees, so I must try to feel privileged to have these two assignments. These opportunities leave little room for creativity. I have come up with countless topics that have been rejected by my professor. They are considered "too out there." I guess she wants to read the same papers over and over again each year. I have figured out one topic and that paper is completely set. I am writing a robotic research paper on the evolution of the PTA.

However, the other paper has hope. I have to research a contemporary program, method or controversial issue in the field of education, based primarily on examination of relevant research studies. I asked if I could discuss the DARE program and future drug use (that was a no), KIPP schools (not enough info), two working parents and teacher-student relationships (not allowed). I am wondering if you think I should propose schools with peace study programs and violence rates. Or is there another topic that fits this area that may be worth looking at?

I truly enjoy all the articles [on testing] you thoughtfully sent me. I wish I could prove that testing causes increased anxiety using eight different research studies, but I fear no one is being funded to prove that these days. If you get the chance, let me know what you think.

I begin my first day of work tomorrow. HERE WE GO!!!! It's time to get all of the life experiences I have been reading about.

Please send my best to your wife and family. You are always in my thoughts, actions and prayers.

Big smile.

Meghan D. Rinehart

Dear Meghan,

A shame that that professor—a real bully it appears—is discouraging rather than encouraging you. I have little taste for assigning research papers, so little in fact that I have never done it—which may explain why I never know where I'll be teaching from year to year.

I am only speculating but one possibility for a program that has been researched a bit is Special Olympics. Though not strictly an education program, it has worked with people—the mentally disabled—who have been marginalized or dismissed by much of society as uneducable. I've been close to the program since its early days in the summer of 1968, through my friendship with Sargent and Eunice Shriver, and could put you in contact with someone at headquarters here. You might Google Special Olympics to see if this works as a paper. Enclosed is a recent column on Eunice, whose daughter, Maria, by the way, is, like you, a Georgetown alum.

On writing about a peace studies program, sure, propose it. A possibility is the Resolving Conflict Creatively Program (RCCP) which has been around since 1985 and is a national effort that has been evaluated over and over—with ample positive evaluations. The founder is Linda Lantieri, whom I've known for some time. I think we were on a panel in New York City a few years back. You might get her book, *Waging Peace in Our Schools* (Beacon) which lays it all out. This would be a productive paper to write because you could do two kinds of research: past and current studies and site visits to schools to interview teachers like Linda.

Tough news about your surgeries. Obviously you ignored all those people who kept telling you to "be careful" when you were playing field hockey. It's to your lasting credit that you did ignore them. The worst utterance, the most negative utterance, that can be said to a child is "be careful." Decoded, it means "be afraid." You can tell which children have been raised by fear-instilling parents, forever cautioning "be careful, be careful." It's similar to parents who tell their one- and two-year-olds "don't touch," when the child, say, touches a lamp on the living room table that might be pushed over. In the child's mind, the "don't touch" message means "don't learn."

Why else is the child touching the lamp, except to learn about it. So the lamp falls over and breaks. Something is learned about gravity, and maybe about cleaning up the mess. A Montessori moment.

So be glad you kept playing hard and were banged up on the playing fields. You've been toughened for life's future hits. Too, you've learned something about medicine—that bodies do heal.

Do give Linda Lantieri's program a try. The research is available, so are the teachers.

Stay well, and swell—

Colman McCarthy

JULY 19, 2008

Dear Professor McCarthy,

Greetings! It's been so long since I have sent you fan mail. I pray you are as well as ever. I just finished my second year of teaching and I continue to live in awe and excitement EVERY DAY! You are and always will be the one who guided me here and blessed me with perspectives I never would have come to see the world from.

I am off to share my energy with new [Montessori] students in sunny California. I will be living in Dana Point. It's halfway between LA and SD. I'll continue my marathons and love for the outdoors in 75 degree weather—365 days a year. I have two bedrooms so you and the Mrs. are welcome ANYTIME!

I want you to truly know that no matter the life situation I find myself in, I honor the lessons you gave me daily. I'm six years a vegetarian because of you. Enclosed is a note from one of my students. They are reciting Mother Teresa's poem "Anyway" all the time and learn about many of the great peacemakers—INCLUDING YOU.

Lots of love,

Meghan D. Rinehart

JULY 28, 2008

Dear Meghan,

Look at all you've done, only three years out of the Georgetown gate at 36th and O: a graduate degree in the field that really matters—Montessori education—plus two years as a teacher, getting fan mail from your students (Eva couldn't be the only one), thriving in southern California and getting good times in the road races. You have much to be proud of.

Immense thanks for your uplifting letter, and all your kind words. I think you know how grateful I was having you in class—that small one for a couple of weeks and then the larger one for a full semester. You brightened up the room both times, and kept me from despairing when assorted dolts trudged in 20 minutes late and fell asleep in the back.

I passed through Dana Point, or at least nearby Rte. 5, when I was doing some stories for the *Post* in Tijuana a few years ago. Maureen O'Connor, then the mayor of San Diego, invited me to go with her early one evening to a place called the Canyon of the Dead—a large expanse at the border where Latin American refugees would gather after slipping through the fences from Mexico. A priest would come and offer Mass, and the mayor would go among the crowds welcoming the anonymous night-walkers. Rather than give a sermon, the priest let Mayor O'Connor be the sermon. Riding back with her to San Diego, I remember her saying, "I was trained by priests and nuns. I wanted to be a nun but they wouldn't let me. They said I didn't have the qualification. I wouldn't take orders!"

Earlier this year, around March, I was up the road in Santa Barbara giving a lecture at the Nuclear Age Peace Foundation—a full-energy nonprofit that ranges from pressuring California universities not to take Pentagon grant money to staying firm with the belief that nuclear war can be stopped only if total disarmament comes about. While I was in Santa Barbara, some teachers at a prep school—Cate—in nearby Carpinteria invited me to do a student assembly and speak in classes. Turns out the students were receptive to the idea of creating a peace studies program. So was one of the teachers, who had a master's in peace studies from Berkeley. I nudged them all, and now there will be a course in place for the fall.

I heard about this just last week, about the same time a teacher from a high school in Dallas—Bishop Dunne Catholic School—where I spoke two years ago called to say that he was starting a peace studies program. So maybe we'll have to do this school by school by school.

That's how it began with Maria Montessori. It was just a hundred years ago that she opened her little classroom in a poor neighborhood in Rome, and then another one and another.

I had three Georgetown students speak in my high school classes last April, after they called to ask if they could come to rally my students to join the boycott against Burger King. The three had taken their spring break among the tomato pickers in the migrant worker fields of south Florida. For years Burger King had been resisting paying a penny a pound more for the picked tomatoes. Taco Bell and McDonald's had agreed to it years before but not Burger King. A penny a pound more was too much of a financial whopper.

It was a similar victory you saw at Georgetown itself when the administration, after a nine-day hunger strike by 27 students, reluctantly agreed to raise the pay of the janitors, cafeteria workers and the other invisible people of the campus. Burger King and Georgetown: poseurs without conscience. During the strike I invited one of the janitors to speak to my classes. He was sweeping the floors in White-Gravenor: just come in and tell the students about your life, I asked. "I'd like to," he said, "but I'm afraid. The administration would find out and I'd be fired." I told him I respected his fear, and then wondered how it came to pass that this honest and earnest man—diligent in doing the university's low-paid dirty work—feared he would be ground down still more by a school run by Jesuit priests.

I imagine Dana Point has some sparkling running trails, and what I don't need to imagine is that you are on them in the full flower of all your athletic graces. Do a seven minute mile for me—one of your slower ones!

All the best and keep giving your best—

Colman McCarthy

∽ ∽ ∽

This letter was accompanied by an invitation to the commencement exercises at Colgate University on Sunday afternoon, May 21, 2006.

MAY 10, 2006

Dear Mr. McCarthy,

Thank you for everything. You have inspired me in so many ways. My degree from Colgate in Peace and Conflict Studies is really because of you. Thank you for imparting a piece of your knowledge and passion for peace to me.

With much love and appreciation.

Laurie Chin

Dear Laurie,

Good going. No. Great going. Large congratulations for graduating as a peace studies major. I've been telling all my high school classes about how you hung in and made it happen. It's been necessary to restrain myself from embellishing the story. I now have you getting up at 5 am to be at the Stone Ridge class at 7 am In a few years it could be 4 am!

You were a rare student, taking the course out of desire and getting no credit for it. As I recall, administrators all but forbade you from being there: the course was for seniors only. You were a junior. To my delight, you came anyway. Audacious. Just think what this means for American education. Students actually deciding for themselves what they want to learn. That's a bud that needs nipping, fast.

I was elated to see you follow through at Colgate. You are generous and thoughtful to send an invitation to the commencement. We should have a visit when you are back home so you can give me the details on Colgate's program. Some have told me it is overly theoretical, others have said the deans aren't really behind it with funding.

Last week some Oberlin students invited me to speak there in the fall, as a way of helping them organize a peace studies program. It will be my second try at Oberlin, having spoken there in 1989 when a math professor assembled a few dozen students to lobby for a program. The effort seemed promising: one math professor pushing for peace is worth a dozen humanities professors. Alas, the next year the math man was denied tenure and off he had to go.

The students? They moved on, too—necessarily so. It's one of my darker conspiracy theories that the reason colleges promote junior year abroad programs is that third-year students cause the most trouble on campuses. They're on the student government, they are writing for the school newspaper, they know where the faculty deadwood is stacked. As freshmen, they're giddy at being away from home. As sophomores, they're starting to focus. By the third year, they're ready to make trouble. As seniors their minds are elsewhere: grad school, job searching, loan worries. So it's only in the focused third year that they can be fire-breathers. Go to Rome, juniors. Go to Paris, juniors. For God's sake, go anywhere.

I'm teaching a couple of college classes this summer. Last year at

Georgetown, a Middle Eastern student was in the class. After initial reticence, she got the hang of it—plenty of debates and opinionating—and became outgoing and intellectually spirited in ways that I imagine she never dared in her schooling back home. She had a tender way of correcting me when I drifted into waywardness. She belonged to her country's royal family. I had had Arab students before—from Bahrain, Kuwait, Saudi Arabia, Yemen, Jordan—but this was a bit different because of her way of life, the privileges of wealth, the security details, the high expectations of being a royal. For our last class she ordered in a catered meal for all of us, well at the other end of Cokes and four Domino's pizzas.

Before leaving for the kingdom, she and her family came to my home for dinner—a rare kind of royal socializing, I was later told by the student's ever-present chaperone. It was an educational moment for my wife and me, both to learn the history of her sand-swept country and how her parents raised so gracious a daughter.

A month later, a royal invitation came to speak at the kingdom's leading university and to help organize a peace studies program. I had to decline, but one of my former Georgetown Law students—Nathaniel Mills, a three-time Olympic speed skater—went in my place and nudged things along. He spent a week speaking in classes and kept suggesting that the university had a chance to become a haven for peace education in the Middle East. Where is it needed more?

Thank you, heartily, for inviting me to your graduation. And unless you get a court order that I desist, I'm going to keep telling my students about you.

Lots of love.

Colman McCarthy

∽ ∽ ∽

Dear Colman,

While it has been a few years since our last contact, I am reaching out to you now as I have been given the green light by the administration here at St. John's Prep [Danvers, Massachusetts] to start the ball rolling on creating a peace studies center here at the school. My task at this point is to do some research on schools that have established such centers, particularly Catholic high schools in the United States.

If you could provide some guidance for me based on your own contributions to setting up such centers I'd be very grateful.

Hope you are well and I look forward to reestablishing contact with you.

Bill Britton

Dear Bill,

Apologies for the delay. I get behind sometimes.

The only way to measure a high school's commitment to peace education is by asking how many courses it offers in peace studies and whether the school has a peace studies department on the same funding level as other academic departments. I've given talks at well over a hundred schools since I've been at this and never came upon a peace studies department. Having a peace studies center at a high school is fine but it sounds fuzzy. Would schools have an algebra center? A science center? Doubtful. They offer full credit-yielding courses.

At Bethesda–Chevy Chase and Wilson currently, and for 25 years at School without Walls until three years ago, I've never had a principal come close to hiring someone to teach peace studies full time. I'm not paid at B-CC, wasn't at Walls and get pocket change at Wilson. Administrators put their money elsewhere—in programs designed to have students well-prepped to join a workforce that needs docile and obedient people readied not to question the country's economic or military policies—as they likely would if they took three or four years of peace courses.

I've been holding memorial services in my classes for dear Pete Seeger, who passed last Monday. Few students had heard of him, sad to report. So I played some of his songs: all verses of "This Land" and "What Did You Learn in School Today," "Bring 'Em Home" and "Where Have All the Flowers Gone." Classrooms at B-CC and Wilson are equipped with access to YouTube, so the songs, and a lot more, were easily pulled up. We also read a few pages from *The Protest Singer*, a meditation on Pete by Alec Wilkinson. I kept thinking how pleasurable it would be to teach a full semester just on the life and times of Seeger, this endearing and pro- foundly relevant man. That's about as likely to slip past a school board's wary eye as a full semester on Woody Guthrie or Dorothy Day or Eugene Debs or Emma Goldman.

Glad to conspire some more. Any time.

Optimally,

Colman McCarthy

P.S. Speaking of conspiring, I've been working with my Wilson students to organize a campaign to change the name of the school. Woodrow Wilson's policies were racist, militaristic and sexist, and it's shameful that a school is named after such a loathsome politician. Imagine if a new high school were to be built and a proposal came forth to name it after someone whose views were racist, militaristic and sexist. No chance. My students have collected a couple of hundred names on a petition to dump the Wilson name, and let students, teachers and the community chose someone who modeled peace, justice and sanity. How about Pete Seeger High?

Index

Abbas, Mahmoud, 149
Abernethy, Bob, 76
Abu Dhabi, 40, 150–51
Act of Conscience, An (Leppzer), 167
Adams, Patch, xviii
Albright, Madeleine, 169
alcohol abuse in college, 21–26
Allen, Amy, 171
Allen High School (TX), 159
Alpert, Merrick, 7
American Friends Service Committee, 169
American University, 16, 35, 80, 112, 120, 127, 138, 155–56, 169
AmeriCorps, xviii, 168
And a Voice To Sing With: A Memoir (Baez), 140
Anderson-Little, Dan, 147–51
Andrews, Megan, 93
Anna Karenina (Tolstoy), 155
anti-war demonstrations, 127–28
Aquinas, Thomas, 124
Aratani, Lori, 91
Arendt, Hannah, xxv
Armstrong, Grace, 9
Army Corps of Engineers, 81
Asian Journals, The (Merton), 171
Augsburg College, 164–65

Bachmann, Michele, 165
Baez, Joan, xvii, xviii, xxii, xxiv, 44, 111, 140
Bailey, Nick, 171

Balch, Emily, xvii, xxiv, xxv
Baltimore Orioles, 104
Balz, Chrissy, 84
banning homework and tests, 39
Barbaro (race horse), 57
Barnard College, 50
Barry, Marion, 168
Beardmore, Meredith, 61–62
Benjamin, Medea, 33
Bernardin, Joseph, 124
Berrigan, Daniel, xvii, 33, 119
Berrigan, Philip, xviii, 119
Berry, Wendell, 132
Bethesda–Chevy Chase High School (MD), xviii, xix, xxi, 10, 38, 43, 50, 91–93, 96–97, 123, 127, 136, 142, 171, 184
birth lottery, winning, 154
Blacklow, Beth, 50–52
Blake High School (MD), 93
Blumenthal, Richard, 7
Boll, Heinrich, 57
Bonaparte, Napolean, xxiv
Boone, Tommy, 23
Boston Red Sox, 105
Boston University, 106
Bourgeois, Roy, 33, 98
Bray, Linda, 3, 4
Britton, Bill, 181–85
Brooklyn Dodgers, 154
Brothers Karamazov (Dostoyevsky), 29
Buchanan, Patrick, 109
Bulson, Sean, 92, 94

Burger King, xix, 29, 180–81
Burning Tree Golf Club (MD), 109
Burriss, Emmanuel, 134
Burton, Dan, 10
Busboys & Poets, 89, 94–95
Bush, George H. W., 77
Buzzell, Colby, 115

caddying, 108
Câmara, Hélder, 52
Canisius College, 101, 103, 163
Card, Andrew, 61–62
Cardinal, Ernesto, xviii
Carter, Jimmy, xix
Cate School (CA), 180
Caterpillar, Inc., 147, 149
Catholic University, 14–17
Catholic Worker, 14, 15, 18, 153
Center for Teaching Peace, 34, 108, 117, 144
Center on Conscience and War, 118
Chappell, Paul, 31, 32
cheating, in school, 39, 137
Cherry Blossom Road Race (DC), 164
Chesla, Lori, 121–22
Chevy Chase Club (MD), 108–11
Chicago Tribune, 146
Chin, Laurie, 181–83
Chomsky, Noam, 97
Christianson, Laura, 164–69
Churchill High School (MD), 160
Clark University, 121
Cleland, Max, 56
Clinton Bill, 11, 12, 109
Code Pink, 33
Cohen, Jacob, 67
Colgate University, 181–82
Collier, Claire, 177
Colorado College, 69, 171
Colorado State University, 69
Columbia Country Club (MD), 109
Confessions of Nat Turner, The (Styron), 101
Confidential Clerk, The (Eliot), 113

Congressional Country Club (MD), 109
Corrections Today, 76
Corrigan, Mairead, xviii
Crispell, Mitchell, 141–43
Crowley, Stephen, 34
C-SPAN, 87
Cultural Leadership Program, 147

Dalai Lama, 41
Dallas Morning News, 162
Daniel, Clifton, 157
Darkness Visible: A Memoir of Madness (Styron), 101
Day, Doris, 15, 40
Day, Dorothy, xvii, 14, 15, 44, 76, 97, 127, 153, 185
Deans, Marie, 72, 74, 77
Dear, John, 119
death penalty, 70–78, 122–24
Death Penalty: An Historial and Theological Survey, The (McGivern), 124
Death Penalty Information Center, 146
death row exonerations, 75
Debs, Eugene, 126, 185
Declarations of Independence (Zinn), 103, 106
DeGioia, John, 91
DeLay, Tom, 109
Dellinger, David, 5
Dellums, Ron, 63
Deming, Barbara, xvii
depression, overcoming, 100
DLA Piper, law firm, 8
Dona, Vicky, 12
Dostoevsky, Feodor, 30
Downs, Hugh, 77
Doyle, Susie, 93
Drinan, Robert, 55, 57
Duke University, 123

E., Sophie, 41–48
Earlham College, xxiv
Eastern Mennonite University, 33
Edmund Burke School (DC), 119

Einstein, Albert, 6, 131, 157
Eisenhower, Dwight, 167
El Mozote massacre (El Salvador), 98
Eliot, T. S., 21, 113
Elizabeth, 173–76
Ellis, Eddie, Jr., 32
Emily, 155–58
Engle, Paul, 47
Esquivel, Adolfo Perez, xviii, 85
Evergreen State University, 30

F., Ariel, 100–101
Fairfield University, 163
Farm Animal Rights Movement, 30, 33
Fay, Mary, 177
fear-based learning, 96
Feith, Douglas, 169
Fitzgerald, Jim, 109–10
Flament, J., 79–81
Flamm, Hannah, xix, xxi
Flores, Lily, xviii, xx
football, 158–59
Foreign Sovereign Immunities Act, 9
Fort Benning (GA), xix, 33–34, 98
Francis (pope), 165
Francis of Assisi, 29
Frazier, Brandon, 156
Free, Zaccai, 33
Friere, Paulo, 52
Furioso, Dante, 87
Furse, Elizabeth, xviii

Gandhi, Arun, 35
Gandhi, Harilal, 157
Gandhi, Mohandas K., xi, 14, 34–35,
    40–42, 44, 46, 76, 93, 131, 139,
    157, 172
Gandhi's Truth (Erkison), 35
Gearan, Mark, 11–12, 63, 80
General Assembly of the Presbyterian
    Church, 147
Georgetown Day School, (DC), 119
Georgetown Preparatory School (MD),
    110

Georgetown University, xviii, 40, 82–83,
    118, 179, 181
  Center on Alcohol Marketing to
    Youth, 21
  Law Center, xviii, 5, 7, 11, 17, 23,
    33, 55–56, 63, 81, 173
  living wage campaign, 83
Georgetown Visitation School (DC), 89
George Washington University, xvii
Geyelin, Philip, 56–57
Giarratano, Joseph, 72–78
Glen Head Elementary School (NY), xxi
Goldberg, Jeffrey, 150–51
Goldman, Emma, xvii
golf club memberships, 109–10
Goshen College, xxiv
Goucher College, xxiv
Guilford College, xxiv
grades, xiv, 17, 37, 39, 52–55, 97
Grant, Ulysses S., xxiv
Grassley, Charles "Chuck," 67
Gray, Tony, 70
Greenspan, Alan, 110
Gugoff, Cassandra, 52–53
Guthrie, Woody, 185

Haig, Alexander, 98
Hallock, Daniel, 12
Hamilton, Anita, xxi
Hamilton, Bill, xxi, xxii
Hamilton, Thomas, xxi, xxii
Hanh, Thich Nhat, 41, 171
Harkin, Tom, 67
Harper, Georgia, 24–26
Harper's magazine, 173
Harris, Sydney, 115
Hartmann, Peter, 31–36, 108–11
Hatfield, Mark, 57
Hehman, Ryan, 15–20
Hell, Healing and Resistance (Hallock),
    120
Hemingway, Ernest, 47
Hesburgh, Theodore, 19, 119
Hewlett-Packard, Inc., 147, 149

Hijazi, Refik, 150
Hiram College, 131
Hiroshima, 101, 103, 157
Hobart & William Smith College, xxiv, 62–63, 81
Hofstra University, 163
Holton-Arms School (MD), 89
Home Run Baseball Camp (DC), 134, 150
homework, 39, 141, 146
Hoya, The (newspaper), 83–84
Hughes, Emmet John, 169
Hughes, Harold, xviii
Hughes, Maggie, 144–47
Humane Society of the United States, 132
Hunt, Amanda, 130
Husar, Bruno, 41

International Herald Tribune, 16
Ismail, Luby, 172

J., 117–20
Jackson, Lena, 82–95
Jacobs, Andy, xviii, 57
James, C. L. R., 86
James, Selma, 86
Japan International Cooperation Agency, 106–7
Jesus, 19, 119, 156, 165
Jewish Voice for Peace, 149
John XXIII (pope), 32
Johnson, Robert, 88

Kahn, Si, xviii
Kaine, Tim, 70–72, 77
Kaptur, Marci, 67
Kast, David, 165
Kast, Nicole, 165
Katz, Olivia, 65–69
Kelly, Kathy, 49
Kelly, Steve, 119
Kennebunk, ME, 157
Kennedy, Edward M., 22, 67

Kennedy, John F., 22
Kennedy, Kerry, 123
Kennedy, Patrick, 67
Kennedy, Robert F., 22, 123
Ketziot prison (Israel), 150
Kim, Joanne, 72
King, Martin Luther, Jr., xxii, 14, 38, 44, 131, 143, 157
Kingdom of God Is Within You, The (Tolstoy), 5, 163
Kirwan, Michael, 15, 16
Kline, Tony, 73
Kozol, Jonathan, 49
Krugman, Paul, 98
Ku Klux Klan, 142

Laden, Osama bin, 146
Lantieri, Linda, 178–79
Laubenstein, Kirk, 62–64
Leahy, Patrick, 67
Lee, Barbara, 67
Lee, Harper, xv, xxvi
Lee, Robert E., xxiv
Lee, Tara, 4–9
Lepore, Jill, 166, 168
Lesevic, Mika, 113–16
Levin, Hannah, 95–98, 166
Levin, Jacob, 166
Library of Congress, 90
Lippmann, Walter, 152
Living Beyond War (Meyers), 133
living wage campaign (Georgetown), 83
Lockheed Martin, Inc., 62–3
Long Island Railroad, 22
Los Angeles Times, 73

Mackey, John, 95
Mahon, Hanna, 21–24, 36
Manalapan High School (NJ), 125–26
Manchester College, xxiv
Manhattan College, xxiv
Mansfield, Katherine, xxvi
Maret School (DC), 33, 119, 172
Marquette Park (IL), 142

Martha's Vineyard Regional High School (MA), 133
Marxist Literary Group, 86
Mayer, Jane, xxii
Mayer, Stephen, 34
McCarthy, Eugene, 162, 165
McCarthy, John, 104, 134
McCarthy, Mav, 45
McCartney, Dan, 128
McCutcheon, John, 44
McDonald's, xix, 180
McDonnell, Robert, 78
McGovern, Jim, 64, 67
McKenna, Horace, 119
McNamara, Robert, 56
McSorley, Richard, 118
Megivern, James, 124
Melcher, John, xviii
Meleski, Aspen, 136, 140
Merhige, Robert, 78
Merrisa, 28–30
Merton, Thomas, 14, 40, 171
Meyer, Bernard, 93
Michael, Eleftherios, 154–55
Middlebury College, 36
Mikulski, Barbara, 67
military spending, 66, 168
Mills, Nathaniel, 183
Moakley, Joseph, 64
Mondale, Walter, 165
Montessori, Maria, 44, 96, 179–80
Montgomery Blair High School (MD), 93
Moody, Claire, 51
Morella, Connie, xviii
Morgan, Ryan, 37, 39–40
Mother Teresa, 63, 105, 122, 179
Motorola Solutions, Inc., 147, 149
Mowbray, Steve, 33
Muller, Bobby, 56, 132
Murder Victims Families for Human Rights, 124
Murphy, Jim, 126

Nader, Ralph, 34, 36, 174
Nagasaki, 101, 103, 157
Napolean, Julie McCarthy, 169
Napolean, Murielle, 169
Nation, The, xvi
National Cathedral School, 81–82, 89
National Catholic Reporter, 24, 80, 156, 161
National Football League, 160
National Student Leadership Conference, 124
NBC Nightly News, 76–77
Nearing, Helen, xvii
Nearing, Scott, xvii
Nelson, Willie, 168
Netanyahu, Benjamin, 149
Neumeyer, Chris, 55–57
Neumeyer, Norris F., Jr., 55–58
New Shoots for Peace (McCarthy and Ur), 44–45, 169
New York Times, xv, xxi, 35–36, 54, 98, 157, 174
New Yorker, 166
Niles West High School (IL), 49
Nixon, Richard, 109
nonviolent self-defense, 138–39
North Carolina A&T University, 33
Northeastern University, 162–63
Northrup, Steve, 70
Northwest High School, 93
Northwood High School, 93
Nuclear Age Peace Foundation, 32, 180
Nunn, Sam, 109

Oak Hill Juvenile Detention Center (MD), xvii
Obama, Barack, 21, 96, 149–50
Oberlin College, 30–31, 34, 36, 69, 108, 110, 182
O'Connor, Flannery, xv
O'Connor, Maureen, 180
On the Duty of Civil Disobedience (Thoreau), 63
O'Neil, Tip, 109

Osumi, Yurina, 101–8
Otis, James, 35–36

pacifism, 66–67, 118, 131, 168
Panama invasion (1983), 5
Panth, Avishek, 93
Patton, George, 6
Peace Corps, xviii, 63, 80–81, 121, 168
    in Benin, 51
    in Bolivia, 10–13
    in Ecuador, 50
    in Mali, 79–80
    in Morocco, 16
Peace Is Possible (Abraham), xvii, 47, 154
peace studies
    classes, 51–52, 58, 91, 95–96, 125,
    127, 129, 160–61
    programs, difficulty in creating, 50,
    94
Pelacanos, George, xviii
People for the Ethical Treatment of
    Animals, 30
People, 75
People's History of the United States, A
    (Zinn), 106
Percy, Walker, 54
Peter, Paul and Mary, 44
Phillips Exeter Academy (NH), xxv,
    37–38
Picciotto, Concepcion, 104, 107
Poplar Springs Animal Sanctuary, 28
post-traumatic stress disorders, 160
Powell, Colin, 120
Powell, Justice Lewis, 74
*Prisoners: A Muslim and Jew Across the
    Middle East Divide* (Goldberg), 150
Protest Singer, The (Wilkinson), 184
Proxmire, William, 7, 139
Public Citizen, 89

Quayle, Dan, 109

R., John, 151–54
Rabinowitz, Stuart, 163
Race to the Top, 96

Rankin, Jeannette, xxiv, xxv, 44, 107
Reagan, Ronald, 77, 88, 104
Red Onion State Prison (VA), 77
Religious Freedom Peace Tax Fund Bill,
    64
Reserve Officer Training Corps (ROTC),
    64
Reyerson, Charity, 33–34
Rhee, Michelle, 134
Rinehart, Meghan D., 177–81
Rinzler, Carol, 137
Roberts, John, 110
Roberts, Sam, 58–60
Rockville High School, 93
Romero, Oscar, xix, xx, 33, 52, 98
Rostenkowski, Dan, 109
Roszak, Theodore, xxv
Rubin, Mark, 70
Russo, Marty, 109

Salinger, J. D., xv
San Francisco Giants, 134
Sanders, Bernie, 67
Saraf, Andrew, 91
Schieber, Shannon, 123
Schieber, Vicki, 122–24
School of the Americas, xix, 33, 98
School Without Walls, 87–88
Schroeder, Patricia, 4
Schumacher, E. F., 98
Schwarz, Henry, 86
Schweitzer, Albert, 168
Scott-Maxwell, Florida, 114
Second Vatican Council, 32
Seeger, Pete, 44, 184
Senate Judiciary Committee, 123
Shallal, Andy, 94
Shanley, Samantha Hubbard, 170–72
Shapiro, Paul, 132
Sharp, Gene, xvii, 6
Shriver, Eunice, 22, 178
Shriver, Maria, 178
Shriver, Mark, xviii
Shriver, R. Sargent, xviii, 12, 51, 80, 178
Shriver, Tim, xviii, 80

Sidwell Friends School (DC) 119
Siena College, 163
Smalley, Melissa, 124–27
Snead, Sam, 111
Socrates, 96, 137
Solutions to Violence (McCarthy), xviii, 30
Sophie's Choice (Styron), 101
Special Olympics, xviii, 81, 178
Spelman College, 106
Spring Hill College, xv, 142
St. Albans, 119
St. John's College, 151
St. John's University, 163
Stanky, Eddie, 154
Stennis, John, 139
Stone, I. F., 135
Stone Ridge School of the Sacred Heart (MD), 80, 97
Strength Through Peace: The Ideas and People of Nonviolence (McCarthy), xvii, 116, 147, 151
Styron, William, 101
suicide, 88, 101
Sullivan, Michael, 159–61
Swartz, Laura, 128–29

T., Sarah, 131–33
Taco Bell, 181
Tatel, Emily, 171
Tattler (school newspaper)
Tenet, George, 169
Terkel, Studs, 103
Thayer, Roger, 133–35
Thich Nhat Hanh, 41, 171
Thoreau, Henry David, 41, 63, 117, 133
Tibbetts, Paul, Jr., 103, 105
Time, 38
To Kill a Mockingbird (Lee), xv
To Love or To Kill: Man vs. Animal (Thomas), 28
Tolstoy, Leo, xvii, 5, 14, 40, 44, 97, 155–57, 163–65
Trimble, Bobby, 22
Truman, Harry S. 103

Truman, Margaret, 103
Tufts University, xxi
Tulane University Law School, 130
Tuscaloosa News, xv
Tutu, Desmond, xxv
Twain, Mark, 40

United States Constitution, 66
United States Court of Appeals, 4th circuit, 9, 74
United States Department of State, 10
United States Department of Veteran's Affairs, 55
United States Military Academy (West Point), xxiv
United States Naval Academy (Annapolis), 3, 5–7, 152
United States Supreme Court, 9, 66, 74
University of Buenos Aires, 85
University of Colorado, 69
University of Iowa Writers Workshop, 47
University of Maryland, xvii, 5, 24, 53, 55, 117
University of Minnesota, 165
University of Missouri, xxiv
University of Notre Dame, xxiv
University of San Diego, xxiv
University of Virginia, 132

Valentine, Bobby, 105
Van Hollen, Chris, xviii
Vanderhaar, Gerard, 136
vegetarian diet, 26, 52, 140–41
Vicky, Dona, 12
Vietnam Veterans Against the War, 120, 132
violence, failures of, 138
Virginia Department of Corrections, 73
Voices for Creative Nonviolence, 49
Vonnegut, Kurt, 57
voting, reasons against, xii–xiii, 65–67

Wack, Paul, 50
Walesa, Lech, 6
Wall Street Journal, 28

Wallace, David Foster, 99, 101
Wallens Ridge State Prison (VA), 78
Walter Johnson High School (MD), 93
Walters, Barbara, 77
Wanner, Susan, 170
war on drugs, Bolivia, 10–11
War Resisters League, 118, 169
war tax refusal, 64
Washington, Earl, Jr., 73–74
Washington Center for Internships and
    Academics, xvii
Washington Nationals, 134
Washington Post, xvi, 36, 38, 46, 54–55,
    78, 81, 91–92, 97, 115–16
Washingtonian, 94
Weber, Michael, 30
Wellstone, Paul, 165
Werner, Fred, 9–14
Wesleyan University, 30, 87
We Who Dared Say No To War (Polner
    and Woods, eds.), 34
Whole Foods, 95
Wilder, L. Douglas, 70, 75, 78
Williams College, 96, 98, 165–66
Williams, Brian, 76

Williams, Jody, xxiv
Williams, Pat, xviii
Wilkinson, Alec, 184
Wilson High School (DC), xviii, 24, 28,
    30, 36, 43, 119, 134
Wolfowitz, Paul, 56
Wolfson, Joe, 37–40
women in combat, 3–5
women victimized by sexual attacks, 138
Women's International League for Peace
    and Freedom, xxv
Woolsey, Lynn, 67
Wyden, Ron, 67

Yale Law Review, 73
Yamaguchi, Tsutomo, 104
Yarrow, Peter, xviii, 120
Your Adolescent: An Owner's Manual
    (Rinzler), 137
Yunus, Muhammad, xviii

Zerkin, Gerald, 74
Zinn, Howard, xviii, 49, 57, 106–7
Zuccotti Park (NY), 152–53